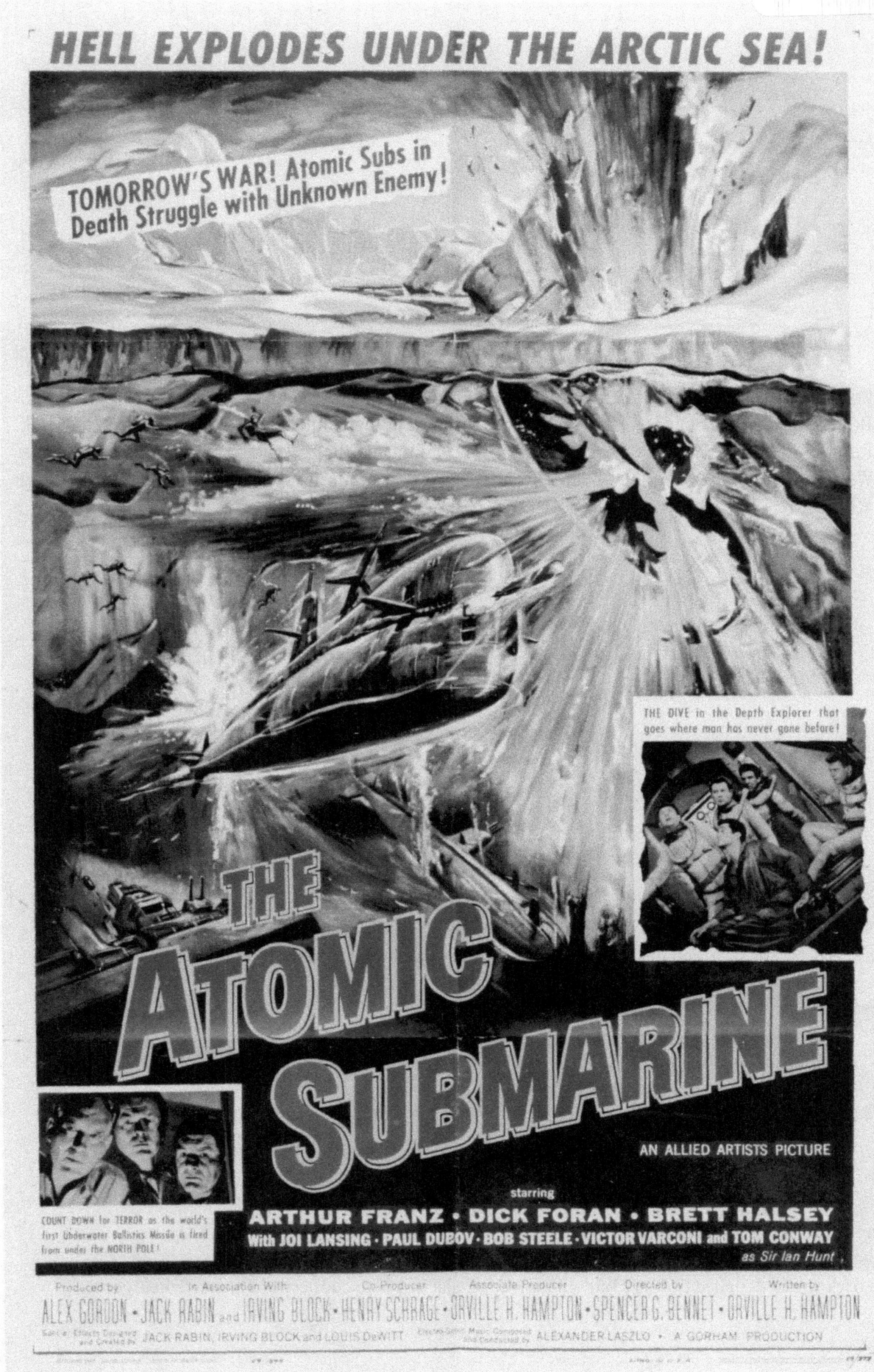

HELL EXPLODES UNDER THE ARCTIC SEA!
TOMORROW'S WAR! Atomic Subs in Death Struggle with Unknown Enemy!
THE DIVE in the Depth Explorer that goes where man has never gone before!
THE ATOMIC SUBMARINE
AN ALLIED ARTISTS PICTURE
COUNT DOWN for TERROR as the world's first Underwater Ballistics Missile is fired from under the NORTH POLE!
starring
ARTHUR FRANZ · DICK FORAN · BRETT HALSEY
With JOI LANSING · PAUL DUBOV · BOB STEELE · VICTOR VARCONI and TOM CONWAY
as Sir Ian Hunt
Produced by ALEX GORDON · In Association With JACK RABIN and IRVING BLOCK · Co-Producer HENRY SCHRAGE · Associate Producer ORVILLE H. HAMPTON · Directed by SPENCER G. BENNET · Written by ORVILLE H. HAMPTON
JACK RABIN, IRVING BLOCK and LOUIS DeWITT
ALEXANDER LASZLO · A GORHAM PRODUCTION

ACKNOWLEDGMENTS

My sincere thanks to Samuel Z. Arkoff, Marty Baumann, Mike Brunas, Bob Burns, Jack Cookerly, Kerry Gammill, Alex Gordon, Richard Gordon, Brett Halsey, Susan Hart, Joe Indusi, Donna Lucas, Tim Lucas, Jack Mathis, Kathleen Mayne, Jim Miller, Robert Neill, Frederick Rappaport, Chris Ed Rock, Robert Rotter, Mary Runser, Rich Scrivani, Tony Timpone, Laura Wagner, Prof. L.M. Wagner of the Atomic Energy Commission (Long Island bureau), Craig Wichman

—Tom Weaver

The Atomic Submarine
© 2018 Tom Weaver. All Rights Reserved.
No part of this book may be reproduced in any form or by any means, electronic, mechanical, digital, photocopying or recording, except for the inclusion in a review, without permission in writing from the publisher.

Published in the USA by:
BearManor Media
P. O. Box 71426
Albany, GA 31708
www.bearmanormedia.com

ISBN 978-1-62933-304-5

Printed in the United States of America.
Book design by Robbie Adkins, www.adkinsconsult.com
Front and back covers designed by Mary Runser. Back cover glacier photo courtesy of Thomas Scheuzger.

The Atomic Submarine Table of Contents

Introduction by Brett Halsey 1

Credits and Synopsis 2

"Disparate Chintz: The Jois of *The Atomic Submarine*" by Richard Heft . . 5

The Atomic Submarine **Production History** by Tom Weaver 9

The Atomic Submarine **Release History** by Dr. Robert J. Kiss 30

"Cyclopean Symphony" by David Schecter 38

Reviews 45

The Script 47

Notes on the Script by Tom Weaver 161

Fun Facts by Tom Weaver 165

Alex Gordon's "In-Depth" Interviews by Tom Weaver 176

"Here Comes Mr. Gordon" by Karen Latham Everson 191

Alex Gordon's "Regular Oldtimers": Edmund Cobb and Frank Lackteen
    by Scott Gallinghouse 196

The Pressbook 218

INTRODUCTION
By Brett Halsey

I am honored to write this introduction to a book on *The Atomic Submarine*.

This film came early in my career and gave me the opportunity to work with and learn from a group of very talented veteran filmmakers. Back in the '50s, B films were made fast, but very efficiently. I am proud to say that with good scripts, dedicated producers, writers, directors, actors and crew, we made some first-rate films that have stood the test of time.

Alex Gordon, Spencer Bennet, Arthur Franz, Dick Foran, Tom Conway, Bob Steele and Victor Varconi have each in their own way made positive contributions to my acting skills which have so far carried me through a career that has spanned over six decades.

Brett Halsey
Laguna Woods, California
January 2018

Before and after: Brett Halsey as Carl Neilsen, pacifist below the Pacific, in 1959's *The Atomic Submarine*, and in a more recent shot. He's also a novelist; his latest page-turner is *West of Hell*.

The Atomic Submarine (1959)

Released by Allied Artists in December 1959
A Gorham Production
72 minutes
Screenwriter & Associate Producer: Orville H. Hampton
Produced by Alex Gordon (In Association with Jack Rabin & Irving Block)
Directed by Spencer G. Bennet
Photography: Gilbert Warrenton
Art Directors: Don Ament & Dan Haller
Assistant to Producer: Ruth Alexander
Editor: William Austin
Production Manager: Edward Morey, Jr.
Assistant Director: Clark Paylow
Set Decorator: Harry Reif
Properties: Max Frankel
Chief Set Electrician: George Satterfield
Sound: Ralph Butler
Production Associate & Dialogue Supervisor: Jack Cash
Wardrobe: Roger J. Weinberg & Norah Sharpe
Makeup: Emile LaVigne
Script Supervisor: Judith Hart
Sound Editor: Marty Greco
Music Editor: Neil Brunnenkant
Special Effects Designed & Created by Jack Rabin, Irving Block & Louis DeWitt
Electro-Sonic Music Composed & Conducted by Alexander Laszlo
Co-Producer: Henry Schrage
Uncredited:
Additional Special Effects: Gene Warren
Saucer Monster Puppeteer: Irving Block
Keyboardist & Electronic Music: Jack Cookerly
Violinist: Elliot Fisher
Poster Artist: Reynold Brown
Per Alex Gordon:
Story Idea: Ruth Alexander, Jack Rabin & Irving Block
Script Input: Alex Gordon
Variety **"Assignments" List, June 19, 1959:**
Assistant Director: Arthur Broidy
Camera Operator: Arthur Lane
Grip: Harry Lewis
Special Effects: Milt Olson

Arthur Franz (*Lt. Comdr. Richard "Reef" Holloway*)
Dick Foran (*Comdr. Dan Wendover*)
Brett Halsey (*Dr. Carl Neilsen*)
Paul Dubov (*Lt. Dave Milburn*)
Bob Steele (*Chief Griffin ["Griff"]*)
Victor Varconi (*Dr. Clifford Kent*)
Joi Lansing (*Julie*)
Selmer Jackson (*Admiral Terhune*)
Jack Mulhall (*Secretary of Defense Justin Murdock*)
Jean Moorhead (*Helen Milburn*)
Richard Tyler (*Don Carney*)
Sid Melton (*Yeoman Chester Tuttle*)
Ken Becker (*Seaman First Class Al Powell*)
Frank Watkins (*Watkins—TV Screen Operator*)
Pat Michaels (*Narrator*)
John Hilliard (*Voice of Saucer Monster*)
And
Tom Conway as *Sir Ian Hunt*
Uncredited:
Everett Creach (*Seaman*)
Edmund Cobb, Frank Lackteen (*Navy Yard Passersby*)

Synopsis

The film is set in the near-future (post-1959) when passenger- and cargo-carrying atomic submarines have established Arctic Ocean routes under the eternal ice of the North Pole. After a number of surface vessels and subs have inexplicably disappeared or been destroyed at the top of the world, Admiral Terhune of the Arctic Defense War Room assigns Commander Dan Wendover of the atomic killer sub *Tiger Shark* to hunt down the cause of these disasters.

At the Arctic Theater War Room conference, Admiral Terhune (Selmer Jackson) introduces Dan Wendover (Dick Foran), "the skipper of the killer atom sub *Tiger Shark*," in such a way that when he finishes, he seems to be expecting applause.

Atomic Submarine ... starts out like a real documentary—admiral's conference, off-screen narration, dispatching of scientists to the arctic sea lanes, to determine the cause of disaster in the polar waters. Sounds arresting, doesn't it? Pretty soon, however, the picture disintegrates into a monster movie....
—Irene Thirer, *The New York Post*

The way Dave gets away with ribbing his superior Holloway, even interfering in his love life, is reminiscent of the easy camaraderie between Kenneth Tobey and his men in *The Thing from Another World*. Maybe Dave knows, and holds over Holloway, the embarrassing story of how he got his nickname "Reef."

At the Bremerton (Washington state) Navy Yard, the *Tiger Shark* is made ready for its mission. Wendover's exec is hawkish "Reef" Holloway and the navigation officer is Dave Milburn. Passengers include Sir Ian Hunt, a Nobel Prize-winning oceanographer; Dr. Kent, one of the *Tiger Shark*'s designers, and Dr. Carl Neilsen, who with his father developed the *Lungfish*, the animated diving bell now stored in the *Tiger Shark*'s keel. Reef practically worships Carl's father, a Navy officer, and knows that Carl's peace-mongering ("Ban the atomic tests! Junk the nuclear subs!") broke the father's heart and prompted him to resign from the Navy. Reef considers Carl a coward; it doesn't take much to light his short fuse whenever Carl's around. (The two characters exchange unpleasantries throughout the movie and yet *Harrison's Reports* wrote, "Brett Halsey is strong as a pal of Franz.")

The *Tiger Shark* is played by what looks like a small children's toy and we frequently see it making its way past strange bumpy masses that are either supposed to be the bottom of the ice crust above or the tops of rock formations below; it's hard to say which, because they don't look like either. Wavy lighting represents sunlight passing through rippling water. The sub is supposed to be beneath the Arctic ice, 12 to 50 feet thick, so I don't know how all this sunlight is getting down there.

The *Tiger Shark* finds itself in an electrical storm center and takes evasive action. Sir Ian notices that every Arctic disaster and strange occurrence takes place 1000 miles from the Pole, a pattern that leads him to believe that they are motivated by some sort of intelligence.

Carl: Well, what on Earth kind of intelligence *is* it, Sir Ian?

Sir Ian: Well, perhaps it's not an intelligence on Earth. Perhaps it's an intelligence from *beyond* the Earth.

An underwater sighting of a saucer-shaped ship "with its rim lighted like a theater marquee" (*The San Diego Union*) makes it clear they're dealing with an extra-terrestrial. The saucer has a turret that they think looks like an eye (it doesn't) and it "throws thunderbolts," so the men dub it *Cyclops*. Dave wonders if this underwater flying saucer carries Little Green Men or Little Green Fish.

Somehow, but we viewers are not trusted to know how, the submariners know that *Cyclops* returns to the Pole after each attack, and they assume that's where it magnetically "recharges." When they learn the location of the newest attack, they get between that spot and the Pole and wait in ambush. Once the saucer appears, they fire "atomic fish" (torpedoes), but a jelly-like substance excreted by the saucer harmlessly "catches" one of them. At Wendover's order, the *Tiger Shark* rams the saucer, its bow piercing the saucer's underside. Locked together, the *Tiger Shark* and *Cyclops* sink to the bottom.

To extricate the sub, Reef suggests using Carl's *Lungfish* to get to the saucer, make their way inside through its "eye" and cut the *Tiger Shark* bow loose with blowtorches. The *Lungfish* sets out with Carl piloting and Reef, Dave and demolition experts Carney and Powell aboard. After it attaches itself to one of the large glassy-looking domes on *Cyclops*' turret, the men open the hatch in the floor, where now instead of the glassy dome there are saucer doors that slide open to create a round entryway. Reef, Dave, Carney and Powell enter and find themselves on elevated walkways and a ramp, completely surrounded by blackness. *Video Watchdog* called these sets "nicely expressionistic." Allied Artists probably called them "nicely economical."

Reef telepathically, the Saucer Monster says that it's been studying various solar systems for planets that can be colonized by creatures like itself – and, of course, the Earth seems "most suitable." Gun in hand, Dave boldly joins Reef at the opening, gets a gander at the one-eyed monster and plinks six bullets into it. The Saucer Monster, unfazed, burns him to death with the light. Reef shoots the monster in the eye with a flare from his Very pistol and rushes back to the *Lungfish*.

With Reef and Carl back aboard the *Tiger Shark*, it reverses engines and pulls loose of *Cyclops*. The Saucer

Every expense spared: The saucer interior is almost nothing but pitch blackness, some lighted walkways and a ramp. Since the Saucer Monster is walloping big, presumably the same size as all its folks back home, one wonders who these walkways were built for.

Between the minimalist-and-then-some sets, Alexander Laszlo's Electro-Sonic Music and the outré events that will follow, *Atomic Submarine* becomes almost dream-like and begins repaying viewer patience up to this point. Carney and Powell start their blowtorch work on the *Tiger Shark* bow while Reef and Dave go off to investigate a commanding voice that only Reef can hear. The atmosphere of the place (or *some*thing) begins to tell on Powell, who abandons his post and starts heading for the egress. Suddenly he is enveloped in a bright light that burns him. Writhing in pain, he hollers for Carney, who comes running; by the time Carney arrives, Powell is fried to a crisp. Carney panics and tries to escape but is caught and crushed by closing saucer doors.

Leaving Dave behind, Reef walks along a walkway to an opening in an enormous sphere and peers in. Within, he sees the saucer's occupant, a giant space creature with restless tentacles at its base, a column-like neck that'd be the pride of any giraffe and, instead of a face, an enormous staring eye that flashes off and on. "Talking" to

Monster reconstitutes its own eye and the saucer takes off like a shot toward the Pole, to recharge and then return to space. Racing against time, Sir Ian and Dr. Kent convert a ballistic rocket into a water-to-air interceptor missile; the *Tiger Shark* finds a hole in the ice crust and awaits *Cyclops*' departure. When the saucer surges up through the crust in preparation for lift-off, Wendover orders the firing of the rocket. After many tense seconds, the missile overtakes the swiftly rising saucer and explodes; ferociously flaming, the saucer drops back to earth. In his script, Orville H. Hampton described this scene as "the 'money' shot – to make or break the picture." The scene does carry a touch of suspense and I'd vote that it "makes" the picture.

Back at the Navy Yard, Reef and Carl, now buds, look up into the night sky, filled with stars of tropical brightness, and wonder which one they have to worry about – will the aliens return? Reef assures Carl that, if they do, they'll get a rough reception.

Disparate Chintz: The Jois of The Atomic Submarine

By Richard Heft

Towards the end of *The Atomic Submarine*, Victor Varconi announces that they must take "one lahst disparate chintz" to kill off the underwater flying saucer that has been their Nemesis for better than a month. In this essay, I plan to examine a few disparate strands of the chintz that is director Spencer Gordon Bennet's finest (?) hour.

Mind you, if you have a deep, overpowering affection for this movie, you are almost certainly (in the words of Commander Reef Holloway) a *mixed-up oddball*, and likely to remain so. I have seen this movie maybe 15 times, always in some state of glee, I have a poster of it on the wall of my house, and I have personally thanked producer Alex Gordon and actor Brett Halsey for their contributions to the aesthetic of the cinema and the safety of the universe. So I'll do what I can to point out the sights to my fellow mixed-up oddballs, even though I didn't win the Nobel Prize for Oceanography like some people.

If you view *Atomic Submarine* for the first time in your life, and the year is 2018, well… sorry, it just sucks to be you, doesn't it? Because if you're a grown-up, *Atomic Submarine* is pretty much rubbish. Cheap sets, leaden script, actors who seem to have staggered half-dead out of an AA meeting and stumbled into their khakis, one guy's allegedly cut in half by a piece of wobbly cardboard that another guy holds open with no trouble, "*My kid can make a better movie than this!*" you'll holler at the screen in impotent fury.

So, what's the case for the defense? Could Perry Mason get the filmmakers off on a double charge of artistic murder and grand theft of 72 minutes of other people's lives? First, you need to get unstuck in time.

Broadly speaking, if you're under 15 years old, there are two kinds of movies: movies for kids and movies for grown-ups. You always can tell the two apart. In movies for grown-ups, adults stand around, drink, smoke, engage in drab conversations about relationships that go on and on and on, they stand and yak their guts out. Grown-up movies tend to have dull actors who loudly proclaim a zero-fun zone, then inhabit that zone with a *thud*: Gregory Peck, Ronald Reagan, Rock Hudson, whoever, he'll stand earnestly in front of some damn picture window and *demand to know, dammit*, if some Hollywood whore's love will last a lifetime. Then he

"U a friend or UFO?": Reef Holloway Meets the Spacemonster. Notice that the wall of the Saucer Monster's sphere looks membranous.

looks away from the window and glumly sees that Ava Gardner is off screwing the director of photography, and he'll have to marry Celeste Holm. Makes you want to stay a kid forever, if all life has to offer is crap like that.

Movies for kids, however, are a whole 'nother story. The producers have vaguely figured out that kids are a tough audience and demand results. Or if not results, dinosaurs, and lots of them. Vampires, werewolves, death rays, alligator pits and alligator people, voodoo, Italian musclemen, rock people, brain eaters, haunted houses, giant insects, sea creatures with attitude problems, and if you get very lucky, Abbott and Costello. If you see a picture window, there's a giant locust outside it, and it wants to eat your mom. These are the hallmarks of a kid's movie: a kick-ass plot where civilization is in serious jeopardy and a Large Monstrosity is about to triumph over sniveling, pathetically tiny Humanity.

The Atomic Submarine, with all due respect to its flaws, gets the fucking job done. It's set in a wild, lonely place where your dad won't yell at you because your chores aren't finished and you better eat your green beans tonight. Under the North Pole ice cap is where nobody the hell ever visits, except those poor bastards on the *Tiger Shark*, and they're stuck there for a solid hour-twelve. *Something* is down there blowing up submarines, and a pack of leathery character actors has been assembled to settle the score. If cinema history teaches us anything, it teaches us to trust leathery character actors. There are grown men, heading towards senility, who have spent their entire lives believing that long-dead Morris Ankrum is running the American military, and I am proud to be numbered among them.

And the telepathic One-Bug-Eyed Monster who regrows his own eye! Hide behind the sofa *now*, before it sees you! Too late, punk, Cyclops sees everything, and

Polar opposites! Reef (Arthur Franz) has a lot of hard bark on him, and a lot of hard barking *in* him, and regularly lays into the pouty Carl (Brett Halsey).

after it reduces Arthur Franz to a bubbling pile of irradiated ham, it'll come for your dog!

But in order to share the joy, you have to make that imaginative voyage in time – not so much back to 1959, the year the film was copyrighted, but back in emotional time, before the VHS and the DVD, before Netflix, back when crappity-ass sci-fi movies were seen on weekend afternoons (preferably with a cold bottle of Orange Crush in your mitt), while your parents did Parent Stuff in another room, and other kids all over the megalopolis watched silently in communion with you. If you can't make that emotional voyage and strip away the barnacles of the last few decades and slide back into that room with the shag rug and the faux wood paneling and the rabbit-eared black-and-white TV set, the joys of *Atomic Submarine* may be elusive indeed.

Okay, there's the case for the defense. Whatever we all mean by that ambiguous word "compelling" (it's like pornography, we know it when we see it), *Atomic Submarine* always compels; Bennet's favorite bit of blocking is to have five humorless guys standing in a row, watching their "visio radarscopes," and the sight of those geezers fretting silently always gets me where I live.

The case for the prosecution is there to be made as well, and since I'm an even-handed geek, let's go down the line and pick out a few offenders.

I'll start by pointing out one moment of cringeworthy embarrassment: when Arthur Franz effectively genuflects, kisses the fingers of screenwriter Orville Hampton, and proclaims that Halsey's shopworn anti-war foolosophizing is "even brilliant." Stop that, Orville. Just stop.

Fortunately, Hampton pivots and gives us the genuinely jaw-dropping "These are my work clothes" address to the Spineless Intellectual (like the Creature, they walk among us), a speech that might have made Luis Buñuel smile in curdled pleasure and wish that ants were crawling out of Reef Holloway's nose.

And while I'm bonking Hampton's head against a metaphoric wall, I'll point out that I'm now 61 years old and I'm in no danger whatsoever of setting foot on a passenger-carrying sub-polar atomic submarine! What are the initials of the man who promised us that yearned-for advance in cruise-ship technology? OHH!

Arthur Franz's performance is much attacked, and I'll add a few points to the anti-Franzian chorus. He evidently decided that Reef Holloway was a truculent dullard and played him that way throughout; there's some evidence that Franz was not dissimilar from Reef, and many people perhaps sighed happily when he abandoned Hollywood and moved to a sheep farm in New Zealand. The Unabomber would have done the same if he'd had the money.

Reef's effort to seduce Joi Lansing seems halfhearted (and you call yourself an *actor*, Arthur!), but once he shakes off that gloomy mask of lechery (it's not his style), he's in full speechifying mode, denouncing Carl Neilsen with remarkably slender evidence. (If Carl's dear old dad chucked in his Navy career because Carl couldn't keep his mushy liberal mouth shut, how did we ever win World War II?) Franz is grim company throughout, but there's a well-buried joke in his character arc. While Reef is clearly proud of the *Tiger Shark*'s ability to project power well beyond the continental limits of the U.S.A., he meets his opposite number in Cyclops – an interstellar imperialist who wants to colonize Earth – and *does not like him!* Arthur actually has a grace note at the tail end of the movie: After the saucer explodes and Dick Foran announces via the squawk box, "We got him," Franz sags into a chair, radiating exhaustion and *surprise* as the adrenaline visibly drains away. Nice moment, Arthur.

Victor Varconi plays the curiously named "Clifford Kent," when he's clearly from behind the Iron Curtain, should be named Dr. Hans-Karl Gustavhousen, and might as well have **INTERNATIONAL SPY** tattooed across his forehead. For some reason known only to Orville Hampton, Reef Holloway, who can smell a traitor from 30 feet out, never seizes the opportunity to slam Cliff the Commie against a bulkhead and whale the truth out of him. Maybe that scene was cut; Varconi has a good-sized lump on one side of his forehead..

It's hard to explain this, but while watching *Atomic Submarine*, it's possible to simultaneously think "Tom Conway really classes up this joint" and "That poor rummy!" It's also possible to watch *Atomic Submarine* and muse aloud if Dick Foran talked out of the side of his mouth because his paycheck was too tiny and Dick only wanted to put on half a show for cheapshit Allied Artists. The other hypothesis is, Dick talked only out of the left side of his mouth in order to counter the right-wing tilt of the project. Man, I'm giving Dick Foran credit for subtlety here!

[This paragraph was going to be a bunch of mean-spirited, bitter wisecracks about one of the minor players in *Atomic Submarine* – but Saintly Tom Weaver talked me out of it, so that skipload of manure I was gonna dump on poor Sid Melton's grave will go on my front lawn instead.]

Balancing off this parade of aging men whose careers have been shattered against the jagged Reefs of Holloway, I mean Hollywood (sorry, just impossible to resist), is the lubricious fertility of Joi Lansing, who is forever young (though just a bit puffy-faced here). As a pre-teen, of course, I considered her scene the Predestined Mushy Stuff that had to be brushed aside in order to get underway for the frigid Arctic. Now, however, she gives the somewhat homoerotic core text of *Atomic Submarine* something it badly needs: an Atomic Blonde with a great rack. Her scene is abominably written and stiffly acted, but I love the rearing stallion behind the couch, proof positive that someone in the art department had a sense of humor.

Another unique pleasure to be had: Some people believe that a voiceover narrator should be warm, wry, human, omniscient but compassionate, Mason Adams selling us a load of Smucker's. Well, fuck that, the rest of us want to hear the Lord God Jehovah roaring **Doom** down on our sorry heads, and *The Atomic Submarine* gives us two such voices, alas, neither of them belonging to the Doomster himself, Art Gilmore. Pat Michaels does a better-than-capable job of delivering such gems as "It was foolish, it was insane, it was fantastic." But John Hilliard is magisterial as the snottily disdainful Cyclops voice, and his contempt for humanity is so full of priss and vinegar that his performance livens up the third act immeasurably. *Of course*!

In summation: This is the kind of movie that Katharine Hepburn would only make in Hell – and one can hope that in some tatty corner of Satan's busy Inferno, Kate and Arthur and Joi and Spencer are furiously sweating away on some half-assed set, spending eternity on the never-ending production of *Atomic Submarine II: I Have Returned, Commander*. (I'd actually go and see that movie. If you bought this book, you'd be sitting in the same row.)

Cyclops pushes its way up through the polar crust of ice and prepares for blast-off.

This book is a rearguard action, of course, a desperate effort to stop the remorseless forward drive of popular culture, to force the Cyclops to look backward over its shoulder and gaze with wistful delight at the drifting *Tiger Shark* and its inhabitants, most of them dead now. (As of this writing, Brett Halsey still lives! To God, there is no zero!) Eventually, the collective American esthetic, whatever it may become, will regard *Atomic Submarine* with the same bored disinterest it now gives to *The Avenging Conscience* and *The Battle at Elderbush Gulch*. And what will devotees of *The Atomic Submarine* (if any are left) say on that dreadful day? "*Fortunes of war!*"

The Atomic Submarine Production History

By Tom Weaver

When I was a kid and *The Atomic Submarine* was a staple in the lineup of local New York TV's monster movie showcases, I wondered why the title didn't reference the movie's flying saucer (*floating* saucer?) or its Kong-sized one-eyed space monster. The explanation, I decided (with nothing to back it up of course), was that the first atomic submarine must have been hot off the assembly line in 1960 when the movie was new – or possibly still a thing of the future – and that therefore, the title *The Atomic Submarine* once had all the excitement and science fiction flavor the doctor ordered.

Wrong! Turns out that the first atomic submarine, the *Nautilus*, set sail in 1954 ... after its construction had been extensively covered in the press since *1951*. And there'd been talk of harnessing the atom to drive undersea vessels since *1945*, the year America unleashed its atomic bull and Japan got the horns. Going back even further, a nuclear power research group was supposedly organized by the naval research laboratory in 1940. It's amusing to consider that among the U.S. naval personnel predicting atom subs in the '40s were men (Admiral Chester Nimitz, for one) who were born and grew up in the 1800s! So much for atom subs being a new concept in the 1960s.

Gone Fission!

At the close of World War II, there were those who felt that that global conflict had been a war of scientists, and a feeling that all subsequent wars surely *would* be. U.S. scientists had prevailed in World War II; would that be the case in the future? In November 1945, Harvey Hayes, a civilian scientist with the U.S. Navy Department, appeared before a group of Rotarians and predicted ... with admirable accuracy ... that it would probably be just seven or eight years (i.e., 1952 or 1953) before submarines were operated by atomic energy. According to the newspaper *The Binghamton Press*, Hayes foresaw atom subs reaching speeds of 50 knots an hour underwater, more than 11 times the present (1945) underwater speed of submarine raiders. "It looks as though the navy is being driven under the water," Hayes told a Rotarian who had asked about atomic energy and submarine warfare. "When that time comes, we probably will have developed an atomic bomb for fighting atomic submarines. Such bombs naturally would have to be dropped from the air because no ship could drop them and get away fast enough to escape destruction."

The following March, at a joint air defense conference in Washington D.C., Vice Admiral Arthur W. Radford said that submarine aircraft carriers, atomically powered and capable of remaining underwater for months, were a possibility. May 1946 news items revealed that Admiral Nimitz was predicting that within months, there would be "super-submarines" equipped to fire rockets with atomic-bomb warheads. According to one press item, "Gas-turbine engines and atomic power, our Navy predicts, may enable submarines to replace surface ships for bombarding distant targets, pinpoint shelling and covering troop landings." In 1947, Charles Andrew Lockwood Jr., former submarine force commander for the Pacific fleet, said that the first nation to develop an atomic submarine would be in the best position to win the next war.

In November 1947, another vice admiral made a speech about the Navy's research into atomic submarine propulsion. According to newspaper columnist Henry McLemore, this admiral "did everything but reveal the blueprints of the project." With annoyance – and humor – McLemore ranted in his column that he someday planned to find out why the U.S. government routinely revealed its military secrets to the world. "I am not quite sure just who I will interview for this information, but I am inclined to believe my final choice will be a circus pinhead, as I feel that no normal man could possibly give me the answer." He continued:

Atoms aweigh! The *Nautilus* was considered "the first constructive use" that knowledge of the atom had been put to, all previous efforts having been dedicated to destruction.

It seems to me that someone should tell our military that Russia, although not nearly as rich as the U.S., still has enough money to buy a few American papers each day and thereby find out what we are doing in the way of preparing for another war. …I may be crazy but I believe that Russia's secrecy makes sense. Why let a potential enemy know what you are doing and give him the chance of either being a copy-cat or concocting an antidote?

What makes the whole thing even sillier is the fool secrecy which the military clamps on minor matters. …I would be willing to bet that while the Navy blabbers about the atomic submarine, if you went to Washington and tried to find the average girdle size of the WAVES you would be told that such information was restricted or secret.

…What is the use of screening Washington for Communists if everything that matters in a military way is given to the world in press releases and speeches? Why not let the samovar boys have to work to get the information? Russia wouldn't even let us in on the secret if one of their bearded scientists invented a new and deadlier fly swatter. Russia works on the theory that when war comes, it isn't a bad idea to have a few tricks up your sleeve.

Of course the government announcements kept coming, including a 1948 preview of a future in which a submarine, underwater, could fire rockets that would "leap into the air and roar skyward," as in *Atomic Submarine*'s finale. Newspaper readers must have thought a certain Jules Verne tale was on the verge of coming to life as they learned that, in addition to setting record speeds, atomic submarines would have unlimited underwater range and descend to greater depth; they could *stay* down longer; and they could run "virtually forever" without refueling.

In June 1952 when construction of the *Nautilus* began at the Electric Boat division of General Dynamics Corp. in Groton, Connecticut, there was a ceremony where speaker President Harry Truman said the vessel would be "a working power plant for peace." And it *was* intended as such, if by "power plant for peace" you mean pitiless killer sub. The public probably already knew or at least sensed this: A United Press story from November 1950 promised in its lead paragraph, "The atomic-powered submarine of the future will be a wolf of the seas that can prowl at great distances after its prey rather than wait like a spider for a victim to approach." Charles A. Lockwood, who directed Dubya Dubya Two's underwater war against Japan, called the atom sub the "deadliest underwater killer ever conceived." The service publication *All Hands* added a touch of humor, pointing out that atom subs would go farther and stay submerged longer, then adding, "This would make for happy hunting."

But even if the *Nautilus could* stay in Davy Jones' Locker indefinitely, could the members of its crew? The human factor was the subject of a September 1952 United Press article ("Navy's 'Supermen' Recruited for New Atomic Submarine") which revealed that men were already being secretly prepared, "with the most thorough training in naval history," for their days and nights – and weeks and months – aboard her. Since no craft can be stronger than her crew, in January 1953 the length of time that men could stand the strain of underwater duty without relief was tested in New London, Connecticut: Two dozen volunteers were sealed aboard the submarine *Haddock* (tied to a wharf, not submerged). The men performed atom sub duties and spent their time off watching TV, listening to the radio and "eating well." At the end of two months bottled up, the experiment (called Operation Hideout) came to an end. An Associated Press story compared the men emerging from the sub to "bears after hibernation, [hunting] the pale spring sun."

There was talk of a *super* atomic submarine in the summer of 1953, the Navy proposing a craft twice as large as the still-under-construction *Nautilus* and the *Seawolf* (a sister ship, similar in

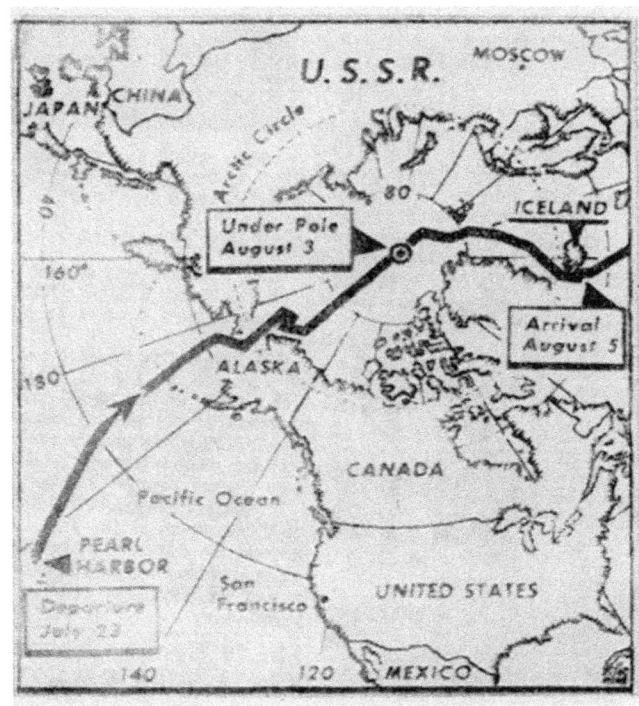

This map showing the under-the-North-Pole route of the *Nautilus* appeared in August 1958 newspapers.

design to the *Nautilus* but with a different type of atomic engine). But there was instant blowback within Navy submarine circles, as some felt that a sub that size would be a sitting duck for enemy attack. Twenty-first century Monster Kids will no doubt think of *Atomic Submarine* when reading breathless 1950s newspaper items that reported that the *Nautilus* would be able to use sonar to probe under the masses of icebergs and thick ice fields that make

FLOTUS Mamie Eisenhower christened the *Nautilus* and then she (the *Nautilus*, not Mamie) slid down into the Thames River. When her rudder fin touched the water, atomic power came of age: the world's first use of nuclear fission for propulsion.

up the frozen sea at the northern top of the world. In a preview of the coming U.S.-Russia "space race," lawmakers alluded to the possibility of a race between the two countries to develop the first atomic-powered sub.

> Who knows if, in another 100 years, we may not see a second *Nautilus*? – Capt. Nemo in *Twenty Thousand Leagues Under the Sea*

According to Brett Halsey, Alex Gordon (seen here in a mid-1950s photo) "wasn't a producer per se on the set [of *Atomic Submarine*], he was more like a cheerleader. He was encouraging and helpful, always had a smile. Always projected a positive-ness that was catching. Everybody liked to be around Alex."

Nemo was close with that prediction. *Twenty Thousand Leagues* was first published as a magazine serial in 1869; the U.S.S. *Nautilus* was launched 85 years later, on January 21, 1954, at the Electric Boat Yard in Groton. Twenty thousand people – one for each of Jules Verne's leagues – were on hand that misty New England morning as First Lady Mamie Eisenhower shattered the traditional bottle of champagne across her bow (see photo on previous page).

Enter Alex Gordon

Look up Alex Gordon in any of the books and you'll find him listed as a movie producer. But producing 18 movies in the period 1952-65 seems like a minor accomplishment alongside the nearly 75 years he devoted to being an all-in movie *fan*. Alex wrote in the January 28, 1959, *Variety*:

> Being born [in London] in 1922 I saw my first movie in 1928 (Mr. and Mrs. Martin Johnson's *Simba*). Since then, I have kept a complete record of every feature picture I have ever seen, and the grand total as of Dec. 31, 1958, is 20,072, which includes serials (each complete serial counted as one feature). My average has been 724 pictures a year, which included screenings of 35mm and 16mm prints of old silent and talking pictures I had missed or which were produced before 1928.
>
> When I finally left a movie theater long enough to get married in 1957, my wife luckily turned out to be a movie enthusiast too, although I had to "educate" her to westerns and serials as she preferred dramas and sophisticated comedies.
>
> We still see an average of 15 features every week, which includes approximately 10 in theaters and five or six on the late television shows.
>
> My all-time record for one month is 159 features (in November 1947, my first month in the U.S.A.) when I had a lot of catching up to do in 42nd Street, New York, on pictures I had missed during the war, mainly westerns and all-night movies which were not shown in England at the time.
>
> I used to travel well over 100 miles every week to see the westerns of Gene Autry and Buck Jones, which were rarely shown in London's larger theaters, and often waited in line, sometimes three hours, to see them. During my five years in the British Army, while stationed in England, I managed to time my 24-hour furloughs to travel up to London and catch the trade-shows of these westerns.
>
> …My greatest delight in now being a producer is to be able to use in my pictures many of the wonderful character actors I have always admired in movies when I was just a plain movie fan.

Samuel Z. Arkoff was president and Gordon vice-president of Golden State Productions, which made movies for American International release. For the first several years, Golden State served up low-budget Westerns, teenage exploitation, melodramas and monster flicks; in the latter category were *Day the World Ended* (1956), an early AIP hit, plus *The She-Creature* (1956)

Alex with Lloyd Bridges, the star of his first AIP Western, *Apache Woman* (1955).

and *Voodoo Woman* (1957). Right from the start of his producing career, Gordon looked to stock his casts with many of the players whose work he'd enjoyed in vintage films – often in small, unbilled parts but sometimes, to Arkoff's dismay, in major roles. Arkoff felt, and he was probably right, that these people couldn't draw a dollar with a green crayon. *Variety* (May 18, 1956) carried a press squib about the casting of his upcoming *The She-Creature*, "Producer Alex Gordon Reverses 'New Faces' Trend in Film Talent":

> While most film producers are on a "new faces" kick, indie producer Alex Gordon has decided to reverse the gears.
>
> Yesterday he cast seven silent film stars to essay roles of society people in the Golden State production *The She-Creature*. Vets include May McAvoy, Snub Pollard, Barry Norton, Franklyn Farnum, Eva Novak, Bess Flowers and Stuart Holmes.

In addition to these folks who had disappeared from movie history, Gordon had Chester Morris in the *She-Creature* lead, Tom Conway in a top role, past-her-prime leading lady Cathy Downs as the second female lead, plus such old soldiers as Frieda Inescort, Frank Jenks, El Brendel and his wife Flo Bert, Jack Mulhall, Edward Earle, Edmund Cobb and more. AIP had its eye on the teen market and yet Gordon was hiring players who might not be familiar to the average teen's *parents* (Edward Earle was crowned King of the Movies in a contest in *1922!*). Watching some of these actors in Gordon's pictures is like catching a glimpse beyond the veil. In 1987, when I talked to Arkoff about Gordon's loyalty to players out of the Silver Screen Trivial Pursuit "Older Than Dirt" edition, I sensed that he was still bristling, three decades after the fact, about some of Alex's casting choices:

> Well, for Christ's sake, Alex loved old actors – he used to drag these old actors around, and I sometimes thought he went out to the graveyards to find 'em! …I wasn't against them, I just was against building a picture around 'em. Let me give you an example: When he brought around Anna Sten and used her in a movie called *Runaway Daughters* [1956], he thought that was a great coup. I thought it was a *coup de grace*! She meant nothing – nobody in the fornicating audience had the slightest idea of who Anna Sten was! …He also used to bring Raymond Hatton around a lot. Well, I remembered Raymond Hatton, he used to play in pictures with Wallace Beery. But at that point the young audience didn't even know who Wallace Beery was, and *he* was the *big* star!
>
> I had nothing against oldtime actors; if Alex wanted to put an older actor into a role, fine, but don't try to base your pictures on them, particularly when you're trying to go for a young audience. I am not ashamed to say that I didn't want to play to empty theaters.

In 1957, Golden State added war movies to their lineup starting with *Jet Attack*, a Korean War action drama scripted by Golden State first-timer Orville H. Hampton. Truth be told, there *wasn't* a lot of action, unless you count behind-the-scenes: This was the movie where Gordon and Arkoff's differences over older actors reached the flashpoint level. According to Mark Thomas McGee's book *Faster and Furiouser*, Gordon found that he could hire Audrey Totter for the female lead for $3000 a week, a good price considering the caliber of movies she made in the '40s at MGM, Warners

Alex with "AIP's Elizabeth Taylor," actress Marla English. She toplined Alex's *The She-Creature*, *Runaway Daughters* and *Voodoo Woman*.

and other studios. "Anybody *but* Audrey Totter," Arkoff decreed. Gordon went behind Arkoff's back and signed her anyway, and told this to Arkoff while they (and others) were walking from a restaurant back to AIP's offices. Gordon recalled:

> He got furious and he shoved me and the next thing I knew I was on the ground. I wasn't hurt really. I was more shocked than anything. I got up and without saying anything I went to my office. …Then Arkoff came in and he apologized. He said, "I know I shouldn't have hit you but sometimes you make me so goddamn mad." And I said, "But Sam, over Audrey Totter?"

For months, Golden State's upcoming picture *Submarine Seahawk* (originally titled *Submarine X2*) was occasionally mentioned in the Hollywood trade papers. The July 21, 1958, *Variety* carried the news that AIP president James H. Nicholson and his veep Arkoff were giving this Gordon production the highest budget in the firm's history, $275,000.

Just two days later, in the pre-dawn hours of July 23, an event of historical importance took place: The *Nautilus* left the Pearl Harbor naval base surrounded by as much secrecy as water, sailing "up toward the rolling, grinding fringe of pack ice in the Arctic – and then on under it" (Associated Press). The thickness of the polar ice above averaged about 12 feet, but in some places it was more than 50 feet. As indicated by the map on page 11, the *Nautilus*' subsurface voyage took it from the Pacific to the Atlantic, and then down between Greenland and Iceland. There a helicopter picked up skipper William R. Anderson, who planed to Washington D.C. and had a Legion of Merit pinned to his coat by President Dwight D. Eisenhower; the *Nautilus*' 116-man crew received a presidential unit citation. The story of the *Nautilus*' pioneering journey, accompanied by photos of Anderson receiving his medal, appeared "above the fold" in newspapers across the country on August 9. The abovementioned AP story speculated that this submarine feat was "counterfire to the propaganda Russia made of her victory in launching the first Sputnik," and pointed out:

> [W]hile President Eisenhower oriented his remarks to the peaceful possibilities of the route, it remains a fact that the *Nautilus* is a combat vessel.
>
> If she can roam under the polar ice, so can the ballistic missile-firing Polaris submarines now building.

According to another contemporary news story, the *Nautilus*' historic cruise "means that deadly, missile-carrying nuclear subs can be switched strategically between the two oceans in less than half the time formerly required." And, returning to Sputnik, it pointed out, "[S]ome sources saw the U.S. leadership in nuclear submersibles as offsetting the psychological and military threats posed by Russia's present advantages in the satellite-missile field." (In August 1959, the U.S. had six nuclear subs built, 13 under construction and seven more authorized. Russia: goose egg.)

Alex Gordon was a fan of submarine movies, and on the verge of making one with a World War II setting: Golden State's *Submarine Seahawk*. Then on August 12, just three days after the story of the *Nautilus*' epic under-ice voyage was front-page news, *The Hollywood Reporter* announced that Gordon was planning a feature about it and had registered the title *Atomic Submarine*. Additionally, he had arranged for the special effects and miniatures to be done by Jack Rabin, Irving Block and Louis DeWitt, who would act as co-producers.

"I forget now how I first met Rabin and Block—I think they came to me, because I was identified with some special effects pictures," Gordon told me in 2002. "They said they had an idea of a combination of a submarine picture and a horror picture. So we were discussing it, and they said that they would come in for a very good price and do a lot of special effects on deferment and so on." I asked Gordon if Rabin and Block had an actual storyline, on paper, at their first meeting, and he recalled,

> They *did* have sort of a very rough outline of what they had in mind, about some underwater monster-creature-alien, an atomic submarine and so on, but they didn't have it in script form or anything like that. Their idea was submitted to us in person, they didn't have an agent, they were their own representatives. But Hampton and I had already thought of making a science fiction-horror atomic submarine picture, because with that and *The Beetle* [a *Them!*-inspired movie about a giant beetle, scripted by Hampton, never made], we figured we'd have two horror pictures. So Rabin and Block had just the basic idea of some kind of an alien creature, and they felt they could do a good job on doing miniatures on that. Hampton agreed with that idea and then *he* put both ideas together and wrote the script, with my input.

When I interviewed Gordon on the audio commentary track of the *Atomic Submarine* DVD (Criterion, 2007), he remembered the chain of events slightly differently, and added one more story contributor:

> When the *Nautilus* story broke, my wife [Ruth] suggested, "Why not *another* submarine picture, but making it *The Atomic Submarine*. And not just a straightforward, factual submarine picture again, but working in maybe a science fiction angle." I thought, "Well, *that's* a great idea, to make a science fiction-horror film." And just about that time, Jack Rabin, Irving Block and Louie DeWitt, a trio that was working on special effects for science fiction-horror films, came to me … and suggested that they had an idea for an underwater submarine horror type of

Nautilus commander W.R. Anderson shows the route the atom sub took on her first transpolar undersea voyage

Jersey Boys: A decade apart, Arthur Franz was born in Perth Amboy, New Jersey, Dick Foran in Flemington, less than an hour away.

> picture, with an alien creature that did not work from above the Earth, but below the ocean, as a different kind of a gimmick for a horror film. I thought that was a great idea. And Orville Hampton, who was quite an experienced writer of low-budget pictures, I talked to him about

this idea and he thought it was excellent and said that he would whip up a script on spec that we could submit to possible distribution companies, releasing outlets and so on, and see if we could set this up. So he knocked it out pretty fast, with some input from Rabin and Block....

Gordon's input included naming the title submarine *Tiger Shark*. This was a nod to one of his favorite movies, the 1932 Edward G. Robinson picture of that same name, and to the mysterious villain in the 1935 Mascot serial *The Fighting Marines*.

If Gordon was right about his wife Ruth's suggestion of an atom sub-sci-fi-horror picture being inspired by the news of the *Nautilus*' submerged sea voyage, then everything must have happened *very* quickly. As mentioned above, the *Nautilus* story broke on August 9, 1958, and by August 12 *The Hollywood Reporter* was reporting that Gordon had already registered the title *The Atomic Submarine*.

Orville H. Hampton doesn't mention Rabin *or* Block *or* Mrs. Gordon in his *Fangoria* #154 account of his contributions to the picture. What he recalled for interviewer Christopher Koetting:

> I went down to the naval base at San Diego and talked to a crew about the ins and outs of the new hi-tech subs. All the "fantastic" ideas [in the *Atomic* script] came from that and stuff I read. But it was reading about flying saucer sightings that gave me the angle for the picture. In all the articles, there weren't any UFO landings. So I asked myself, "Why don't we see them land? If they're all out there being sighted, then where do they go?" Since I was doing a lot of scuba diving in those days—I had the first scuba rig manufactured in the U.S.—I came up with the idea that they were based underwater: Theirs was a marine world.

Hampton doubled-down on his contention that *he* dreamed up Unidentified *Floating* Objects when he added, "[*The Atomic Submarine*] must've struck a chord—30 years later they stole **my idea** for *The Abyss!*"

Born in 1917, a product of Rockford, Illinois, Hampton had his first "show biz" experiences in the Army during World War II, when he wrote and staged shows to entertain the troops. After his discharge, he beelined to Hollywood and wrote scripts on spec until he got a job with indie producer Robert L. Lippert (writing scripts and working as a story editor and script supervisor). On-screen in Lippert's *Rocketship X-M* (1950), he gets an "Additional Dialogue" credit, but he told Koetting that his contribution was much more: He claimed that, from "the bones" of "an absolutely unshootable script," he drafted an entirely new one, but at producer-director Kurt Neumann's request, he let Neumann have sole screen credit for the script. Again per Hampton, he did much rewriting of the script of *Lost Continent* (1951) during production. Just some of Hampton's other genre credits: *The Alligator People* (1959) for Lippert and *The Four Skulls of Jonathan Drake* (1959), *The Flight That Disappeared* (1961), *Jack the Giant Killer* (1962) and *Beauty and the Beast* (1962) for producer Edward Small. For Alex Gordon, Hampton had already written *Jet Attack* and *Submarine Seahawk*. In the credits of movies he didn't think would be up to snuff, Hampton used his *nom de shame* Owen Harris. For the interracial marriage drama *One Potato, Two Potato* (1964), he and co-writer Raphael Hayes received an Academy Award nomination. "I bet I've written more pictures than I've actually seen," Hampton joshed (?) to Paul Woodbine, who interviewed him for *Filmfax* magazine. He died in 1997.

An August 14, 1958, *Variety* item included a list of movies Alex Gordon was planning for the future: *The FBI's War Against Crime*, screenplayed by Gordon and Mildred Gordon, and Edgar Allan Poe's *Mask* [*sic*] *of the Red Death* would both be produced under his independent banner. The squib went on to mention that he was currently prepping *Atomic Submarine Attack* [*sic*], "yarn based on the historic voyage of the *Nautilus*." The next day's *Variety* mentioned in the front-page blurb "Polar Pix Planned" that producer Charles H. Schneer was also looking to cash in on the history-making news written by the *Nautilus* and had registered with the MPAA the titles *Beneath the North Pole*, *The First Passage Under the North Pole* and *Under the Arctic Ice*.

> What, no *I Was a Teen-ager Under the Arctic Ice*?
> —columnist Erskine Johnson, September 2, 1958

Submarine Seahawk went before the cameras on October 9, 1958. Gordon's last Golden State production was also one of his best, production-wise, with former stuntman, now veteran director Spencer Gordon Bennet at the helm (pardon the pun) and special effects stock footage from two old Warner Brothers pictures adding excitement. (In one interview, Gordon told me the two pictures were *Air Force* and *Destination Tokyo* [both 1943]; in another interview, he said they were *Destination Tokyo* and *Action in the North Atlantic*, also 1943.)

Set late in World War II, *Submarine Seahawk* logs the aquatic exploits of the "pigboat" *Seahawk*. Captained by the aloof and unpopular John Bentley, staunch Paul

AIP claimed that *Submarine Seahawk* was budgeted at $275,000. For the company's sake, let's hope they were fibbing (which they surely were): As of April 1972, *Seahawk* showed a cumulative gross of $253,000.

Atomic Submarine director Spencer G. Bennet in a gag shot from the Republic Serial Factory, probably 1943 or '44: Cliffhanger writers Royal Cole and Ronald Davidson show Bennet (upside down in chair) how they want a fight scene done. Associate producer W.J. O'Sullivan is the mortified onlooker.

ALEX GORDON PRODUCTIONS

In Release
"SUBMARINE SEAHAWK"

In Preparation
"ATOMIC SUBMARINE"
Screenplay by Orville H. Hampton

"WAR AGAINST CRIME"
Screenplay by The Gordons

Edgar Allan Poe's
"MASK OF THE RED DEATH"
Adapted for the screen by Ruth Alexander
Screenplay by The Gordons

An ad from the February 16, 1959, issue of *Boxoffice*.

Maxwell and inexperienced operations officer Brett Halsey, the *Seahawk* scours the seas in search of a secret reserve force of Japanese warships. Itching for action, neurotic Halsey cannot accept the fact that theirs is a reconnaissance mission with no opportunity for combat. He vents his frustration by criticizing the captain; he maintains that the captain is scared (so that no one will think that he, Halsey, is). As the *Seahawk* stealthily approaches the Jap task force, Halsey cracks under the strain and forcibly takes command of the conning tower in a scene rightly described by *Variety*'s Powe as "strongly incredible." He's pacified by Bentley, sedated and placed under guard. In the rousing finale, a waiting U.S. task force, alerted to the warships' position by the *Seahawk*, moves in and deals a devastating blow to Japanese sea strength.

When I did an on-camera interview with Brett Halsey for Criterion's *Atomic Submarine* DVD, he said of his *Submarine Seahawk-Atomic Submarine* director Bennet, "He was very, very efficient. He was a friendly man, but he wasn't 'one of the guys.' He was too busy thinking of the next shot. When you shoot a feature in six days, you have no time for horsing around."

From the October 20, 1958, *Variety*:

> *The Beetle*, science fiction yarn involving a maximum of special effects, will be the fourth property on indie producer Alex Gordon's film slate. Negotiations are underway for Orville Hampton to screenplay and Jack Rabin and Irving Block to create the effects, with pic expected to roll next spring on an estimated $250,000 budget.
>
> No release has been set for *Beetle* or Gordon's other three upcoming indie projects – *Atomic Submarine*, *War Against Crime* and *Mask of the Red Death*.

Toward the end of October, both *The Hollywood Reporter* and *Variety* mentioned that Gordon had moved *The Beetle*'s starting date to February 1, 1959, immediately following *The Atomic Submarine*, which was slated to roll on January 5. On December 12, 1958, the same two papers revealed that Gordon, having completed the dubbing on *Submarine Seahawk*, had ended his association with AIP, a company where he'd worked since its inception. From my 2002 Gordon interview:

> **Gordon:** [AIP was] now making deals with many other producers, and I was being sort of shoved into the background a little bit. And also, they expected *me* to come up with some of the financing for my pictures. I wasn't really in that end of it, I didn't think that I *should* be responsible for that, because AIP was putting the money that my past AIP pictures had made into pictures that I was *not* involved with.
>
> **Weaver:** Your parting of the ways with AIP wasn't 100 percent pleasant. Did you have an "I'll show them" attitude in the back of your mind when you went off on your own to make movies?
>
> **Gordon:** It wasn't really an "I'll show them" attitude, I just wanted out. And I wanted to try to do better, try to "upgrade" a little bit. At that point, the AIP experience was water under the bridge.

The abovementioned December 12 squibs also mentioned that Gordon and Allied Artists were in negotiations about *The Atomic Submarine*. Gordon would be joined in his new company, *Variety* reported, by art director Don Ament and production manager Bartlett A. Carré; the former had worked on most of Gordon's AIPs, the latter *all* of them. Ultimately, Carré did not work on *Atomic Submarine*.

My 2002 interview with Gordon, in which he talked about making a co-production deal with Allied Artists, finding financiers, etc., begins on page 176 of this book. The trades reported that the *Atomic Submarine* would shove off (begin production) on January 5; later it became February 12 and then March 9. Cameras would not roll until June 18.

Veritably on the eve of the start of production, *Variety* announced the ambitious course that Gordon had charted for himself over the next 18 months: 12 pictures including *War Against Crime*, *Mask of the Red Death* ("adapted by Ruth Alexander, Alex's wife and veepee of the company"), *Killer Smog* ("an original by Dale Wasserman," who later wrote the play version of *One Flew Over the Cuckoo's Nest*), *Mystery Bomber* ("based on the current newspaper stories about the B-24 found in the Libyan Desert"), *Pick-Up on Vice Street* ("a police-action melodrama") and *Chicago Crime Boss*. The item also mentioned upcoming sci-fis to be made in connection with Jack Rabin and Irving Block, *Project X*, *The Beetle* "and several untitled properties." Other papers had reported his plan to make a sci-fi called *The Boneless Man* and his completion of the script of a sci-fi Western, *Cowboy from Outer Space*. Not one of these movies was ever made.

> Alex Gordon has four old-timers in *Atomic Submarine*—Victor Varconi, once a DeMille star; Jack Mulhall, Bob Steele and Frank Lackteen. The director probably goes back farthest of all. He is Spencer G. Bennet, who has directed more than 100 serials, beginning with *The Perils of Pauline* in 1913.
> —columnist Philip K. Scheuer, June 23, 1959

Actually, Bennet (who, by the way, did not direct *100* serials and did not direct *The Perils of Pauline*) wasn't Gordon's first choice. Gordon told me he initially wanted Edward L. Cahn, "and we *did* go to him, Orville Hampton and I. But he was exclusive with Edward Small by then, so we got Spencer Bennet. I was very happy with Bennet, who was a good friend and a wonderful, likable man. And he worked fast! He was not as good a director as Eddie Cahn, I think, because he didn't direct the actors at all. If they spoke their lines, that was it [*laughs*]—that was good enough for him!"

Brett Halsey in our 2002 *Fangoria* interview: "[Bennet and I] didn't have much of a personal relationship, but I felt that I learned a lot from him. He didn't waste any time, but he wasn't pushy about it. He knew exactly what to do. And he was also good with working with the actors. When you're in a hurry, as all these movies were, it's seldom that the director would have time to work with his actors."

Bennet explained why he *had* to work the way he did in his foreword to Gene Fernett's 1973 book *Hollywood's Poverty Row, 1930-1950*:

> I recall the '30s and '40s as a trying time, particularly for film directors who were making pictures for independent production units, since that was where I did so much work. Working with low budgets, short schedules and harried producers, the independent film director was really caught in the middle! He had to know how to "cut his picture in the camera," for example, in order to reduce laboratory costs, and to conserve film. He had to use inexpensive, yet capable, players in order to cut down the number of takes, too. My serial experience qualified me to overcome such problems, and more besides; for instance, I made the mistake of always bringing my pictures in on time, just because I thought it proper to do so. Unfortunately, producers came to take advantage of this, shortening schedules on my films to where it was practically impossible to produce a product which did not suffer as a result. But like most personnel at the independent units, I tried. All in all, they were colorful days, and their problems do not make me less proud to have been a part of that era, when we turned out pictures that were clean and entertaining.

A submarine beneath polar ice would *not* be conducive as a setting for the full duration of any serial and yet *Atomic Submarine*, with regularly placed cliffhanger-worthy situations (the underwater electrical storm, the falling iceberg ice, the submarine-saucer collision) does sometimes give off the same vibe as a featurized serial.

Gordon being Gordon, the industrious digger-upper of players from the past, he relished the *Atomic Submarine* casting process. From my interview with him:

> I always did my own casting on *all* my pictures, down to the bit parts and extras and everything. Allied Artists, however, had a casting director

Continued on page 22

 # We all live in atomic submarine...

Arthur Franz as "Reef" Holloway, whom the script calls "a handsome, capable, relaxed Annapolis-type."

Dick Foran as Comdr. Wendover, "a hard-bitten, intelligent young-old man of about forty. Years of responsibility have made him older mentally than physically."

Brett Halsey as Carl Nielsen. "[He] has the look of an ascetic – thin, sensitive features, a nervous, intense manner – the 'egghead' appearance."

Tom Conway as Sir Ian Hunt, "English, winner of the Nobel Prize for Oceanography."

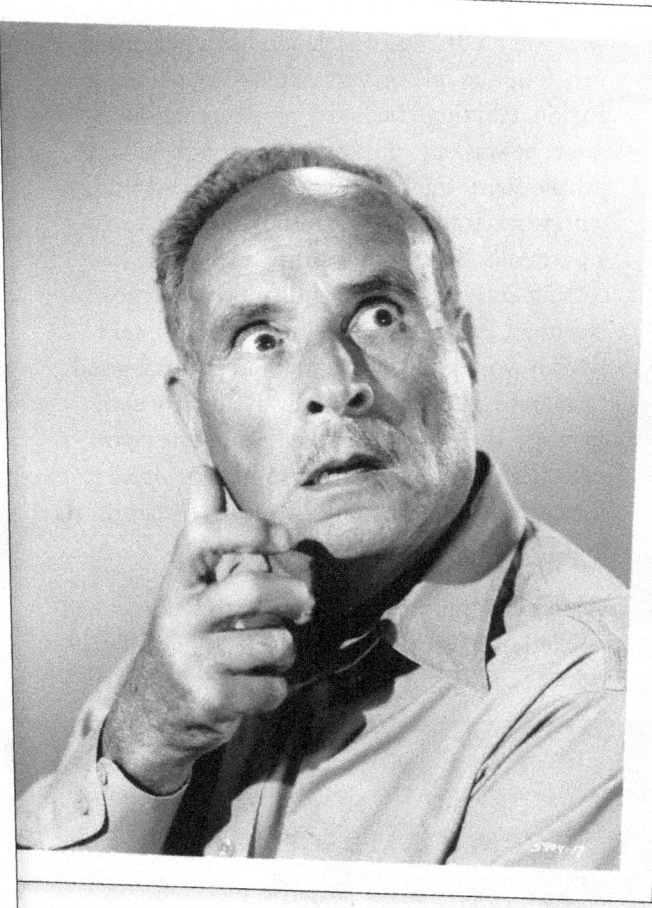

Victor Varconi as Dr. Clifford Kent, "a practical, 'egghead' scientist."

Paul Dubov as Lt. Dave Milburn, "ex-Naval Academy halfback and inter-collegiate boxing champion, hard-nosed and trigger-tempered."

Continued from page 19

who was a rather miserable kind of a person, very tough to talk to, very unpleasant, named Joe Rivkin. Although he had a good reputation in the trade, he was one of those rough, tough-talking people (with the bad language and everything) who worked for several studios. And he took a particular delight in wanting to impose his casting choices, which I didn't like. George Burrows, Broidy's second-in-command, said Rivkin would do the casting and get us a good cast, and I said, "No, no. I always do my own casting." Burrows said, "Well, you better work *with* Rivkin, then, because we have to *approve* the cast." By that, I think he meant the leads, the first four or five people.

Well, I thought of John Agar, with whom I had worked on *Flesh and the Spur* [1957] and *Jet Attack* [1958], but his agent quoted too high a price. So then I took Marshall Thompson and Arthur Franz to lunch. They were close friends [of each other]. I knew Marshall Thompson because he had done several pictures with my brother Dick, so I got in touch with him and with Franz and I had lunch with them at Frascati's on the Sunset Strip, a great French-Belgian restaurant I liked. I told them, "I would love to have *both* of you in the picture [Franz as Lt. Comdr. Holloway, Thompson as Comdr. Wendover], but unfortunately in this particular case I can't *afford* to have both of you, I can only have one of you." So Thompson said, "Then take Arthur." He didn't *say* that Arthur wasn't working too much lately and needed the money, but … he inferred it. So I said fine, I'd be delighted to have Franz. And Allied Artists approved Arthur Franz.

How much would actors on the Franz-Thompson level have commanded in 1959?

I think they wanted 1500 each. [In a different, later interview, Gordon said 1000.] We settled for 1000 with Arthur Franz. Then, for the other parts, I began looking through various agents' books. I didn't think of Dick Foran right away, but when I saw his picture, and they said that he would work for a week for a thousand dollars [as Comdr. Wendover], I thought, "That's pretty good!" And he'd already worked in an Allied Artists picture or two, so they approved him. As it turned out, I had much more fun talking to Dick Foran than I would have with Marshall Thompson, who was a rather reserved type and not all that interested in his old pictures and all that. Brett Halsey they all thought was a very good idea, too—I'd used him in *Submarine Seahawk*. He was a very nice guy who was going at the time with Italian actress Luciana Paluzzi. Allied thought his was a very good name, that was fine.

Did Luciana Paluzzi visit the set?

She visited quite a bit. I don't know if she didn't trust Brett with the ladies [*laughs*] but, yes, she *did* visit quite a bit and she also came to a showing of it and was very complimentary. She was very, very nice-looking, very much Americanized, and they seemed to be very happy together when they were on the set.

Variety's resident humorist George E. Phair wrote on August 15, 1958, "[T]here will be a race to project a movie under the North Pole. Currently leading the under-ice fleet is *Atomic Submarine*. It will be pretty tough, heating up story in that temperature." Pictured: Atomic Submariners Dick Foran, Arthur Franz and Paul Dubov hold brave faces while looking at danger.

Anyway, then I came to my famous "supporting casting." Paul Dubov, Allied didn't care; he had worked very well with us on several other pictures, including *Day the World Ended* and *The She-Creature*, and was always on time and knew his lines and everything. So that was great. Bob Steele they also didn't object to; that role was further down the castlist, they thought he was okay. I liked Bob Steele and used him wherever I could. When I suggested Victor Varconi, they sort of did a double-take [*laughs*], but they didn't object. Of course, I was thinking of Varconi back to when he was playing Admiral Nelson in *The Divine Lady* [1929], things like that. So *he* was accepted. Jean Moorhead had been in my picture *Motorcycle Gang* [1957], a very attractive girl, very nice. Joi Lansing was someone Rivkin proposed, and I gave way to him. I was told that she was Frank Sinatra's girlfriend—or one of many [*laughs*]—and she'd work one day for 250 bucks. They probably wanted to use her in order to keep in good with Sinatra and especially the William Morris Agency, who represented her.

I said, "That's fine," even though 250 bucks was a lot of money for us—we would have ordinarily paid a hundred bucks for that role. She turned out to be a *very* sweet girl, didn't bother us at all, had no airs. The guy who did the saucer voice [John Hilliard] I think may have been suggested by Spencer Bennet, our director. I think Spence knew him and had used him on some narration at Columbia, or wherever.

And, getting special "and" billing, Tom Conway.

Tom Conway I *loved*—he was a terrific guy, a terrific actor, and he had a great sense of humor. I'd already used him in *The She-Creature* and *Voodoo Woman* [1957], and I had *started Runaway Daughters* [1956] with him but then, unfortunately, he got sick and we had to replace him with John Litel. In a way, I felt I owed him another picture, because we made a multiple deal with his agent Wallace Middleton, and Conway had even flown over from England especially to do *The She-Creature* for us, when we were in trouble. So I really wanted to use Tom wherever I could. (And, also, he needed the money.) So I got *him* in it, and of course he was a *very* good name for Allied Artists.

As always with you, familiar faces even in the tiniest parts.

Selmer Jackson, who played the admiral—of course, nobody could object to him, he'd played so many Army and Navy men! Jack Mulhall was an old pal of mine and I tried to get him in wherever I could. Sid Melton was somebody that Henry Schrage wanted, so I threw him a bone. I *hated* Sid Melton on-screen, the kind of roles that he always played—the loudmouth. I didn't think he was the least bit funny. And he was also the kind who, on the set, wouldn't leave you alone for a *moment*—he was always suggesting bits of business and additional dialogue and so on. He was a nice guy personally but it was just *too much*, he was always after you!

Edmund Cobb and Frank Lackteen were two actors I used whenever I could, and I *told* Joe Rivkin, "Of course I always use Edmund Cobb and Frank Lackteen." He knew who they were and he said, "You can't have them on the submarine, they're

A lovely profile all the way down: platinum blonde Joi Lansing, who played Reef's girl Julie. With Alex Gordon casting the movie, it's surprising that the role didn't go to Anna Sten or Bess Flowers!

In the (not-so) great Vintage War Movie tradition, every crew must have a clown. In *Atomic Submarine* it's Sid Melton (right) as Chester, "rumor-monger of the *Tiger Shark*," seen here contending with the gruff Griff (Bob Steele). Alex Gordon: "I hated Sid Melton on screen"!

much too old." I said, "I know that, I'm just gonna have 'em like as extras, walking by in the submarine yard." He said, "That's ridiculous, that's throwing money away. We'd have to pay them $100 each [an actor's minimum one-day salary], and nobody'll even recognize them. If anybody is to walk by, it can be an extra at 20 bucks." I said, "Well, I *insist* on having them in there." This was really going to

Arthur Franz said of his niche in '50s Hollywood, "There was an 'Arthur Franz mold' [square nice-guys] that was variously filled by myself or Richard Carlson or Richard Denning with as much distinction as there is from one Oreo cookie to another."

be an issue, you know! I told him I would pay it out of my own pocket, but to no avail. He said [*flatly*], "No. I'm going to tell Steve Broidy that that's a waste of money."

So the next morning at six o'clock, I was outside the Allied Artists gate, in the brush there, waiting to "ambush" Steve Broidy. I knew that at nine o'clock, Broidy was going to come in. I waited from six o'clock 'til five to nine—and it was cold! And as Broidy's chauffeur-driven car drew up and stopped at the gate, I got on the running board of the car. I had my courage back—I was now fighting for somebody *else*, not for myself. I said, "Mr. Broidy, before anything else, before you go to your office, I've got a problem that I've got to solve and it means a lot to me. Do you mind if I walk with you to your office?" He said okay. So Broidy walked in with me as the driver put the car away, and I said, "Look, this is so stupid, we're arguing here about a situation of Edmund Cobb and Frank Lackteen ..." He knew them from Monogram Pictures. "I use them in virtually every picture. It's a question of [Lackteen and Cobb] working as actors, not as extras, so it's a hundred bucks each. I will pay that out of my money, but I want them in this picture." Broidy said [*in a weary voice*], "Why is Rivkin making all this fuss about it? *Certainly* you can use them. As soon as I get to the office, I'll call him and tell him to ... to shut up!" [*Laughs*] So after that, I felt a little better about Broidy, I felt, "Okay, he *is* all right to sit on the Board of Directors of those humanitarian organizations—he's not as bad as I thought at first.

On June 18, 1959, Dick Foran's 49th birthday, *The Atomic Submarine* got underway at Allied Artists. Gordon told me it took eight days but he wrote in his *Fangoria* #48 column "The Pit and the Pen" that it was six. (Brett Halsey also remembered six.) Gordon was used to this kind of on-the-double filmmaking from his AIP years.

Whether six or eight, d.p. Gilbert Warrenton had his work cut out for him. Three decades prior, Warrenton was behind the camera on such well-remembered films as *The Cat and the Canary*, *The Man Who Laughs* and *Show Boat*, but by the 1930s he was already toiling for Monogram, and then Lippert and AIP in later years. He was even one of the photographers of *Mesa of Lost Women* (1953). "What was great about him," Gordon told me, "was the fact that he took just as much care shooting [*Atomic Submarine*] with umpteen setups a day as he did on some of the *big* pictures he'd worked on. This was something that always impressed me about Hollywood crews: For the most part, they took just as much care with B pictures as they did with much bigger pictures. To them, there was pride in their work and, whether it was a big picture or a small picture, they wanted it to have that gloss and that perfection."

An exchange from my 2002 interview with Brett Halsey:

Weaver: Most of your *Atomic Submarine* scenes were with Arthur Franz.

Halsey: Is he still alive?

Weaver: Yes, but I'd love to hear about him off the record. [With Franz dead, it's now *on* the record.]

Halsey: Arthur Franz was a nice man, but my impression was…he was bitter about his career. That he wasn't a happy man. I think he felt he should have had a much bigger career, and that working in [movies like *The Atomic Submarine*] was a real comedown for him. He was very professional and there was no problem…but I just didn't feel I was working with a happy person.

Weaver: He's a world-class grouch. Which is too bad.

Halsey: Yeah, 'cause he was a good actor. But…I didn't *care* [that he seemed unhappy to be there]. If a person was open and friendly, then, yes, he and I would become friendly. But if he was closed, well, to hell with it! You don't have *time* for babying personalities.

"Arthur Franz was a strange man," Gordon told me. He continued:

He was "up" on his dialogue, he never kept you waiting, and he said all his lines and everything, hardly ever fluffed. But he wanted to come and see the rushes—and even bring his kids to see the rushes! I said, "I'm sorry, Arthur. Allied Artists does not allow actors to see rushes"—I made it appear that it was all Allied. If Allied had allowed it, I would have *maybe* given way, I don't know, because he was so emphatic about it. But I didn't like the idea of actors seeing rushes either, because they may want to do something

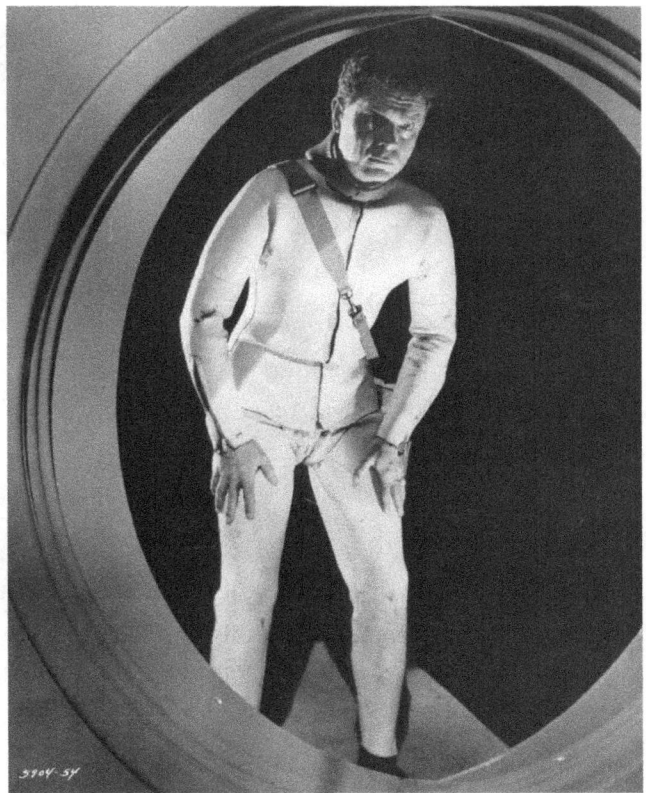

I'll tell you before you read the next sentence that it's not a typo: Arthur Franz died before his 22nd birthday. He was born February 29, 1920 – Leap Year – and had his first birthday on February 29, 1924. By the time he died in 2006, he'd had 21 birthdays.

over again, so on and so forth. As I said, Franz would do all his stuff very professionally, but then if I wanted to sort of approach him on something, sometimes he'd shun me and sit down all alone on the stairs, waiting for his next shot. It wasn't easy to have little conversations with him, like with the others. So he was not too friendly, but I thought he came off well in the picture.

Even if Gordon's name hadn't appeared in the credits of *The Atomic Submarine*, at least a few card-carrying Monster Kids would surely have sensed his fine hand in it, with Halsey and director Bennet returning from *Submarine Seahawk*, Gordon regulars Tom Conway and Paul Dubov in prominent parts (the latter with conspicuous "And" billing), Cobb and Lackteen making drive-by appearances, and giddy-up B-Western stars Dick Foran and Bob Steele in way-out-of-their-line roles as head men aboard a nuclear sub. It's an almost surreal moment when we see atomic torpedoes being launched by Poverty Row cowboy Steele and pint-sized movie funnyman Sid Melton!

Adapt an Intercontinental Ballistic Missile? Betcha two to one Victor Varconi (left) couldn't even *pronounce* Intercontinental Ballistic Missile!

Neither Tom Conway nor Victor Varconi fill the bill as a Colossus of science. The sleepy-eyed, phlegmatic Conway plays a Nobel Prize winner for oceanography (there *is* no Nobel Prize for oceanography), but because we fans know him so well from his dapper roles in the *Falcon* series, the Val Lewtons, etc., it's hard to believe he ever got close to any fish that wasn't on a plate. Alex Gordon reached *way* down into the has-bin for Varconi, whose atom sub designer Dr. Kent doesn't look like someone who could tackle a daily newspaper's Sudoku puzzle, much less solve the mysteries of the atom. He sounds like a real *paisan* when he pronounces "magnetic" mag-ga-*net*-tic.

Variety's Glen did a good job of describing the general level of acting in *Atomic Submarine*:

> None of the featured players have marquee value but most have records of competence, e.g.: Arthur Franz, Dick Foran, Brett Halsey, Tom Conway, Paul Dubov, Bob Steele, Victor Varconi, Joi Lansing. In this film, director Spencer G. Bennet has them smiling incongruously, floundering in stage waits and moving without haste or seeming concern as alarm bells clang disaster.

Wanda Hale of the *New York Daily News* had the same beef with the acting, describing the players as "all doing nothing but looking through the monitor and talking a great deal about what to do if and when they sight the nemesis. [They] are merely figures moving around and talking too much."

Brett Halsey enjoyed the company he kept on the *Atomic Submarine* sets. "Working with Dick Foran, who was such a big B Western star when I was a kid, was a thrill," he said in our *Fangoria* interview. "I would get a real charge out of working with people like Dick Foran and Bob Steele, who was another cowboy star from the old days. [Steele] was playing a really small part in *Atomic Submarine* and I was playing a starring part, and I felt like, "This is *wrong*. This is *Bob Steele* – my God, I must have seen 40 or 50 of his movies!"

The Atomic Submarine wrapped in late June. On September 4, editor William Austin checked in at Allied Artists to begin cutting the Rabin-Block-DeWitt special effects footage into the movie. At that time, Gordon wanted him to cut in a lot less than he did: The producer was bitterly disappointed with the Saucer Monster ("fit to be tied," as *he* put it), to the point where he didn't want it in the movie, and told Steve Broidy, "I don't think we ought to show the monster, I think we ought to just suggest it." (The whole story is on pages 180 and 181.) Forty-three years later, Gordon had cooled off a bit, telling me,

> In view of the cost of the picture … I think probably the effects were as good as they could be. I must say that in all honesty, I was not *altogether* satisfied, and did not think we got 100 percent our money's worth. I do *think* that Rabin and Block … I won't say "skimmed off the top," I don't want to say *that*, but I think they inflated their expenses a little bit.
>
> …I think the reason Rabin and Block wouldn't show me the monster in advance was that they knew that if I saw it, I would blow my top. *But*, they figured that once I saw it on-screen, with the lighting and everything, I would think it was all right. Actually, they were right in a way. Especially when you see the picture on TV or DVD. The monster actually doesn't look at all bad on the small screen.

Variety reviewer Glen called the Saucer Monster – "a clump of tentacles and weeds with one Cyclops eye on a central stock — …quite satisfactory." In my opinion, it's so grotesque that it works fine in a movie like this; the flickering lights and superimposed rippling effect add to the weirdness. According to the article

"Special Effects Designed and Created by: Jack Rabin & Irving Block" (*Fantascene* #2) by Robert and Dennis Skotak, the creature "was built around Block's arm which was inserted up into a hollow sphere lined with foil. The base of the monster (in actuality Block's elbow) was encircled by a row of rubber tentacles which he manipulated with wires." Talking to the Skotaks about the monocular monstrosity, Block brought up an ancient legend: "Odysseus has to defeat [the Cyclops], and the only way to do that is to poke his eye out. That wasn't a very good film ... but there were many, many interesting things in that film."

In a booklet that came with Criterion's DVD of *The Atomic Submarine* (part of their 2007 "Monsters and Madmen" collection), Bruce Eder wrote that *Atomic* scripter Hampton

> forged a story and script that managed to get references to Homer's *Odyssey* (as well as Hesiod's *Theogony*) into the same scene with a discussion about flying saucers. ...[T]he adventure of the *Tiger Shark*'s crew aboard the alien vessel, as they are "devoured" one by one, is a close-enough parallel to Homer and the fate of Odysseus' men in the cave of Polyphemus.

In his book *Keep Watching the Skies!*, Bill Warren called the Saucer Monster "unusual and imaginative, and in some senses is the best thing about the film, giving it a peculiar air of alienness just when it needs it the most."

If Gordon was going to see red about anything, it should have been the effects men's submarine and saucer. Never before have miniatures looked more miniature; the subs are almost at the level of the plastic "baking powder submarine" toys which descended and rose in kids' sinks and bathtubs back in the day. Photographed dry-for-wet, the subs and saucers have to be a *bit* bigger than they appear, because the subs have spinning propellers and the saucer is lit from within.

Jack Rabin told the Skotaks that *The Atomic Submarine* was "a horrible picture" before adding, "I never saw it completed, though." He went on:

> I built a submarine that cost a fortune! It worked. What I did to duplicate water: In the back room I made a whole channel of crazy-looking rocks and took the miniature submarine

Frogman Richard Tyler is about to get fried like a bug under a magnifying glass. Presumably *Atomic Submarine*'s screen-credited makeup man Emile LaVigne did the burn makeup on Tyler (and also Paul Dubov); below is a behind-the-scenes shot of LaVigne giving Laurie Mitchell a cremated kisser in *Queen of Outer Space* (1958).

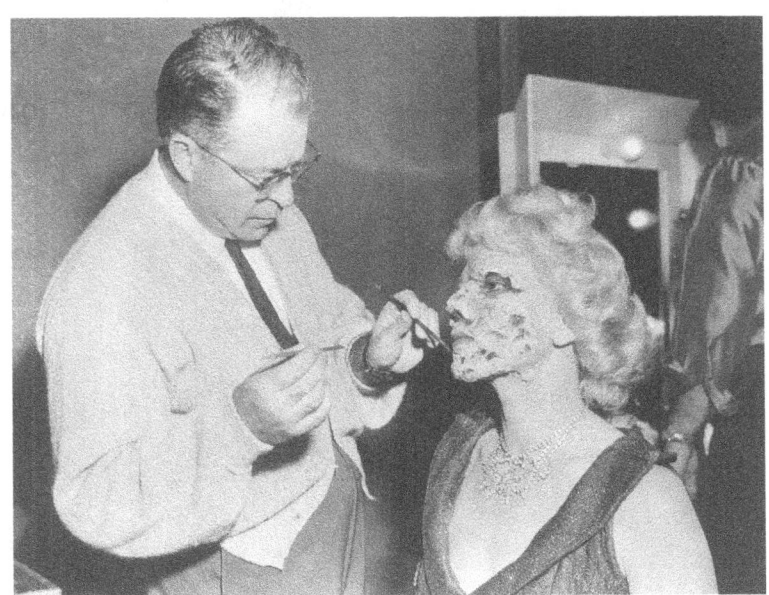

> [a three-foot-long model] along a fine wire on a track above. I put little pieces of aluminum foil atop the water in a large tank, and shined a light on it so that when we jiggled the water, it reflected rays like underwater currents.

Several shots of the sub are quite blurry; this may have been intentional, to give the impression that we are seeing it diffused through water. But this also adds to the impression that the prop is tiny, too small to properly capture even with macrophotography. After the *Tiger Shark* has rammed the saucer, it's funny to hear the narrator call them "two titanic craft," because

Neither posters nor trailer offered any hint that *The Atomic Submarine* was a monster movie. If there was ever a surprise appearance by a monster in an oldie, this is the one.

On September 5, 1959, newscasters John Hilliard and Pat Michaels reported to Ryder Sound Studios to lend their vocal talents to *Atomic Submarine*. Hilliard was the perfect-diction voice of the Saucer Monster, deep, bombastic and mocking, sounding like the super-villain in a Hanna-Barbera superhero cartoon for children. Michaels was the movie's narrator, describing events in documentary fashion *à la* the voiceovers in such flicks as *It Came from Beneath the Sea* (1955) and *Earth vs. the Flying Saucers* (1956), W. Lee Wilder's '50s sci-fis and others. But occasionally he waxes melodramatic:

 The *Tiger Shark* moved across the top of the world, toward her rendezvous with ... *what*?

 [T]he strangest, most fearful voyage ever made by a submarine, atomic or otherwise!

 It was foolish, it was insane, it was fantastic. But it was their only hope. And the *Earth's* only hope!

The narrator talks so often and so long that he practically becomes a just-off-camera character in the story.

"The script of *Atomic Submarine*, of course, isn't the greatest," Alex Gordon told me, "and some of the lines are a little..." Instead of finishing the sentence, he shook his head a little and quietly laughed. The low point, dialogue-wise, might come in the early moments of Reef's

Atomic Submarine narrator Pat Michaels' real job was covering Southern California news for TV, radio and newspapers. Despite lung cancer and other ailments, he produced a weekly digest of neighborhood news right up to just a few weeks before his 2010 death.

even when joined together, two props in one, they look small enough to put in your pocket. (In 1961, a print of *Atomic Submarine* was sent to Japan and, after a screening, it was rejected by the theaters in the Toho circuit because the special effects were so poorly done. The Japanese felt a bad job like this would do harm to them in the future, as local theatergoers would assume this was a Toho production.)

encounter with the Saucer Monster. "So, Commander Holloway ... as you Earth inhabitants would express it: We meet, face to face," says the colossal nightmare creature; the double-tough Reef, not horrorstruck for even a moment, comes out with the childish zinger: "That's a *face*?" Orville H. Hampton later wrote scores of Hanna-Barbera cartoons (*Scooby-Doo, Super Friends*, etc.) and I'd be willing to bet that was a good fit for him.

You'd never know there *was* a monster in *Atomic Submarine* going by its posters, trailer and pressbook. In its past history, Allied Artists had no shortage of shabby-looking monsters (Tabanga the walking tree, the Crab Monsters, the see-through 50 Foot Woman, etc.) and they were apparently unembarrassed by those bargain basement beasties. But they shunted the Saucer Monster aside completely in all *Atomic Submarine* promotional materials. They also kept the flying saucer "hush-hush super-secret," exploitation-wise. It *is* on the posters, but underwater, and at quite an angle, and in the midst of a fiery explosion, so that the average Joe looking at the poster probably couldn't tell it *was* a saucer without being *told*. Text-wise, even the pressbook's synopsis and its other allusions to the movie's story avoid "flying saucer" and call the *Tiger Shark*'s undersea nemesis "a new type of enemy craft," "a weapon about which [the submariners] know very little," a "strange circular craft," etc. The trailer narrator calls the destroyer of polar shipping a "dreadful unseen adversary." All the press material I've seen give the impression it's a story of submarine combat, with an unkept promise of futuristic twists (poster ad line: "The shocking news that flames Tomorrow's War under the Arctic Ice!"). The non-sci-fi title adds to the suspicion of planned deception. *Variety*'s Glen wrote:

> The importance to the film of the monster and the untidy deaths it inflicts on some mariners would indicate the film's title isn't apt — suggesting as it does a story about present-day war craft.

Because *Atomic Submarine*'s ads all make it look like a conventional subs-at-war story, one wonders if the ticket-buyers included any Navy men expecting another

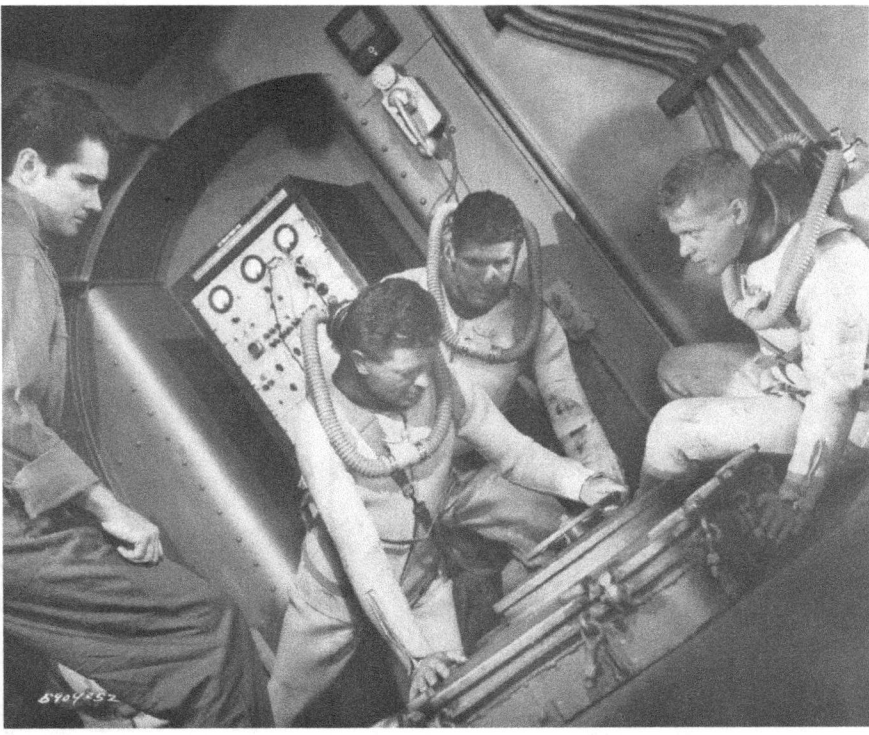

The on-camera *Lungfish* must be bigger than what Orville H. Hampton pictured when he scripted, because he describes a shot inside as a "TIGHT – (AND WE MEAN TIGHT) GROUP SHOT." Pictured: Brett Halsey, Arthur Franz, Richard Tyler and Ken Becker, all with plenty of "personal space."

Run Silent, Run Deep or *The Enemy Below*. Imagine how these fellows' hearts sank when the monster appeared and they realized they'd been lured into a kiddie matinee-level sci-fi movie. I'm picturing one with egg on his face, to go with the fruit salad on his dress uniform.

> The interstellar mastermind is unimpressively conceived as a large eye in a woolly wig waving a tentacle or two.—*Monthly Film Bulletin*

The Atomic Submarine Release History

By Dr. Robert J. Kiss

Theatrical first run, December 1959 to October 1960

Allied Artists launched *The Atomic Submarine* with a week-long "preview" engagement at the 2115-seat 5th Avenue Theatre in Seattle commencing December 11, 1959. This booking had originally been penciled in for November 29 – a date widely reported in the trade press – but was quietly rescheduled due to the venue's decision to hold over Paramount's *Career* starring Dean Martin and Anthony Franciosa for a second week. The preview engagement proved a somewhat understated affair, presented with little advance publicity and saddled with a second feature that, rather than likewise being a new release, was instead Allied Artists' three-year-old Western *The Young Guns* starring Russ Tamblyn. The theater reported ticket sales that were ten percent below average, which in view of the lackluster circumstances of this initial opening should probably be considered a relative success.

Two days after the conclusion of the Seattle run, the December 19 launch of another atomic submarine, the U.S.S. *Scorpion*, caused a literal and figurative splash as newspaper front pages from coast to coast carried reports on the vessel's dip into the icy waters of the Thames River in Groton, Connecticut, before a crowd of 5000 onlookers. Nothing whatsoever was made of this potential publicity and ballyhoo tie-in as *The Atomic Submarine* opened in a limited number of

All this and Donald Duck too! Ad for the Seattle preview opening on December 11, 1959.

midwestern and southern towns from Christmas Eve 1959. For these engagements, the movie was again double-billed with a second Allied Artists release, either in the form of the British-made thriller *Web of Evidence* (originally *Beyond This Place*) starring Van Johnson, or

In 1960, movie fans who enjoyed seeing Paul Dubov in *The Purple Gang* as professional hit man "Killer" Burke, "a cold, deadly murder machine," could stick around for the second half of the bill and see him as the laugh-a-minute Dave in *Atomic Submarine* (pictured).

of the Italian-made World War II espionage drama *The House of Intrigue* (originally *Londra chiama Polo Nord*) with Curt Jurgens and Dawn Addams.

As 1959 drew to a close, events in Groton once more commanded front-page column inches thanks to the December 30 commissioning of the ballistic missile sub U.S.S. *George Washington*. Just as before, absolutely nothing was made of this in publicity for *The Atomic Submarine*, as Allied Artists set about placing tens of prints into circulation from early January 1960 to serve as a supporting feature for its first-run release of *The Purple Gang*, the Lindsley Parsons-produced drama about Detroit's notoriously violent Prohibition Era mobsters, starring Barry Sullivan. On January 4, 1960, the two features were given a trade preview less than 50 miles inland from Groton, in Hartford, Connecticut, leading to the publication of their earliest reviews in the January 5 edition of the trade paper *Motion Picture Daily*.

The *Purple-Atomic* double bill opened with a volley of major metropolitan engagements throughout New England, foremost amongst which were week-long runs at Boston's 1797-seat Paramount Theatre from January 6 and at Hartford's 1991-seat Allyn Theatre from January 8, in addition to a six-day run at the 700-seat Strand Theatre (now the Jane Pickens Theater & Event Center) in Newport, Rhode Island, from January 7. In all instances, publicity remained focused squarely on the main feature *The Purple Gang*, with *The Atomic Submarine* treated as little more than an incidental footnote to the bill, frequently described merely as a "bonus feature" or "extra feature" and largely ignored by reviewers.

This pattern would be repeated in cities throughout the United States, including at the four-venue opening in San Diego on March 2, the seven-venue opening in Dallas on March 3, and the largest single opening of the double bill at 27 theaters and drive-ins in the Greater Los Angeles area on March 9. The effective dismissal of *The Atomic Submarine* was singularly pronounced in Detroit, where *The Purple Gang* of course held particular local interest. For the keenly anticipated city premiere at the 2200-seat Palms Theatre (now the Fillmore) on January 14, *The Atomic Submarine* was simply left off the bill, and only joined *The Purple Gang* for the remaining 13 days of its two-week engagement. There was also yet another missed opportunity for tie-in publicity and ballyhoo when the nuclear sub U.S.S. *Sargo* grabbed headlines by breaking through the ice at the North Pole and planting the flag of its home state Hawaii there on February 9; the *Purple-Atomic* double bill had opened at two theaters and one drive-in in Honolulu just the day before.

Box office takings in all the abovementioned cities were reported to be merely average, with the exception of the 27-venue opening in Los Angeles, where salacious saturation advertising for *The Purple Gang* – "They matched Al Capone vice-for-vice… kill-for-kill! They ran Detroit with rum-running, highjacking [sic] and murder! They were the top executioners of the underworld! Authentic! Brutally real!" – helped its supporting feature to secure profits that were 35 percent above normal.

The Purple Gang was not programmed together with *The Atomic Submarine* in all major cities. For example, it was served up to Chicagoans as a stand-alone attraction from January 29, while New Yorkers got to see it on a bill with Allied Artists' *The House of Intrigue* during late February and March. In these localities, *The Atomic Submarine* accordingly played second fiddle to a different array of main features. At the Windy City's 980-seat Garrick Theatre, it hitched a two-week ride on Sophia Loren's coattails – or rather, on her barely there hosiery, which constituted a key part of the promotional campaign – when it opened in support of the Midwest premiere of Paramount's *Heller in Pink Tights* from March 25. This

From March 1960, Allied Artists also frequently supplied *The Atomic Submarine* as support for its gimmicky horror flick *The Hypnotic Eye* featuring Jacques Bergerac and the "amazing new audience thrill" of HypnoMagic. The largest single opening of this coupling took place in Pittsburgh, where it ran at 20 venues from June 26. As ever, publicity remained focused almost entirely on the (admittedly eminently ballyhooable) main feature.

By maintaining a flexible, unhurried approach to supplying *The Atomic Submarine* as a supporting feature for a range of different double bills, Allied Artists was able to avoid the substantial costs inherent in striking a sufficient number of prints for a simultaneous nationwide release. The film's distribution consequently proved a protracted, piecemeal process, with a few big cities such as Philadelphia not getting to see the picture until mid-September 1960, and the domestic first run ultimately extending until the end of October. This gradual surfacing of *The Atomic Submarine* around the nation was reflected in its coverage on *Boxoffice Magazine*'s Boxoffice Barometer (a chart recording "the performance of current attractions in the opening week of their first runs" in 20 key U.S. cities). The title popped up on the chart no less than 14 times between February 8 and October 31, 1960, with the final tally according it a national box office performance that was seven percent above average.

Diving to the depths on a double bill

Looking at a sample of 1500 theaters from coast to coast which played *The Atomic Submarine* in first run between December 1959 and October 1960, a colossal 94 percent of engagements took the form of a double bill, with the movie constituting the bottom half of the bill some 91 percent of the time. There should be no doubt, therefore, that seeing *The Atomic Submarine* as a supporting feature on a double bill was absolutely the most common way to have encountered it in theatrical first run.

Fully 69 percent of these double bills paired *The Atomic Submarine* with a second Allied Artists feature, indicating the company's preference for controlling both halves of the bill. At 44.5 percent of engagements, this second Allied Artists feature was *The Purple Gang* – confirming this as the movie's most regular co-feature – followed by *The Hypnotic Eye* at 12.5 percent of double-bill bookings. Allied Artists was also clearly happy to supply *The Atomic Submarine* together with a vast number of other titles from its catalogue, with a further

What lies submerged beneath Sophia Loren? March 25, 1960, opening in Chicago.

engagement scored *The Atomic Submarine* a box office take of 70 percent above average. In New York City, the movie sailed into altogether more kiddie-friendly waters, as it mooch(i)ed into theaters supporting the Buena Vista-Disney live-action release *Toby Tyler, or Ten Weeks with a Circus* starring Kevin Corcoran. Following a ten-day run at Brooklyn's 3250-seat RKO Albee Theatre beginning April 6, the pairing was rolled out to 41 neighborhood theaters across the five boroughs on April 19. This represented the largest single opening of *The Atomic Submarine* anywhere.

1 hypnotic eye + 1 cyclopic eye = an odd pair of spectacles. Twenty-venue opening in Pittsburgh on June 26, 1960.

24 Allied Artists features accounting collectively for 12 percent of double-bill engagements nationwide. All of these additional Allied Artists co-features are arranged alphabetically below; the month mentioned in each case is the earliest in which the pairing was encountered within the sample of 1500 theaters.

March 1960 *The Bat* (Vincent Price)
June 1960 *Battle Flame* (Scott Brady)
April 1960 *The Big Circus* (Victor Mature)
March 1960 *Crime & Punishment, USA* (Mary Murphy)
February 1960 *Dragoon Wells Massacre* (Barry Sullivan)
January 1960 *Face of Fire* (Cameron Mitchell)
October 1960 *Hell to Eternity* (Jeffrey Hunter)
December 1959 *The House of Intrigue* (Curt Jurgens)
February 1960 *House on Haunted Hill* (Vincent Price)
July 1960 *I Passed for White* (Sonya Wilde)
April 1960 *Last of the Badmen* (George Montgomery)
January 1960 *Man from God's Country* (George Montgomery)
March 1960 *Never Love a Stranger* (John Drew Barrymore)
March 1960 *New Orleans After Dark* (Stacy Harris)
February 1960 *The Oklahoman* (Joel McCrea)
August 1960 *Pay or Die!* (Ernest Borgnine)
August 1960 *Queen of Outer Space* (Zsa Zsa Gabor)
July 1960 *Raymie* (David Ladd)
February 1960 *The Rebel Set* (Gregg Palmer)
June 1960 *Seven Guns to Mesa* (Charles Quinlivan)
February 1960 *Snowfire* (Don Megowan)
June 1960 *Spy in the Sky!* (Steve Brodie)
December 1959 *Web of Evidence* (Van Johnson)
December 1959 *The Young Guns* (Russ Tamblyn)

The only movie from another distributor to establish itself as a regular co-feature was the previously mentioned *Toby Tyler*, which played at ten percent of double-bill engagements of *The Atomic Submarine*. Although this coupling was much more common on the East Coast, bookings were nevertheless attested as far west as Portola, California.

The remaining 21 percent of double-bill engagements nationwide were filled by 70 different features from distributors other than Allied Artists. Most of these pairings are indicative of exhibitors who aimed to furnish a so-called "balanced program" comprising works from two distinct genres, which they considered to possess a broader general appeal than a genre-matched bill. The few instances in which *The Atomic Submarine* ended up on all-sci-fi bills supporting the likes of *The Angry Red Planet*, *4D Man* or *The Time Machine* seem to have been the product of misdirection, with exhibitors in search of a balanced program booking *The Atomic Submarine* in the erroneous belief that it was a straightforward action movie. This was an easy mistake to make, since Allied Artists' campaign foregrounded the film's action content while almost completely disregarding its substantial sci-fi elements.

Still not as angry as the theater owner who discovered he'd unwittingly booked two sci-fi movies. April 6, 1960, opening in Oshkosh, Wisconsin.

(There could be no such excuse, however, for the handful of theaters that presented patrons with a double dose of atomic submarines by playing the title in support of *On the Beach*!)

All of the 70 additional co-features from other distributors attested within the sample are listed alphabetically below, with the month mentioned again the earliest in which the pairing was encountered.

June 1960 *The Adventures of Huckleberry Finn* (Tony Randall; MGM)
April 1960 *The Angry Red Planet* (Gerald Mohr; AIP)
August 1960 *The Apartment* (Jack Lemmon; United Artists)
April 1960 *Battle of the Coral Sea* (Cliff Robertson; Columbia)
June 1960 *Because They're Young* (Dick Clark; Columbia)
August 1960 *The Bellboy* (Jerry Lewis; Paramount)
March 1960 *Blood and Steel* (John Lupton; 20th Century-Fox)
April 1960 *The Boy and the Pirates* (Charles Herbert; United Artists)
March 1960 *The Bramble Bush* (Richard Burton; Warner Bros.)
January 1960 *But Not for Me* (Clark Gable; Paramount)
March 1960 *Cash McCall* (James Garner; Warner Bros.)
June 1960 *Circus of Horrors* (Anton Diffring; AIP)
May 1960 *Circus Stars* (Oleg Popov; Paramount)
May 1960 *Counterplot* (Forrest Tucker; United Artists)
April 1960 *Cry Tough* (John Saxon; United Artists)
April 1960 *Day of the Outlaw* (Robert Ryan; United Artists)
January 1960 *The Deep Six* (Alan Ladd; Warner Bros.)
March 1960 *A Dog of Flanders* (David Ladd; 20th Century-Fox)
May 1960 *Flying Leathernecks* (John Wayne; Universal-RKO reissue)
February 1960 *For the First Time* (Mario Lanza; MGM)
July 1960 *Forbidden Island* (Jon Hall; Columbia)
June 1960 *4D Man* (Robert Lansing; Universal)
May 1960 *Four Fast Guns* (James Craig; Universal)
October 1960 *From the Terrace* (Paul Newman; 20th Century-Fox)
January 1960 *The Gene Krupa Story* (Sal Mineo; Columbia)
February 1960 *Gold Raiders* (George O'Brien; United Artists reissue)
March 1960 *The Gunfight at Dodge City* (Joel McCrea; United Artists)
April 1960 *Guns of the Timberland* (Alan Ladd; Warner Bros.)
June 1960 *Hannibal* (Victor Mature; Warner Bros.)
March 1960 *Heller in Pink Tights* (Sophia Loren; Paramount)
July 1960 *Hercules Unchained* (Steve Reeves; Warner Bros.)

March 1960 *Here Come the Jets* (Steve Brodie; 20th Century-Fox)
April 1960 *Home from the Hill* (Robert Mitchum; MGM)
March 1960 *I Mobster* (Steve Cochran; 20th Century-Fox)
May 1960 *Jack the Ripper* (Lee Patterson; Paramount)
April 1960 *The Jayhawkers!* (Jeff Chandler; Paramount)
April 1960 *Kidnapped* (Peter Finch; Buena Vista-Disney)
January 1960 *The Last Angry Man* (Paul Muni; Columbia)
February 1960 *The Last of the Fast Guns* (Jock Mahoney; Universal)
February 1960 *The Matchmaker* (Shirley Booth; Paramount)
April 1960 *Missile to the Moon* (Richard Travis; Astor)
February 1960 *The Mouse that Roared* (Peter Sellers; Columbia)
April 1960 *On the Beach* (Gregory Peck; United Artists)
May 1960 *Once More, with Feeling!* (Yul Brynner; Columbia)
May 1960 *Our Man in Havana* (Alec Guinness; Columbia)
July 1960 *The Rat Race* (Tony Curtis; Paramount)
February 1960 *The Rise and Fall of Legs Diamond* (Ray Danton; Warner Bros.)
April 1960 *The Rookie* (Tommy Noonan; 20th Century-Fox)
January 1960 *Run for Cover* (James Cagney; Paramount)
March 1960 *Samson and Delilah* (Hedy Lamarr; Paramount reissue)
February 1960 *Seven Thieves* (Edward G. Robinson; 20th Century-Fox)
February 1960 *Sierra Baron* (Brian Keith; 20th Century-Fox)
May 1960 *Solomon and Sheba* (Yul Brynner; United Artists)
January 1960 *The Story on Page One* (Rita Hayworth; 20th Century-Fox)
September 1960 *Strangers When We Meet* (Kirk Douglas; Columbia)
September 1960 *Studs Lonigan* (Christopher Knight; United Artists)
April 1960 *A Summer Place* (Richard Egan; Warner Bros.)
April 1960 *The Sword and the Cross* (Gianna Maria Canale; Valiant Films)
April 1960 *Tall Story* (Anthony Perkins; Warner Bros.)
September 1960 *Tarzan the Magnificent* (Gordon Scott; Paramount)
June 1960 *These Thousand Hills* (Don Murray; 20th Century-Fox)
March 1960 *Three Stooges Fun-o-rama* (Three Stooges; Columbia)
September 1960 *The Time Machine* (Rod Taylor; MGM)
June 1960 *Vice Raid* (Mamie Van Doren; United Artists)
May 1960 *Visit to a Small Planet* (Jerry Lewis; Paramount)
April 1960 *Wake Me When It's Over* (Ernie Kovacs; 20th Century-Fox)
January 1960 *When Hell Broke Loose* (Charles Bronson; Paramount)
May 1960 *The Wind Cannot Read* (Dirk Bogarde; 20th Century-Fox)
May 1960 *Yesterday's Enemy* (Stanley Baker; Columbia)
January 1960 *The Young Stranger* (James MacArthur; Universal-RKO)

Nyuk-nyuk-dive! Unlikely companions for the *Tiger Shark*'s February 12, 1960, arrival in Green Bay, Wisconsin.

Uncommon forms of first-run presentation

Just six percent of first-run engagements within the sample of 1500 theaters took a form other than a double bill.

At the forefront of these uncommon exhibition practices were the 4.5 percent of theaters that could get away with screening *The Atomic Submarine* as a stand-alone feature. Patrons of these establishments would have been used to this form of presentation, though, since these venues were located within very small communities – what one might refer to as "one-theater towns" – where a lack of competition had long since established single bills as the norm. A lone exception was the 911-seat Garden Theater in Charleston, South Carolina, whose owners elected to try and double ticket sales by running *The Atomic Submarine* and *The Purple Gang* as stand-alone features for four days each, rather than booking them together as a single attraction.

At the other end of the spectrum, a little under 1.5 percent of first-run engagements of *The Atomic Submarine* showed the picture on a triple bill. The venues involved on this occasion were located in heavily built-up areas where multiple theaters were playing *The Atomic Submarine* on a double bill; in an attempt to stand out from these direct competitors, theater-owners augmented their programs with a third feature, usually in the form of a cheap western or a rerun of a popular recent hit.

The least widespread – though surely also the most memorable – of these variant first-run viewing possibilities was attested at just two major venues nationwide, where *The Atomic Submarine* was exhibited together with a live music show. At the Howard Theatre in Washington, D.C., known at the time as a rhythm and blues hot spot, the movie played for seven days from March 11, 1960, in support of an outstanding line-up that included Jimmy Jones performing his million-seller "Handy Man," the Ernie Fields Orchestra with its international hit version of "In the Mood," Marv Johnson with his top ten single "You Got What It Takes" and Bo Diddley beep-beeping his way through "Road Runner." A few days later, for four performances on Sunday, March 20, the 3600-seat Paramount Downtown Theater in Los Angeles presented *The Atomic Submarine* in support of a "Giant Rock and Roll Stage Show" that featured teen idol Bobby Rydell, the Little Dippers (i.e., the Anita Kerr Singers) singing "Forever" (#9 on the *Billboard Hot 100* at the time), pop duo Skip & Flip at the height of their fame and Richard ("Louie Louie") Berry performing "Have Love, Will Travel." One can't help but wonder how the film's Electro-Sonic compositions by Alexander Laszlo went over at these musically minded screenings.

Beyond the first run but never out of sight

The Atomic Submarine continued to receive steady employment as a supporting feature at second-run houses in 1960-61. Its myriad co-features during this phase of its theatrical life ran the gamut from the Soviet-made animated feature *The Snow Queen*, via such Oscar-nominated fare as *Cat on a Hot Tin Roof* and *The Big Fisherman*, to Robert Youngson's silent era compilation *When Comedy Was King* and a number of horror titles including Roger Corman's *House of Usher* and Hammer's *The Curse of Frankenstein*, *The Mummy* and *The Brides of Dracula*. At discount theaters and $1-per-carload drive-ins, *The Atomic Submarine* could furthermore be encountered on triple, quadruple and even quintuple bills.

The film was then swiftly sold to television, making its small-screen debut in a *Movie at 5* slot on WWLP-TV (broadcasting from Springfield, Illinois) on March 3, 1962. By the end of the year, it had aired on stations throughout the U.S., reaching Los Angeles in an 8:30 p.m. *Chiller* slot on KTTV on May 5, and the East Coast by way of an 11:15 p.m. broadcast over WNYS-TV in Syracuse, New York, on September 15. *The Atomic Submarine* thereafter became a television staple that played regularly during each and every year from 1963 to 1984. There should be no doubt that much of the Monster Kid affection for the title stems from its showings in this medium, with listings columns and TV guides also finally emphasizing its sci-fi content. The feature made its VHS debut on the Monterey Home Video label in December 1985, with a retail price of $39.95. What this all means is that *The Atomic Submarine never* fell out of sight, remaining in circulation throughout the quarter-century following the beginning of its theatrical first run in late 1959.

"One of these must activate the cathode ray tube!" Ad for a February 26, 1964, television showing.

"CYCLOPEAN SYMPHONY"

By David Schecter

The score for 1959's *The Atomic Submarine* isn't atypical in the way that *Forbidden Planet*'s entirely electronic score was three years earlier, but its consistent blending of acoustic and electronic instrumentation sets it far apart from almost every soundtrack of the era. Two exceptions are Paul Dunlap's *The Angry Red Planet* and *Invisible Invaders*, both also from 1959. The two Dunlap scores are much simpler than *Atomic Submarine*'s, and they use fewer electronic effects. But both share an important connection with *The Atomic Submarine*, as the same musician handled the electronics on all three movies.

While other scores from the 1950s and '60s occasionally featured electronics along with their conventional orchestration, they generally used a single type of electronic sound to add a futuristic layer to the rest of the ensemble. These include the use of Theremin (Bernard Herrmann's *The Day the Earth Stood Still*, Ferde Grofé's *Rocketship X-M*, William Lava's *Phantom from Space*), electric violin (Paul Sawtell and Bert Shefter's *Kronos* and *It! The Terror from Beyond Space*, and Irving Gertz's *The Alligator People*), and oscillator-electro-Theremin (Jack Marshall's *The Giant Gila Monster*).

What sets *Atomic Submarine*'s score apart from others is the sheer amount and variety of electronics in it. The wide range of electronic tonalities in *Atomic Submarine* makes the orchestra seem much larger than it actually is. In addition, the electronic instruments in the other pictures usually only accompanied fantastic images such as spaceships, robots or monsters. There are a few instances when only conventional instrumentation

is heard in *Atomic Submarine*, but for the most part, even scenes that don't contain any outlandish visuals are musically colored in some electronic fashion.

Coupled with the many claustrophobic visuals set aboard both the *Tiger Shark* submarine and the *Cyclops* flying saucer, the music contributes to a consistent and all-enveloping sense of weirdness and confinement in a singular cinematic universe. The soundtrack portends such electronic-acoustic intermingling during the 1960s and '70s in the hands of composers like Jerry Goldsmith (*The Satan Bug, The Illustrated Man*), Leonard Rosenman (*Beneath the Planet of the Apes*), Fred Myrow (*Soylent Green*) and Jerry Fielding (*Demon Seed*), with many additional such scores being created as synthesizers became more popular.

The Atomic Submarine's unique soundtrack was written by Alexander Laszlo. Born Sandor Totis, the composer-conductor-pianist-music publisher-inventor was born in Budapest, Hungary, on November 22, 1895. He taught piano and composition while still a teenager, and later studied piano at the Franz Liszt Academy of Music. Laszlo worked as a pianist in Berlin's Blüthner Orchestra at the age of 20, and toured as a concert pianist in Germany and elsewhere in Europe during the 1920s. He was a music director and professor of film music in Berlin, and graduated from the Budapest Academy of Music. Laszlo studied with Hungarian pianist-composer Árpád Szendy, composer Victor von Herzfeld and others. He received his PhD from the University of Munich in 1924, later serving as a professor of film music there, as well as at the German Stage and Film School. He supposedly adapted his professional name as a tribute to Hungarian film producer Alexander Laszlo Korda.

Laszlo invented Colorlight, in which a piano or organ generated colored illumination through projected slides. It was premiered at a music festival in Kiel, Germany, in 1924. The process was labeled "Die Farblichtmusik" (color-light music), and Laszlo wrote books on the subject, traveling throughout Germany to popularize this new art form. He also served as music director at the Munich Cinema Art Studios, was the head of the music department at the Hungarian Film Office, and executive-produced documentary films for the Hungarian government from 1933 to 1938. Laszlo composed music for movies in Budapest and in other European countries, but with the rise of Nazism in 1938, he immigrated to the United States, where he served as a music professor at Chicago's Institute of Design.

He became a member of ASCAP (American Society of Composers, Authors and Publishers) in 1942 and an American citizen in 1944, arriving in Hollywood that same year. Laszlo began composing for studios including Paramount, Columbia and Republic, and he wrote music for *The Amazing Mr. X, Attack of the Giant Leeches, Black Magic, Follow That Woman, Forbidden Island, Ghost of the China Sea, The Glass Alibi, The Great Flamarion, Hot Cargo, Night of the Blood Beast, One Body Too Many, Scared Stiff, Strange Impersonation, Submarine Seahawk, Tarzan's Magic Fountain, Yankee Fakir* and other motion pictures. He also performed as a soloist at the Hollywood Bowl, served as music director for NBC Radio, and scored industrial films.

Laszlo assembled two music libraries (Guild-Universal Music Program Aid Library and Structural Music), promoting them for radio and television uses. He had already composed much of this music for earlier projects, recording many of the cues in Germany with the Frankenland State Symphony Orchestra. Some of the music was re-used in the TV shows *Biff Baker, U.S.A., The George Burns and Gracie Allen Show, The Donna Reed Show, Leave It to Beaver, The Life and Legend of Wyatt Earp, The Lone Wolf, My Little Margie, Racket Squad, Rocky Jones—Space Ranger, The Stu Erwin Show* (*Trouble with Father*), *This Is Your Life, Wagon Train, Wanted: Dead or Alive, Whirlybirds* and others. Cues from his libraries also became a part of Capitol's "Hi-Q" library, where they were heard in productions like *The Hideous Sun Demon*.

A few of Laszlo's songs and instrumental works include "Fairytale (dance)," "11 Preludes," "Sonatina," "Improvisations on 'Oh Susannah'" for symphony orchestra, "Mechanized Forces" for orchestra, "Hollywood Concerto" and "Pacific Tryptych." His daughter and his first wife, Arleen, died of cancer; his second wife, Emmy, was a physician. In 1955, Laszlo was diagnosed with leukemia, and although he was told he only had about two more years to live, he lived for another 15 years, passing away on November 17, 1970, in Los Angeles. Many of the composer's scores are archived at the American Heritage Collection at the University of Wyoming in Laramie.

The Atomic Submarine was a low-budget picture, which should be obvious to anyone observing the cut-rate unblinking monster and the submarine and flying saucer models. However, the filmmakers should be applauded for the sheer chutzpah of including endless special effects shots, which provide much of the charm of the picture, including icebergs that appear to be constructed with aluminum foil. The score follows a similar throw-it-all-out-there-for-the-audience-to-enjoy approach, with the wide range of musical effects being employed without much restraint. Although the music was recorded on-the-cheap, the various futuristic-sounding gizmos fill in a lot of the "blanks" caused by the limited number of musicians, adding production value to the soundtrack. The general musical approach is consistent throughout, and the score holds together very well during the movie's 72-minute length. The soundtrack probably wasn't completed when the film's trailer was made, as the ad features some swashbuckling and other conventional action music that shares nothing in common with Laszlo's creation.

Laszlo's ensemble consisted of about ten players: harp, piano, minimal brass (perhaps a total of three instruments including trumpet and trombone), strings (maybe violin, viola and cello), percussion (with snare drum, celesta, vibraphone), guitar and electronics galore (including organ, electric violin and oscillator). Even without the electronics, Laszlo's composing and arranging skills allowed him to get the most mileage out of his limited instrumentation.

The musician who turned *The Atomic Submarine*'s score into something special was Jack Cookerly. An important figure in electronic music both inside and outside the film music world, the keyboardist-inventor-composer was already orchestrating for Walter Lantz Studios when he graduated in 1949 with a music degree from Occidental College in Los Angeles. After arranging for CBS Radio and playing keyboards with various jazz groups, he become a Hollywood studio musician, playing keyboards for hundreds of productions, including the television shows *Alfred Hitchcock Presents, The Beverly Hillbillies, Dr. Kildare, The Flintstones, Hawaii Five-0, Naked City, Thriller, The Twilight Zone* and *The Wild Wild West*, and movies such as *The Colossus of New York* and *The Space Children*. In the mid-1950s he began orchestrating and then composing for many studios, and his music can be heard in television series like *Combat!, Death Valley Days, Father Knows Best, The Fugitive, The Gumby Show, Hollywood and the Stars, I Spy, In Search of…, Lassie, Maverick, Mister Ed, Mutual of Omaha's Wild Kingdom, My Three Sons, National Geographic Specials, The Rifleman, Sesame Street* and *The Untouchables*, and motion pictures such as *Invasion of the Star Creatures, Omega Syndrome, Shoot Out at Big Sag* and *This Is Elvis*.

Jack Cookerly's "Magic Box" and other musical paraphernalia, used by the keyboardist to create many of his electronic sounds.

In 1954, Cookerly developed the first music synthesizer to be used in motion pictures and television, and he designed many synthesized sound effects that became a part of the original *Star Trek* TV series. He helped devise a number of important inventions pertaining to electronic music, including an electronic circuit that added full harmony to a single organ note. Cookerly also invented the first electronic guitar, and took part in the development of the first computer-controlled electronic organ. In 1979, his inventions became a part of every electronic keyboard that featured interactive player control. Cookerly passed away in Oregon on September 13, 2017.

A few years before *The Atomic Submarine*, Cookerly had created a special organ-like contraption that arranger Nelson Riddle nicknamed "The Magic Box." Cookerly's homemade electronic instrument was built using the gutted insides of a walnut Hammond Chord Organ, retaining only the case, keyboard and speaker. He rebuilt the electronics so the instrument could generate new sounds hitherto unknown in Hollywood or anywhere else on the planet. The inventor eventually added other keyboards and electronics to his creation, also hooking up an external Leslie speaker which could further modify the sounds by producing tremolo and pitch variations. Cookerly recalled somebody describing his setup as "orange crates and a lot of tubes." In a number of movies, he used his "Magic Box" in tandem with an electric violin that was processed through the keyboard, allowing him to produce mysterious and otherworldly sound effects that were musical enough to serve as part of the orchestra. He featured this particular approach on *It! The Terror from Beyond Space*, *Missile to the Moon* and *The Cosmic Man*, as well as in the aforementioned musical effects-heavy *The Angry Red Planet* and *Invisible Invaders*.

With his Magic Box, Cookerly was a sort of one-man electronic band, able to supply an incredible breadth of music and musical sound effects to *The Atomic Submarine*, including processed electric violin melodies played by Elliot Fisher, various "bloops" and "bleeps" and other futuristic-sounding tonalities that add to the strangeness of the cinematic proceedings. As a result, the melding of acoustic and electronic instruments is as important an ingredient in the picture as are the plot and the ubiquitous special effects.

Because Laszlo was probably unaware of all the different sounds Cookerly could provide, it's likely that the keyboardist auditioned many of these effects prior to Laszlo writing the score. It's possible that some of Cookerly's contributions weren't written down in Laszlo's score, and the musician was instead winging various things during the recording sessions. Because of the small number of musicians present, after listening to the orchestra and electronics rehearse together for the first time, it would have been possible to make some quick changes to the compositions before they were recorded. Cookerly sometimes stayed a bit longer after recording sessions in order to provide some additional sounds, but because he remembered that no overdubbing was done on *The Atomic Submarine*'s music, any such extras would have only affected the parts of the score that were solely electronic.

The Atomic Submarine's score was so low-budget that Laszlo conducted and recorded it in his own Sherman Oaks, California, house on a hill. Cookerly recalled that Elliot Fisher was performing on his electric violin while sitting on a four-legged stool in Laszlo's living room. He was playing a weird vibrato on the string instrument when he looked up and saw Laszlo conducting as if he were leading a major symphonic performance, whereas it was just a handful of players creating some extremely bizarre music in his own house. Fisher started laughing so hard he fell backwards off his stool, went right through the patio screen door and landed in the backyard.

There are 32 cues in the movie, totaling just over 39 minutes of music. It's likely that one of the cues wasn't written for *The Atomic Submarine*, instead coming from Laszlo's music library. An odd touch is that the titles of nine of the first 15 cues contain the word "Telling," as in "Telling the Story Further," "Telling More About the Story" and "Telling Complications of Story." Either Laszlo or somebody compiling the cue sheet did not have a particularly extensive vocabulary.

The score doesn't employ many motifs beyond a five-note theme (often played on brass) that seems to represent the *Tiger Shark* submarine or possibly its travels, although certain electronic sounds get associated with specific events. Laszlo repeats some very brief phrases in a number of cues, which is an easier way of creating music than writing longer and more complex melodies. However, he often keeps his repetitions fresh by altering his instrumental combinations – in many cases thanks to the electronics. The composer employs some basic film music approaches such as ascending the scale to create tension and increasing the tempo to raise dramatic intensity. These tools are pretty rudimentary, but seeing as Laszlo had minimal orchestral forces at his disposal, he was more reliant on such basic tricks to get as much impact out of his score as possible. Rather than relying on too many musical-to-visual "hits," his score instead broadly paints the overall drama in a particular sequence. Since it's doubtful the composer had a professional screening room in his home studio, the score was most likely conducted and recorded without the movie being shown. Performing the music without viewing the picture would have made recording precise hits a more difficult task. Neil Brunnenkant was the movie's music editor, and it would have been his responsibility to try to fix any mismatches between music and film.

Laszlo obviously wanted his score to call attention to itself, as opposed to serving as subtle background accompaniment, a wise choice when a monster that can regenerate its only eye is one of the more subtle aspects of the picture. By having the soundtrack so prominently featured in the movie, the "large-sounding" musical enhancements manage to add a sense of bulk to the model subs and flying saucer. The filmmakers weren't shy about displaying their sci-fi toys, and the composer helped prop them up with powerful musical backing, or at least as powerful as a handful of instruments could manage.

The Atomic Submarine's opening piece is oddly notated on the cue sheet as "Main Title Time to Come," perhaps an inadvertent addition because it wasn't known how long the piece might be when the composition was originally written. Brass plays the five-note theme, and from the very beginning, low electronics can be heard lurking in the background, quickly building in pitch and intensity while piano adds to the sense of danger. Rhythmic, agitated strings then enter, followed by electric violin contributing some seemingly random phrases. After a sprinkling from piano offers a break from the action, an oscillator provides a rising sound effect. The brass returns along with some electronic "pings" playing variations of the main theme, with further brass, piano and some new electronic sounds winding up this decidedly unusual initial musical statement. The immediate blending of acoustic and electronic instruments sets the framework for the majority of the score, with the composer's credit of "Electro-Sonic Music Composed and Conducted by Alexander Laszlo" presumably being the only one of its kind in the history of the cinema. A July 2, 1959, notice in *Variety* mentioned that Laszlo's score was instead called "Electrophonic music," which "consists of audio-vibrations created exclusively by direct electronic devices and instruments." In other words, it was electronic music given a catchy name to make it seem more impressive.

"Telling the Story" segues from the previous cue, again combining the conventional with the fantastic, beginning with harp and brass that's soon bolstered by the addition of electric violin. The music weds the realistic with the science fictionistic as the narration describes a world where "great passenger- and cargo-carrying atomic submarines glided by the dozens" under the Arctic Ocean. The acoustic instrumentation helps convince the viewer that he is witnessing reality, while the electronics tries to persuade us to accept the extraordinary elements as part of this reality. Even when the scene switches from a matter-of-fact topside view to the waterworld below, the music continues using both acoustic and electronic sources. This way, both reality and fantasy are brought together in one world, where they remain for the duration of the picture.

Piano plays a prominent role in the score, with its low notes accompanying the sighting of the submarine *U.S.A.S. Sturgeon* in "Climax of Destruction." Electric violin and other futuristic sounds creep in even more when *Cyclops* is spotted in the distance, the bizarre music informing us that this is no ordinary adversary. As the sub meets its doom, the screams and squeals from the electronics blur the line between music and sound effects. "Telling Disaster," a short transitional cue that takes us to Washington, D.C., uses brass and snare drum to emphasize the military aspect of the Bureau of Arctic Defense. A bit of electronics in the otherwise

A Hewlett-Packard audio oscillator, similar to the one Jack Cookerly used to add some futuristic sounds to the *Atomic Submarine* score.

acoustic presentation is heard during a shot of the Pentagon. Considering there is nothing fantastic about any of the visuals in the sequence, this further illustrates how the futuristic elements of the score are usually lurking nearby, regardless of the nature of the drama.

The electronic aspect of the soundtrack even manifests itself when Lt. Comdr. Holloway woos Julie in the hotel room, as the cue "No Time to Waste (Slow Fox)" features prominent organ, along with electric guitar and vibraphone. While we would classify such a piece as "lounge music" today, this was a typical way of scoring such romantic sequences at the time. The guitar was used in only a few cues, and it's likely that the vibraphone was courtesy of Jack Cookerly, who owned one that he had made some alterations to. The eight-second "Navy Yard," which immediately follows the previous piece, is one of the rare cues that doesn't contain electronics. Brass, snare drum and harp signal the transition from Holloway's hotel room.

Harp and electric guitar help highlight the *Tiger Shark* departing on its mission. The music sounds more Hawaiian than science fiction, but as the submarine clears Puget Sound and heads for the open sea, electric violin portends strange things to come. The next time the submarine is glimpsed, the acoustic accompaniment is similar, but more electronics are incorporated, informing us that the voyage will be even weirder than ever imagined.

As the *Tiger Shark* passes through an underwater electric storm center, various electronics move to the forefront, and when she heads to the top of the world, piano, brass (playing the five-note theme among other things) and electric violin add some drama to the proceedings. Faster brassy versions of the main theme and ascending organ tonalities signal an iceberg breaking up. When the submarine's route is shown via a top-of-the-world map and an animated cartoon line, "Telling About More Disasters" offers brass, harp and electric violin, with electronic punctuations from the keyboard.

As the "Radiation Level" suddenly changes, harp and celesta play alongside various electronic music contributions including electric violin, with the sound effects-type accompaniment emphasizing the radiation as well as the presence of *Cyclops*. A low electronic drone is among a number of devices that musically depicts the torpedoes being fired at the flying saucer. "Ram It" uses strings, organ and brass, with variations of the main theme rising in pitch as the submarine plows into the extraterrestrial craft. When the two vehicles are "On the Bottom," locked in a death grip, the peculiar situation is colored by harp and vibraphone.

The unusual music in "Floating to Nowhere" and "Floating to Nowhere, Part 2" informs us that we're going to enter an even more fantastic part of the film. Along with piano, "bloops" and "bleeps" from the Magic Box provide otherworldly sonic enhancement as the *Lungfish* diving bell approaches the disabled saucer. The electronics heard in this sequence are similar to some of the sounds Cookerly created for the same year's *The Cosmic Man*.

When part of the crew goes "Inside the UFO," piano figures, celesta and electronics add up to a sound effectsy musical background, with hints of the main theme, but not the complete version, which is an interesting touch. Laszlo might have done this because the theme is associated with the submarine. A low, furtive electronic sound is introduced that will become associated with the alien and his telepathic powers.

The low sound returns when the crew works on separating the *Tiger Shark* from the saucer. The only mention of sound or music in *The Atomic Submarine*'s revised May 15, 1959, screenplay reads: "As he works, a weird SOUND OSCILLATION – varying wildly in pitch – sweeps over scene. Reef reacts, startled. The

Jack Cookerly and his wife Arnette in September 2010.

SOUND COMES AGAIN..." Whether Cookerly or Laszlo ever saw the screenplay or knew about this particular description isn't known, but the sound effect in this part of the movie doesn't vary in pitch, instead remaining in the low registers, which adds to the creepiness of the situation.

Because the sub and saucer are linked, Laszlo did not alter his music when the scene shifts from inside the saucer to the interior of the submarine and back again, even though there are different characters in each vehicle dealing with different situations. A change of locale in a movie will often elicit a corresponding change in music, but it's likely the composer's approach was a clever way of letting us know that everyone was in the same boat due to the crafts being connected.

"Light-Waves Kill" adds what sounds like a modernistic piano cadenza (a virtuoso solo passage within a classical composition) to Cookerly's sound effects, with screaming electronics emphasizing Powell being radiation-burned to death; the music, makeup and use of negative footage effectively conjures his ghastly demise. When Carney runs from Powell's burned body and is killed by closing doors, the electronics top even what came before. Swirling dissonances accompany the piano onslaught, while electric violin further emphasizes his horrific end.

"Voice from UFO" and "Declaration of UFO" use low sounds to accompany the presence of *Cyclops* amidst brass fanfares, harp and sundry electronic offerings, with the same musical approach that illustrated

Powell's radiation death similarly covering Dave's. "Escape from UFO" continues the cadenza-like piano approach, with various electronics, harp glissandos and brassy outbursts adding to the frenetic musical accompaniment. As the *Lungfish* rejoins the submarine in "Floating to Port," the diving bell's journey is again depicted by "bloops" and "bleeps."

"Prepare the ICBM" raises tension with electric violin rising in pitch while being accompanied by additional futuristic sounds – including an oscillator's whine. Strings, organ and piano highlight "Rise and Destruction of UFO," with brass playing variations of the main theme as the missile pursues and eventually blows up the escaping saucer.

"Hurrah They Come—March," is heard just before the end of the movie as Holloway and Carl contemplate humanity's future and whether we'll ever again have to deal with one-eyed puppet monsters. Featuring a marching band, this cue was probably a recording that Laszlo had done for a previous project, or else it was written and recorded in the past by someone else, as it uses a full band rather than the instruments employed in the rest of the score. It was an odd choice for closing music, because even though they're supposedly at the Bremerton Navy Yard, there's no Navy band in sight.

More appropriate is "End Title End of UFO," a short coda that throws in an oscillator along with the rest of Laszlo's ensemble. It's a fitting end to a singular score that meshes conventional and unconventional sounds into a cohesive whole – creating a soundtrack that is often noticed even by those who normally don't pay much attention to film music.

REVIEWS

Boxoffice: [T]his is a highly imaginative science fiction offering with a climactic sally into the field of the horror play. As a supporting piece on the nether side of dual programs, it should prove acceptable entertainment for the not too critical ticket-buyer. During its early sequences, the film is about as exciting as a meeting of the Tuesday Afternoon Discussion Club. That's because too much footage and dialogue is devoted to creating the situation upon which the yarn is predicated. At midmark, however, it picks up speed and generates a fair helping of spine-tingling and suspense. Special effects…are generally adequate and in a few instances are ingeniously devised. But they, too, lose some of their impact because of long periods of conversation liberally larded with the usual scientific double talk.

The Los Angeles Times (from its two-sentence review): Orville Hampton's script tries moderately hard but ends up routine anyway.

Motion Picture Daily: The straight-a-way story thankfully ignores the trifles and irrelevancies that can conceivably slow down any theme bordering on the patriotic….

Variety: The exploitation value of the title is about all this one has to recommend it, though it's based on a fairly good science fiction monster story idea. The directing is sluggish, special photography loses effectiveness by repetition of scenes and the screenplay wanders aimlessly. …Some of the special effects are good, but one atomic vessel passes the same iceberg at least three times. …A typical error found in Orville Hampton's hasty script is to have learned scientists solemnly proclaiming that the Magnetic North Pole is identical with the Geographical North Pole.

Monthly Film Bulletin: A moderately ingenious idea, ruined by indifferent acting, poor special effects and a lumbering script….

Harrison's Reports: [This] tale of seagoing danger and derring-do makes lively program entertainment. And business should be abetted by the title and current interest in things naval and atomic. …Direction by Spencer G. Bennet keeps the film on course most of the way and wisely concentrates on the action. The special effects are quite good [*sic*]….

The San Diego Union: This one has a cast of competent actors, but unfortunately they are handicapped by awkward pauses between lines and actions so they meander through the film's most tense moments and in general do not seem very impressed by it all.

New York Daily News: It's a dull voyage to the North Pole, what with the crew and experts sent along to see what they can see, all doing little but looking through the monitor and talking a great deal about what to do if and when they sight the nemesis.

The New York Post: Unhappily, [the children's movie *Toby Tyler*] is co-billed with *Atomic Submarine*, a horror-filled pseudo documentary. We would suggest that elders time their moviegoing for the children and skip the second feature.

The New York Times: Credit the Allied Artists entry with some erratic but genuine suspense, a beguiling assortment of miniature, grotto-like settings and a good, eerie musical score. Then forget it.

The Courier-Journal (Louisville KY): The film is presented with a running commentary, which was used, undoubtedly, to make the whole goofy business seem factual.

Buffalo Courier-Express: Scenes often are repetitious and the screenplay tends to wander. Arthur Franz, Dick Foran, Bob Steele and Tom Conway are the best known

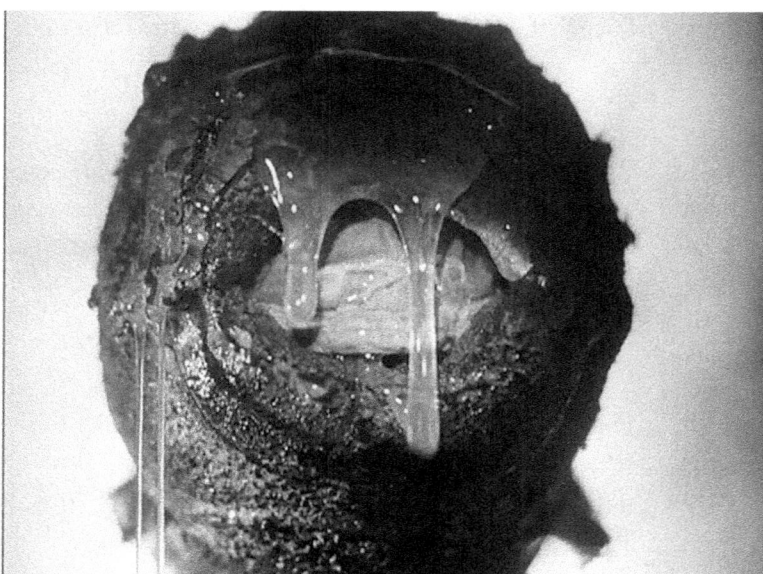

players, all competent but in a sluggish yarn marked by numerous errors.

Kinematograph Weekly: In spite of some ingenious special effects, the film has an inexpensive air and the script contains more untidy improbabilities than is usual with such fancies. The central idea that flying saucers are never seen to land because they hide in the ocean is intriguing and the actual encounters between man and monsters is handled quite well, but the script is halting and the direction does not move swiftly enough to cover inconsistencies or trim the loose ends.

Video Watchdog: [I]ts wretchedness retains a certain charm that isn't entirely rooted in nostalgia.

"The Astounding B Monster" (website): For our money, it's producer Alex Gordon's most enjoyable film.... A cast that only good ol' Gordon could assemble ... the only one missing is Marla English. (Instead there's Joi Lansing, so who's complaining?) The plot is 14 karat sci-fi corn, and we mean that in the most affectionate sense. A furry cyclops of an alien has burrowed his saucer beneath the polar ice cap and it's up to the intrepid crew of the *Tiger Shark* to blast him in the ice hole. I like this movie and I don't care what you say.

The Script

(Revised - 5/15/59)

"ATOMIC SUBMARINE"

Screenplay by

ORVILLE H. HAMPTON

PRODUCER

ALEX GORDON

DIRECTOR

SPENCER G. BENNET

IN ASSOCIATION WITH	PRODUCTION MANAGER
JACK RABIN & IRVING BLOCK	EDWARD MOREY, JR.

GORHAM-RAYLOCK PRODUCTIONS

6322 Franklin Avenue
Hollywood 28, Calif.

HO. 9-7728

ASSOCIATES

Henry Schrage
Orville H. Hampton

"ATOMIC SUBMARINE"

AHEAD OF TITLES - PROLOGUE

FADE IN:

1   STOCK SHOT - NORTH POLE AREA - DAY

With, possibly, radically-designed jet planes flying over the Arctic wastes.

>NARRATOR
>It cost Commander Robert Peary twenty years of unremitting hardship and misery to reach the North Pole, finally, in 1909.

DISSOLVE TO:

2   ANOTHER STOCK SHOT - ARCTIC WASTES - DAY

>NARRATOR
>It would have astounded Peary to learn that, by the late 1950's and early 60's, the vast, frozen top-of-the-world he pioneered had become a vital highway for world travel and commerce. Not just in the skies...

DISSOLVE TO:

3   SPECIAL EFFECT SHOT - UNDER ICE - SUBMARINE ROUTE

>NARRATOR
>...but also deep under the ice, in the frigid, five-million-square-mile depths of the Arctic Ocean.

4   SPECIAL EFFECT SHOT - CARGO SUB STURGEON - DAY

The huge, heavy vessel glides smoothly along, between underwater mountains, following the well-beaten Polar route.

(CONTINUED)

4   (CONTINUED)

                    NARRATOR
          Here great passenger and cargo-
          carrying atomic submarines glided
          by the dozens, back and forth
          across the Pole, until a series
          of mysterious undersea disasters
          threatened to close the Arctic
          route forever.

5   SPECIAL EFFECT SHOT - CLOSE SHOT - STURGEON

        As it glides, very close, PAST CAMERA, so we can read
        the name: U.S.A.S. STURGEON (United States Atom Sub
        Sturgeon) on the bow. We may spot the closed-circuit
        TV camera on the surface of the conning tower.

                    NARRATOR
          The decisive moment came May 3, at
          1315 hours, when the undersea
          atomic liner, Sturgeon, largest of
          them all, reached 87 degrees, 10
          minutes north latitude - only a
          few miles from the North Pole it-
          self!

6   SPECIAL EFFECT SHOT - UNDERWATER ICE CAVE - DAY

        In the depths of it appears a distant, faint ball of
        glowing light. The ball begins moving toward CAMERA,
        slowly, becoming larger and larger. There may be a
        FAINT, WEIRD ELECTRICAL HUM just audible from it.

7   SPECIAL EFFECT SHOT - CARGO SUB STURGEON

        It moves ahead, unconscious of impending doom, the Peep-
        Peep of its sonar impulses now gradually increasing in
        pitch, Doppler effect, as they echo back from the
        approaching blob of light.

8   SPECIAL EFFECT SHOT - THE SAUCER - DAY

        Dimly seen, a vague, indistinct shape (thru this sequence
        -- it approaches -- a huge, oval-shaped disc, with what
        seems to be a revolving turret, or lighthouse, on top.
        The Peep-Peep of the Sturgeon sonar has now risen to a
        frantic scream, and the MAGNETIC, LOW-FREQUENCY HUM from
        the saucer becomes louder and louder.

9   SPECIAL EFFECT SHOT - PAN SHOT WITH STURGEON

The great atom sub glides past camera, but now, as we are shooting from her stern over the bow, we see the screws halt, then go into reverse, and she begins to back away, back TOWARD CAMERA. Then, in the b.g., we see the saucer, the great, eerie 'eye' or whatever it is, looming like a searchlight on her top, and the oval shape seeming like a great mass of glowing energy. The saucer is easily overtaking the reversed Sturgeon, when:

10 SPECIAL EFFECT SHOT - THE SAUCER

It moves to a position nearly filling screen, when...

A great bolt of sheer high-frequency energy - like an undersea lightning bolt - stabs out from somewhere in the saucer, and lances out TOWARD CAMERA.

11 SPECIAL EFFECT SHOT - THE SAUCER AND STURGEON

The great, stabbing bolt of energy impinges on the hull of the Sturgeon, and for an instant, the entire sub seems to glow with radiant light. Then, in closer details, we see the effects...

12 SPECIAL EFFECT SHOT - BOW OF STURGEON

It seems to melt away (or collapse) like a shell of paraffin over a fire. The water boils and hisses about it.

13 SPECIAL EFFECT SHOT - CONNING TOWER

The radio antenna, the periscope, the mast, the tower itself - all seem to melt, and collapse.

14 SPECIAL EFFECT SHOT - THE STURGEON

What is left of the Sturgeon, glowing and hissing, still red hot, begins rising to the surface, towards the ice-layer.

15 SPECIAL EFFECT SHOT - THE SAUCER

It reverses, draws back into the ice-cave from which it issued.

16 SPECIAL EFFECT SHOT - ABOVE ICE - DAY

And now, she seems to be rising in a tremendous crunching, grinding, writhing activity. Finally, it breaks completely, and for a moment, the red-hot hull of the Sturgeon is visible in the cracking, grinding masses of ice. Then, a larger hiss of steam, and finally a ROAR of earthquake volume, a fireball, then a mushroom cloud. The atomic reactor of the Sturgeon has blown up, the ship is vaporized to nothingness. As the atomic cloud rises up toward camera...

17 SCREEN WHIRLS OPTICALLY INTO A SPIRAL BLUR

and then

DISSOLVES TO:

18 INSERT - CLOSEUP - NEWSPAPER FRONT PAGE

This comes WHIRLING INTO VIEW, then WHIRLING STOPS and we can read the headline in the CAPITAL TIMES.

>   CLOSE ARCTIC SEA LANE
>   AFTER EPIC DISASTER!!
>   - - -
>   Mysterious Loss of Sturgeon,
>   Latest in Series of Polar
>   Tragedies, Prompts
>   Drastic Action.

DISSOLVE TO:

19 EXT. STOCK SHOTS - WASHINGTON

Preferably of the Pentagon. A helicopter shot of it would be most readily identifiable.

> NARRATOR
> According to the official reports, the next phase of the life-and-death drama occurred May 10, in Washington --

DISSOLVE TO:

20 INSERT - CLOSEUP PANELED DOOR

On which is lettered:

(CONTINUED)

20 (CONTINUED)

        BUREAU OF ARCTIC DEFENSE
               WAR ROOM
        NO ADMITTANCE WITHOUT
               SPECIAL
        SECURITY CLEARANCE

              NARRATOR
  -- at a hush-hush, super-secret
  meeting in the Arctic theater
  war room.

21 INT. WAR ROOM - DAY - MATTE SHOT - EST. SHOT

    This room is, more than anything else, a system of maps and charts - a huge detail of the Arctic ocean occupying an entire wall behind the conference table. On it are small, magnetic models of submarines, defense stations, etc. Also, to one side, is a huge globe of the world, on a revolving stand. File cabinets, rolled maps and charts, shelves of references, navigation guides, etc. All business; no time wasted on decoration. There is an electric lock on the door; no one can 'burst in' on the excuse of making a mistake.

22 CLOSE SHOT - ADMIRAL TERHUNE

    The burly, grim-faced Admiral, in uniform, is at the head of the conference table. There is an intercom on a small stand beside his position at the table. The Admiral has a sheaf of reports and photographs, also a stack of mimeographed 'briefs' at his elbow. No nonsense; Terhune speaks in clipped, brief phrases, almost as if he has digested sentences down to short, terse bursts before 'releasing' them from his lips. The Admiral's lips are moving as we first see him, but we do not hear his speech until the Narrator is finished.

              NARRATOR
  Admiral Terhune, in charge of the
  Arctic Theater for the Joint Chiefs,
  well knew the effect the 'leak' of
  any of the explosive information
  would have on the world civilian
  population. So the Admiral was
  determined: There would _be_ no
  leaks!

REVISED 5-26-59   "ATOMIC SUBMARINE"

23 FULL SHOT - PAST CONFERENCE TABLE - TOWARD DOOR

And now we see Admiral Terhune in the close f.g., and the other participants of the meeting - DR. CLIFFORD KENT, a practical, 'egghead' scientist, Chief of Scientific Research and Weapons Development; SIR IAN HUNT, English, winner of the Nobel prize for Oceanography, and Defense Secretary Murdock, distinguished, white-haired.

There is a KNOCK. Admiral Terhune presses the button, the lock BUZZES, and the door opens.

COMMANDER WENDOVER steps inside. He is a hard-bitten, intelligent young-old man of about forty. Years of responsibility have made him older mentally than physically. He is the highest type of the professional navy man, the elite of the new craft, the atomic submarine.

                    WENDOVER
              Admiral Terhune!

24 PANNING WITH WENDOVER

He manages a smile, puts out his hand as he crosses to the Admiral's place at the table, in a TIGHT GROUP SHOT with the other men.

                    ADMIRAL
              (addressing the men at the table)
              Gentlemen, this is the man we've
              been waiting for - Skipper of the
              atom killer sub, Tiger Shark -
              Commander Dan Wendover.
                  (indicating)
              This is Justin Murdock, Secretary
              of Defense...
                    WENDOVER
              Mr. Murdock...
                    MURDOCK
              Commander.
                    ADMIRAL
              And I know you've heard of Dr.
              Clifford Kent, Dan - -

Wendover puts out his hand and the scientist takes it.

                    KENT
              Commander.
                    ADMIRAL
              Dr. Kent had a lot to do with the
              development and design of your boat.
                  (continued)

                                        (CONTINUED)

REVISED 5-26-59   "ATOMIC SUBMARINE"   7.

24 (CONTINUED)

                    MURDOCK
                      (indicating)
              Sir Ian Hunt just flew in from
              London.

                    WENDOVER
                      (impressed)
              Are you the Doctor Hunt - Nobel
              prize winner for Oceanography?

                    SIR IAN
                      (smiling)
              Let's say I took the bows for a
              team of brilliant associates.

    They take their seats at the table. Terhune indicates
    a place for Wendover; meanwhile, he pulls a sheet of
    paper from a file folder in front of him. Looking at
    them all in turn to command attention, the Admiral says:

                    ADMIRAL
              Gentlemen, to begin, let me read
              you just one line from a detailed
              staff study prepared for the Joint
              Chiefs: "In our judgment, these Arctic
              disasters may prove the gravest
              emergency in all history."

25 REACTION SHOT - PANNING OVER FACES

    As part of the above line carries over scene.

                    MURDOCK O.S.
              Any comments on that statement?

26 CLOSE TWO - SIR IAN AND KENT

    Sir Ian, in typical English underplay fashion, comments:

                    SIR IAN
              Bit on the fanciful side, isn't it,
              Sir?

27 GROUP SHOT

    The Admiral smiles wryly, murmurs:

                                            (CONTINUED)

27   (CONTINUED)

                    ADMIRAL
           Possibly, possibly.
                (then, a new thought,
                taking another paper
                from the folder)
           Let me read you a partial list
           of observed phenomena:
           1. Complete disruption of communica-
           tions with Dew line warning stations.
           2. Destruction of four surface
           vessels, largest, 10,000 tons.
           3. Radioactivity in Arctic waters,
           floe ice and bergs.
           4. Peculiar television images preceding
           each distress call.
           5. Seven Polar atom subs, vanished
           without a trace!
                (a grim smile)
           "Fanciful" did you say, Sir Ian?

28   REACTION SHOTS - CLOSEUPS - MEN

     To INTERCUT above, while Admiral reads.

29   TIGHT GROUP

     The Admiral looks up expectantly into the faces.

                    ADMIRAL
           Now we come to you, Dan. You
           skipper the Tiger Shark, the
           most advanced, the deadliest
           killer sub in the fleet. Right
           now she's undergoing emergency,
           around the clock modification in
           the Bremerton navy yard.

     The Admiral pulls a cross-section of the Tiger Shark
     from his pile of documents, uses a pencil to indicate
     his point as he says:

                    ADMIRAL (cont'd)
           The orders call for special obser-
           vation and testing instruments
           here...

30   INSERT - CLOSEUP - DIAGRAM OF SUB

     As the Admiral's pencil, as a pointer, follows his
     words, he explains:

                              (CONTINUED)

30   (CONTINUED)

                    ADMIRAL O.S.
            Removal of all but two atomic
            torpedos. Special launching
            equipment for water-to-air
            ballistic missiles. A special
            escape hatch in the keel for the
            Lungfish.

31   GROUP SHOT - FAVORING WENDOVER AND ADMIRAL

        As Wendover frowns, puzzled.

                    WENDOVER
            'The Lungfish?'

                    ADMIRAL
            A special deep-exploration device
            - sort of an animated diving bell.
            Captain Siguard Nielsen developed
            it, after he retired, if you remem-
            ber?
                    (tossing the diagram
                    back on the pile)
            He'll be going with you -
                    (then, indicating
                    the other two
                    scientists)
            - along with Dr. Kent, and Sir Ian.

32   CAMERA ROLLS IN SLOWLY FOR TIGHT TWO OF THE ADMIRAL
        AND WENDOVER

        Wendover's face becoming more and more grim as the
        Admiral explains:

                    ADMIRAL
            Special orders are being cut
            recalling your entire crew
            from leave, effective at once.
            There's a fast jet at National
            Airport waiting to fly you,
            Dr. Kent and Sir Ian to Seattle.

33   CAMERA MOVES IN FOR BIG HEAD OF WENDOVER

        as the Admiral concludes:

                                              (CONTINUED)

REVISED 5-26-59   "ATOMIC SUBMARINE"
                                                          10.

33   (CONTINUED)

                         ADMIRAL O.S.
               The Mission of the Tiger Shark is
               to hunt down and identify the cause
               of these Arctic disasters. If humanly
               possible, you will remove it!

                                          SLOW DISSOLVE TO:

33-A STOCK SHOT - SEATTLE - PREFERABLY HIGH PANORAMA - NIGHT

                                               DISSOLVE TO:

REVISED 5-26-59   "ATOMIC SUBMARINE"
                                                          10-A.

33-B   INT. REEF'S APARTMENT - NIGHT

        A modern bachelor apartment - living room and bedroom
        combination, nicely furnished, with a kitchenette
        behind a pass-through bar at the other end of the room.
        This doubles as a bar for mixing drinks. Empty
        glasses and the remnants of snacks are scattered about.

33-C   APARTMENT DOOR - THREE SHOT - DAVE HELEN REEF

        LIEUTENANT DAVE MILBURN, ex-Naval Academy halfback
        and inter-collegiate boxing champion, hard-nosed and
        trigger-tempered, is reluctantly taking leave from
        Reef's party. His pretty, placid wife, HELEN, is
        indeavoring to get him through the open door and cut
        his 'farewell scene' short. Dave is slightly, but
        not objectionably, high. REEF HOLLOWAY, a handsome,
        capable, relaxed Annapolis -type, is smiling amiably
        and bantering with Dave, all the while trying to
        usher him out with determined speed. But it is not
        easy to get Dave through the door. He is chattering
        constantly, in a lecturing tone, to someone inside
        the apartment o.s.

                        DAVE
                   (earnestly)
                ...Not that I don't think our
                Lieutenant Commander Holloway is
                the finest exec in the sub fleet,
                Julie...and not that he isn't the
                best friend I have -

                        HELEN
                   (pulling Dave by his arm)
                Come on, Dave. You talk too much.

                        DAVE
                Quiet, Little Mother!
                   (back to Julie o.s.)
                I feel it behooves me to warn
                you -

33-D   FULL SHOT - JULIE

        perched on the arm of an overstuffed chair, in all
        her lush female magnificence - contoured and
        accoutered elegantly - with fine legs, long and sexy.
        Julie is drool-bait, especially for an undersea
        sailor who only comes up for air and 'so forth'
        every three months. Julie smiles to herself as she
        listens to Dave's slightly thick, but earnest advice.

                        DAVE
                   (continuing, o.s.)
                Our friend Reef is no less than
                Number One Howl of the entire sub
                Wolf Pack. Nuclear powered! When
                it comes to women, he has a built-in
                sonar detector that -

REVISED 5-26-59   "ATOMIC SUBMARINE"   10-B-C-D.
33-E   THREE SHOT - REEF DAVE HELEN - APARTMENT DOOR

Reef is trying to crowd Dave through the door from behind while Helen is tugging away at him from the outer portion of the doorway.

> REEF
> Now, Dave Old Buddy, you know
> you're exaggerating -
> (to Helen)
> What do you think of this husband
> of yours? On most boats a certain
> loyalty exists between the Exec and
> his Navigation and Firing Officer.
> (he sighs tragically)
> But unfortunately, in the case of
> Lieutenant Dave Milburn of the Tiger
> Shark and myself -
>
> DAVE
> (fighting his way back
> inside, militantly)
> But Julie's a nice girl, and I've
> seen you work. She deserves a fighting
> chance!
>
> REEF
> Helen. I appeal to you -
>
> HELEN
> (clutching Dave by both
> shoulders and staring him in
> the eye)
> Dave! Look at me! I am the mother
> of your three children! Now _please_
> take me home to them. At once!

Dave smiles weakly, now feeling the drinks, bows heroically to the room at large, and exits scene under Helen's guiding arm. Reef closes the door behind them with an elaborate sigh, then CAMERA PANS WITH HIM into scene with Julie. She looks up at him impishly and smiles:

> JULIE
> Dave _is_ exaggerating. Just think, a
> man spends three months in a deep freeze.
> It'd take his whole shore leave just to
> thaw him out. By that time, he's ready
> to report back!
>
> REEF
> It won't take _me_ long to defrost -
> not around _you!_

The moment is pregnant with anticipation as Reef meets the unspoken challenge in Julie's eyes as we

                                        DISSOLVE TO:

REVISED 5-26-59 "ATOMIC SUBMARINE" 10-E

30-F TIGHT TWO SHOT - BIG HEADS - REEF AND JULIE

In a deep, torried kiss on the couch. Eyes closed, they enthusiastically plumb the depths of feeling, then, at last, reluctantly, they break apart. Julie sighs deeply. Reef shakes his head, like a boxer who has sustained a knockout punch, trying to clear it. CAMERA PULLS BACK for MED. TWO. Julie, unable to speak for a moment, throws a quick look at Reef, who seems to be gulping for air, then she reaches for a cigarette from a box on the coffee table. She drops two or three as she fumbles for one and finally gets it in her mouth.

Reef picks up a table lighter, strikes it, holds it to her cigarette. But his arm is trembling so he cannot hold it steady. Finally, Julie grasps his wrist, holds the flame steady, then contrives to bring the tip of the cigarette in contact with it. She leans back, takes a deep drag, only now dares to speak.

    JULIE
   (ruefully)
  What was I saying...about thawing
  out icebergs?

Reef manages a tiny smile. Then he observes:

    REEF
  You never can tell about icebergs. Only one-ninth above water.

Julie weighs this, then studies Reef appraisingly:

    JULIE
  After that kiss - I'd say that's
  about right.

Reef snuggles closer to her, slips an arm about her waist, murmurs:

       (CONTINUED)

33-M (CONTINUED)

>   REEF
> Do you feel anything?

>   JULIE
>   (incredulous, dis-
>   traught)
> Are you kidding???

She takes a couple of rapid puffs, reaches for her drink, takes a long pull at it.

>   REEF
> I mean - that this is the be-
> ginning of something - that it
> wasn't just...accidental, our
> getting together?

>   JULIE
>   (wryly)
> Original!
>   (staring off, as
>   if to recall)
> Isn't the next chorus something
> about: 'Let's not waste one
> precious golden moment - any
> second, there could be a knock
> on the door, and - '

Reef covers her mouth with his fingertips, murmurs:

>   REEF
> Stranger things have happened,
> you know. I've had leaves can-
> celled like -

He snaps his fingers. Now Julie covers his lips, murmurs with unmistakable import:

>   JULIE
> Then by all means, let's not
> waste time!

And she kisses him - hard, enthusiastically. Immediately, happily, Reef enters into the spirit of the thing.

10-G

34   (OMITTED)

34-A   INSERT - CLOSEUP GLOVED HAND - AT DOOR OF REEF'S
        APARTMENT

        A uniform glove. It comes up to the bell, which is beneath a card reading: LT. COMM. RICH. L. HOLLOWAY, U.S.N. The gloved finger punches the bell.

35   INT. REEF'S APARTMENT - NIGHT - TIGHT TWO - REEF AND
        JULIE

        Still kissing. Julie murmurs:

                        JULIE
                I hear a bell.

        Eyes closed, Reef murmurs:

                        REEF
                I hear a whole carillon of 'em!

        And he kisses her again.

36   INT. HALL OUTSIDE REEF'S APARTMENT - NIGHT - INSERT -
        CLOSE PAN - WITH HAND

        As it leaves the bell, begins BANGING on the door insistently.

37   INT. REEF'S APARTMENT - NIGHT - TWO SHOT - JULIE AND
        REEF

        Again, frowning, she listens:

                        JULIE
                What's that pounding?

        Reef, eyes still closed, takes her hand, places it over his heart.

                        REEF
                    (murmurs)
                Need I say more?

        And he kisses her again. The POUNDING STOPS.

REVISED 5-26-59   "ATOMIC SUBMARINE"   10-H

38 OVER SHOULDERS OF REEF AND JULIE - DOWN AT FLOOR

And now Julie, looking over Reef's shoulder, sees an envelope pushed under the door from the hall outside. She reacts, taps him on the shoulder.

              JULIE
           (insistently)
    Reef - look!

Reluctantly, he turns, sees the envelope. He frowns at her. With extreme reluctance, he goes to the door, stoops down, picks up the envelope, removes the contents. Julie waits anxiously.

Suddenly, Reef grasps the significance, slaps his forehead in exasperation.

              REEF
    Oh no!

              JULIE
           (alarmed)
    What's wrong?

She jumps up, goes over to him, grasps his wrist, looks at the papers. She, too, reacts, as Reef tragically slaps his forehead again, looks regretfully at her - this lovely, willing morsel.

              REEF
    Oh no!

And he is almost crying as we -

                          SLOW DISSOLVE TO:

38-A STOCK SHOT - A NAVY YARD - NIGHT

                                  CUT TO:

REVISED 5-26-59　　　　　"ATOMIC SUBMARINE"　　　　11

39　EXT. NAVY YARD - NIGHT - CLOSEUP SIGN ON BUILDING

>   BREMERTON NAVY YARD
>   DOCKS 1-6
>   No Admittance Except to Authorized
>   U.S. Navy Personnel

CAMERA PANS OFF SIGN to pick up jeep which pulls up to the front of the gate leading to the pier. Reef Holloway, very grim-faced, very disgusted, climbs out, takes his sea bag from the vehicle. The jeep pulls away. Reef, shaking his head regretfully, starts toward the Marine guard at the door.

OMIT 40

40A　NAVY YARD - AT GATE

CHIEF OF THE BOAT 'GRIFF' GRIFFIN, an 'old Navy' man with clipboard, is checking off seamen, one by one, as they pass through the gate, murmuring their names and passing on the submarine o.s.

As Reef approaches, LIEUT. DAVE MILBURN intercepts him.

>   DAVE
>   Reef!
>
>   REEF
>   (glumly)
>   So they caught up with you, too?

40B　TWO SHOT - DAVE & REEF

>   DAVE
>   (sadly)
>   At the worst possible moment.
>   Tomorrow is Janie's birthday.
>   Poor little kid has looked forward
>   for two months to having her Daddy
>   home. Now -
>
>   REEF
>   (unimpressed)
>   That's the worst possible moment?
>
>   DAVE
>   (frowning)
>   What could be worse than disappoint-
>   ing a little girl?
>
>   REEF
>   (flatly)
>   Disappointing a big girl!

(CONTINUED)

REVISED 5-26-59   "ATOMIC SUBMARINE"   11-A

40B (CONTINUED)

Dave, with a wicked grin, takes this big.

> DAVE
> Julie!
> (he laughs cruelly, unsympathetically)

Reef throws him a dirty, betrayed look.

40C PANNING WITH THEM - PAST GRIFF

As they start through the gate past Griff, who acknowledges them. Dave laughs heartily, claps Reef sympathetically on the shoulder.

> DAVE
> Tough, old buddy! Really tough!

DISSOLVE TO:

41 INT. CONTROL ROOM - GROUP SHOT - WENDOVER HUNT KENT

As Dave and Reef come down ladder and greet Wendover.

> REEF
> (puzzled)
> Thought you were going to Washington, Skipper.

> WENDOVER
> I did go. Just back.
> (then)
> Reef, these are a couple of our passengers - Sir Ian Hunt, and Dr. Clifford Kent. My exec, Commander Richard Holloway.

> REEF
> (shaking hands)
> I met Dr. Kent, once.

> KENT
> Nice to see you again, Commander.

> REEF
> (puzzled)
> Are you men going with us? What for? Where -

> WENDOVER
> (non-committally)
> We'll discuss that later.

REVISED 5-26-59   "ATOMIC SUBMARINE"

42   PAN WITH WENDOVER TO SEAMAN

                    WENDOVER
            Tell Chief Griffin to report to
            me as soon as the crew is aboard.

The seaman acknowledges the order and exits.

                    WENDOVER
                (to Kent and Sir Ian)
            My yeoman will show you to your
            quarters.

                    SIR IAN
            Thank you.

One of the seamen leads the way out bulkhead door
to the wardroom.

42A   EXT. NAVY YARD - AT GATE (as in 40-A)

The seaman who reported Wendover's message is just
exiting scene. Griffin is checking names off on his
roster as YEOMAN CHESTER TUTTLE, rumor-monger of the
Tiger Shark, approaches the Chief.

                    CHESTER
            What's the scoop, Griff? Hauled
            out in the middle of the night - all
            leaves cancelled. We goin' to war,
            or what?

                    GRIFF
                (logically)
            Don't you worry, Chester. When the
            Skipper wants you to know what's going
            on, he'll tell you. Okay?

                    CHESTER
                (not satisfied)
            I don't like it. This is all mighty
            funny -

                    GRIFF
                (non-commitally)
            Isn't it, though?
                (then, motioning with his
                 pencil)
            Suppose you get aboard, anyway, huh?

Disgruntled, Chester passes through the gate, as Griff
checks him off on the roster and grins after him.

REVISED 5-26-59   "ATOMIC SUBMARINE"   13-14

43   INT. CONTROL ROOM - NIGHT

       Here is the 'brain' of the sub - the controls, the
       TV monitors, the sonar sets, the 'Christmas Tree' panel
       of warning lights, etc.

44   FULL SHOT - THE CON

       Dave Milburn is already busy checking the equipment.
       The other seamen are preparing the boat for sea. Reef
       turns to Wendover.

                         REEF
                 I think I'll stow my gear.

       But Wendover, with a peculiar look, frowns, and says:

                         WENDOVER
                 I'm - afraid I have some bad
                 news for you, Reef -
                     (as Reef looks at him)
                 You'll have to share quarters,
                 this trip.

                         REEF
                     (frowns, puzzled)
                 Who with?

                         WENDOVER
                 Dr. Neilsen. He'll be - -

                                              (CONTINUED)

15.

44   (CONTINUED)

> REEF
> (grins)
> 'Doctor' Neilsen? When did <u>that</u> happen?

> WENDOVER
> (puzzled)
> Huh?

> REEF
> (cheerfully)
> It'll be all right. We're old friends!

Now Reef is down below deck level. Wendover turns towards Dave. Wendover shrugs helplessly. Dave returns it.

> WENDOVER
> (checking the plot board)
> Get ready. We shove off as soon as Griff reports all the crew aboard.

> DAVE
> Right, Skipper.

He goes to work, as Wendover smiles peculiarly at the bulkhead door through which Reef just passed.

45   INT. PASSAGEWAY - NIGHT - PAN SHOT - WITH REEF - OVERLAP ACTION ABOVE

As he climbs down a ladder into FRAME, then PAN WITH HIM as he eases past a couple of seamen and arrives at the entrance to the exec compartment. He frowns as he sees a sign by entrance.

46   INSERT - CLOSEUP - THE SIGN

It is only stuck on by scotch tape, below the normal exec sign. It reads: DR. NEILSEN.

47   CLOSE SHOT - REEF

He hesitates only a second, knocks, then pushes drapes aside.

48   INT. EXEC COMPARTMENT - NIGHT - MED. CLOSE - REEF

As he enters, smiling cheerfully:

          REEF
I understand we'll be sharing
quarters, Skipper -
     (but then, his grin
     fades, becomes a look
     of disgust, loathing)
Carl! You - !

49   TWO SHOT - REEF AND CARL NEILSEN

CARL NEILSEN has the look of an ascetic - thin, sensitive features, a nervous, intense manner - the 'egghead' appearance. He turns, reacts to Reef's presence. He is smoking a cigarette in rapid, nervous puffs. Reef sinks, disgusted onto the bunk.

          REEF
I should have suspected, when
I heard that 'Doctor.' I thought
it was your father.

          CARL
It was supposed to be. Dad had
a heart attack, two days ago.

          REEF
     (alarmed)
How is he - ?

          CARL
It was moderate. He'll be
all right.
     (then)
But it was out of the question,
his coming along.

          REEF
     (disgusted)
And they thought *you* could replace the Skipper?

Carl displays a trace of anger for the first time.

          CARL
There was no choice. Dad and I
developed the Lungfish together.
Except for him, I'm the only one
qualified to dive in it.

(CONTINUED)

49   (CONTINUED)

                    REEF
           You could train someone else.

                    CARL
           Not in two days.
                (then, earnestly)
           Look: Do you think I wanted
           to come? If it didn't mean
           so much to Dad - proving his
           depth-explorer - it's the last
           thing I'd want!

Reef's lip curls contemptuously. He mutters slowly, angrily:

                    REEF
           That I can believe!

Carl drops his eyes at the intensity of Reef's stare. He turns to his gear, begins unpacking his essentials. Reef shakes his head vaguely, worriedly.

                                        DISSOLVE TO:

50
thru   (OMITTED)
53

54   EXT. SUBMARINE DOCK - NIGHT - STOCK SHOT OR SPECIAL
       EFFECT - SUBMARINE LEAVING DOCK

       It makes a turn in the channel, then heads up the
       Sound, past Seattle, toward the open sea.

                                        (CONTINUED)

54   (CONTINUED)

                    NARRATOR
          The Tiger Shark left her dock
          at Bremerton at 0335 hours, the
          morning of May 11, on what was
          to prove the strangest, most
          fearful voyage ever made by a
          submarine, atomic or otherwise.

                                        WIPE TO:

55   INT. CAPTAIN'S COMPARTMENT - NIGHT - CLOSE SHOT -
     WENDOVER AT DESK

     He carefully opens a compartment of his desk, locked
     by a combination lock, takes out the log book and the
     sealed orders for the voyage. Then, replacing the
     orders in the compartment, he takes a pen and begins
     making an entry in the log.

                    NARRATOR
          Simultaneously with the 'Shark's'
          departure, and with his crew still
          in the dark concerning their secret,
          fateful mission, Skipper Wendover
          made the first notation in the log...

56   INSERT - CLOSEUP - THE LOG BOOK

     As Wendover's hand writes, carefully and precisely:
     MAY 11 - 0335 HOURS. DEPARTED BREMERTON DOCK, FULL
     CREW - SPECIAL PASSENGERS KENT, HUNT,
     NEILSEN. WILL BRIEF CREW IN TWO HOURS
     AFTER CLEARING SOUND...

                    NARRATOR
          ...The men would remain un-briefed
          for two hours, until the Tiger
          Shark cleared Puget Sound and was
          headed for the open sea...

                                        DISSOLVE TO:

57   INT. CREW DINING ROOM - NIGHT - FULL SHOT - THE
     DINING HALL

     Which has a series of long tables and benches, re-
     movable when the room is to be used for other pur-
     poses. To one side is the pass-through to the galley,

                                        (CONTINUED)

REVISED 5-26-59   "ATOMIC SUBMARINE"

57   (CONTINUED)

where there is always a cook on duty to feed and coffee men coming off watch. There are several crew members drinking coffee at the tables now. We see CPO Griff Griffin enter, almost stumble and fall over a huge pile of equipment on the floor - aqualungs, face masks, tanks, fins, rubber suits, etc. - sharkman outfits. Griff explodes:

> GRIFF
> Who the devil belongs to this... gear?

> POWELL O.S.
> We do, Chief.

And AL POWELL, a long, lean drink-of-water, and his partner, DON CARNEY, shorter, stockier, an ill-assorted pair, step into scene, looking somewhat uneasily at the irate Chief.

> GRIFF
> Oh? You two guys - what do you do around here?

> CARNEY
> Underwater demolition. Seamen First Class Powell...
>   (indicating the taller)
> ...and I'm Carney.

> GRIFF
>   (exasperated)
> Yeah, I know - so you're frogmen!

> POWELL
> We're off tin cans. We've looked this pig-boat over from fore-to-aft, but can't seem to find an empty locker to stow our stuff.

> GRIFF
> An empty locker in a sub? Are you kidding?
>   (then, hands on hips)
> This whole deal is making less and less sense to me. What're frogmen doing aboard the Tiger Shark?

(CONTINUED)

57 (CONTINUED)

> CARNEY
> Following orders, like everybody
> else in the navy.
> > (he takes out his
> > and Powell's, hands
> > them to Griff)

Griff examines them, scratches the back of his neck, shakes his head.

> GRIFF
> Beats me.
> > (then, handing
> > back the orders)
> I don't envy you swabbies, swimmin'
> in that North Pole ice water.

> POWELL
> Meantime, where'll we stash these
> gizmos?

Griff gestures for them to pick it up, and follow him.

> GRIFF
> Come on. Maybe we can hide it
> somewhere in the aft torpedo
> room.

Powell and Carney pick up their gear, follow Griff aft.

DISSOLVE TO:

58 EXT. OPEN OCEAN - NIGHT - SPECIAL EFFECT SHOT - TIGER SHARK SNORKEL

The only portion of the sub above water.

> NARRATOR
> Shortly before dawn, the Tiger
> Shark, running submerged at
> better than thirty knots, had
> left the Sound behind and was
> headed for the open sea.

59 INT. PASSAGE TO WARD ROOM - PAN SHOT WITH WENDOVER

as he climbs down a ladder from an upper hatch into the passage to the ward room.

5-27-59   "ATOMIC SUBMARINE"   22-23.

59-A   INT. WARD ROOM OF SUB - NIGHT

The ward room, officers' dining room and "social" area, where the ship's officers, including Reef and Dave, the scientists, Carl Neilsen and Griff, are assembled. Griff has a microphone ready for the Captain, as he enters.

Wendover sits down, as Griff steps back a pace or two. Wendover takes out his sealed orders, opens them, glances through them, then hands them to Reef.

> WENDOVER
> These are our orders, Reef. Better look them over while I fill in the crew.

Reef takes them, and is reading them intently while the Captain is saying into the microphone:

> WENDOVER
> Now hear this: All men of the Tiger Shark. This is the Captain speaking.
>   (he takes a deep breath)
> I know you're wondering about all the mystery –

OMIT 60-62

5-27-59   "ATOMIC SUBMARINE"   24.

63   REACTION SHOTS - ABOUT SUB

In the (a) torpedo room (b) crew dining room (c) control room, as desired, to intercut Wendover's briefing. All the faces are sober, tense.

          WENDOVER O.S.
            (filter)
     Our mission is so dangerous it
     had to be kept completely secret.
     It's our job to find out what
     caused the disasters under the
     Arctic ice. Once we cross the
     Arctic Circle, any command you
     hear will be the real thing,
     remember that!

64   INT. WARD ROOM - NIGHT - MED. GROUP - ABOUT WENDOVER

As he finishes, his face set, solemn, sober.

          WENDOVER
     That's about it. Now you know as
     much as I do - as much as anybody does -
          (a faint, grim smile)
     I assured Washington this was the
     best crew of the best sub in the
     fleet. I know you won't make a
     liar out of me!

Wendover clicks off the mike, hands it to Griff, who solemnly hangs it up. Dave heaves a deep sigh, relieving tension, breathes a solemn:

          DAVE
     Well!

Reef, grim, his face frozen, hands the orders back to Wendover.

          WENDOVER
     What do you think?

          REEF
           (slowly, considering)
     I think I should have joined the
     Air Force!

And the members of the group manage a faint smile.

REVISED 5-26-59   "ATOMIC SUBMARINE"   25.

65   CLOSE SHOT - CARL

Nervously he studies Reef. He is visible just beyond, looks up, meets the glance. Carl turns ostentatiously away.

DISSOLVE TO:

66   MONTAGE SEQUENCE

INSERT - CLOSEUP WENDOVER'S HAND WRITING IN LOG

And the notation: MAY 18, 1200 HOURS, STILL RUNNING DUE NORTH VOYAGE UNEVENTFUL POSITION 165:20 W. LONGITUDE, LATITUDE 58° 10'...

And over the moving hand we:

SUPERIMPOSE:

INSERT - ANIMATED MAP OF POLAR REGION

With a moving course line of the Tiger Shark's voyage from Puget Sound north into Arctic waters. At this point she is possibly about opposite Juneau, but far out in the Pacific.

Over above two scenes:

             NARRATOR
A week later, the Tiger Shark was
still running due north at cruising
speed. So far the voyage was routine,
uneventful. But the nearer they came
to the Arctic Circle...

OMIT 67

67   (CONTINUED)

       Over these scenes:

                    NARRATOR (cont'd)
              ...the more the tension increased,
              the more tiny irritations were
              magnified into bitter feuds...the
              more the crewmen pondered their
              possible fate at the end of the
              voyage...

       FADE BACK IN - SUPERIMPOSED:

68   INSERT - THE ANIMATED POLAR MAP

       With the course line still moving north.

       END OF MONTAGE

                                            FADE OUT:

       FADE IN:

69   INSERT - CLOSEUP - WENDOVER WRITING IN LOG

       And now the entry reads: MAY 20, 0900 HOURS CROSSED
       ARCTIC CIRCLE NEARING DANGER AREA ALL WATCHES DOUBLED...

                    NARRATOR
              On the morning of May 20, the
              Tiger Shark crossed the Arctic
              Circle into the critical area...

                                            DISSOLVE TO:

70   STOCK SHOTS - ARCTIC

       This should consist of moving fields of bergs, avalanches,
       polar bears, walrus, etc.

                                            DISSOLVE TO:

71   SPECIAL EFFECT SHOT - TIGER SHARK

       Running at periscope depth.

REVISED 5-26-59   "ATOMIC SUBMARINE"   27.

72   INT. CONTROL ROOM - DAY - POV - OPTICAL SHOT -
     SPECIAL EFFECTS - CLOSE SHOT TV MONITOR

   As the viewer apparently pans over a field of floating
   icebergs.

                                            DISSOLVE TO:

OMIT
  73
  74
  74A

75   INT. WARD ROOM - DAY - PANNING WITH REEF AND DAVE

   As they come in. Reef stops, glares as he sees Carl,
   sitting at one of the tables, making calculations on a
   pad, sipping coffee. Carl looks up, catches Reef's
   eye. Without a word, he finishes his coffee, picks up
   his material, and goes out. Dave watches this tableau
   curiously. When Carl is gone, Reef goes to the silex,
   pours a cup of coffee for himself and one for Dave.
   Dave joins him, puzzled.

                REEF
             (bitterly)
        You've asked why I stay a bachelor?
        There goes the best reason I know!

                DAVE
             (puzzled)
        Huh?

                REEF
        I might have a son like <u>that!</u>

(Revised - 11/14/58)

76 TWO SHOT - AT TABLE

As Reef and Dave sit down. Dave shakes his head, bewildered.

          DAVE
I don't get it. What's with you two?

Reef sips his coffee.

          REEF
I guess Skipper Neilsen retired before you enrolled at the Academy, didn't he?

          DAVE
I guess.

          REEF
          (sincerely)
One of the finest men, and officers, alive. A real hero - in the best sense of the word - in World War Two. He taught us Engineering and Design. Fought like a demon to develop atom subs.

          DAVE
So?

          REEF
          (bitterly)
So all of a sudden his only son drops out of school, begins making noises like a pacifist. A real egghead, do-gooder, and crackpot! 'Ban the atom tests! Junk the nuclear subs! Spend the military budget for peace!'

          DAVE
          (soberly)
A lot of people think like that.

(CONTINUED)

REVISED 5-26-59   "ATOMIC SUBMARINE"   29-38

76   (CONTINUED)

                    REEF
                (earnestly)
            But they're not Skipper Neilsen's
            son!
                (sadly)
            It broke his heart. Then when some
            newspapers called Carl 'the honest,
            sincere son of a war-mongering father' -
            Captain Neilsen resigned from the Navy.
                (then)
            Oh, he still keeps his hand in - playing
            around with projects like the 'Lungfish' -
            but it broke him, all the same.

                    DAVE
                (broad-mindedly)
            Have you ever talked to Carl - tried
            to see his side?

                    REEF
                (sarcastically)
            'His' side? I've seen it, all right.
            A nice, bright yellow!

    Dave looks questioningly at Reef. Reef drinks his
    coffee rapidly, then exits.

                                        CUT TO:

OMIT
77
78-92

93 INT. TORPEDO ROOM - DAY - TRUCKING OR PANNING - WITH
    REEF

    As he enters, climbs down the ladder to the torpedo
    room, starts forward.

94 MED. FULL - ESCAPE HATCH

    Chester and Powell are working on equipment for the
    little sub, which is stored below the escape hatch and
    will be used to launch it from the belly of the Tiger
    Shark.

    Reef enters, addresses the crewmen.

                    REEF
            Any of you men seen Dr. Neilsen?

    Chester turns.

                    CHESTER
            He's here, Sir.

    Reef turns to the other men.

                    REEF
            Tuttle, would you mind leaving
            us alone for a minute?

    Chester Tuttle looks at Powell, who shrugs.

                    CHESTER
            Sure, Mr. Holloway.

                                            (CONTINUED)

94 (CONTINUED)

He and Powell go o.s. towards the men's dining room. Carl, sensing something, frowns, moves closer to Reef.

95 TWO SHOT

> CARL
> What is it?

> REEF
> (contemptuously)
> Your 'out.'
> (as Carl looks puzzled)
> This came for you.
> (indicating the radiogram)

> CARL
> My father! He's not - ?

> REEF
> Dead?
> (he shakes his head)
> Matter of fact, he's much better. He's left the hospital.

He hands the radiogram to Carl, who scans it eagerly, relaxes, vastly relieved. Then he frowns, puzzled.

> CARL
> What did you mean: I'm 'out?'

> REEF
> Your father can be in Nome, Alaska, tomorrow. We have two choices: Ask them to send him out in a 'copter', and take you off, or the Shark can put back into Nome...

Now Carl reacts angrily, hotly, for the first time.

> CARL
> You 'trade school boys' are all alike, aren't you? Anybody who doesn't happen to think like a little gold-braided puppet is, ipso facto, a coward!

> REEF
> (angrily)
> You said it. But I won't argue -

(CONTINUED)

95 (CONTINUED)

                    CARL
          Wearing a uniform doesn't bestow
          an automatic monopoly on courage,
          Commander! It just so happens I'm
          not a coward - physical or mental -
          and before I'd risk my father's life...

                    REEF
                (interrupting)
          We're all risking our lives!

                    CARL
          That may be. But Dad stays where
          he is, and I'm staying here!

                    REEF
                (studying him)
          You're really a mixed-up oddball,
          aren't you?

                    CARL
          Perhaps. But the idea of willingly
          going to school to spend my life at
          a Paleozoic pastime that should have
          disappeared with the thunder-lizards -
          I'm referring to War - that strikes
          me as the worst cowardice of all -
          being spiritually yellow!

                    REEF
                (sneering)
          You mean nothing is worth fighting
          for?

                    CARL
          Peace - the dignity of man - the
          destiny of the human spirit!
                (hotly)
          Show me a man who says you win those
          by fighting wars, and I'll show you
          an idiot!

                    REEF
                (bitterly)
          You may not win them. But without
          men like your father, to 'degrade'
          himself by fighting to preserve them -
          or as much as we have of them - they'd
          have disappeared, long ago!

Carl reacts to this. The shot, for the first time, has struck home. But then, just as he opens his mouth to say something, there is a TREMENDOUS, RATTLING CRASH...as if

                                         (CONTINUED)

95 (CONTINUED - 2)

the Tiger Shark had shattered a huge, infinite pane of glass under water. The SCENE JUMPS. Reef looks around, terribly alarmed.

          REEF
What the - ?

Now there is the CLANGING of the GQ alarm, and over it, Wendover's voice.

        WENDOVER
         (filter)
Mr. Holloway to the Con, please!
On the double!

96 CUT TO COVER - DIALOGUE ABOVE

97 PAN WITH REEF

He runs to the end of the torpedo room, begins scrambling up the ladder.

98 INT. CONTROL ROOM - DAY - MED. FULL - TOWARD INSTRUMENTS

Present besides the seamen are the Skipper, Dave, Dr. Kent and Sir Ian. The scene is bedlam - the Sonar is screaming weirdly, the SHATTERING CRASHES are repeated over and over, and the scene JUMPS WILDLY. Dave points at the view screen, yells:

          DAVE
The instruments have all gone
crazy! And look at the view
screen!

The scientists peer over his shoulder, absorbed:

         SIR IAN
        (murmurs)
Incredible! Absolutely!

Kent's jaw sets tensely.

99 SPECIAL EFFECT SHOT - VIEW SCREEN AND INSTRUMENTS

This is a wild extravaganza. The radar pattern is jumbled, overlaid with a half-dozen wave-forms. The dials and lights flicker and glow with utter insanity. And the view screen - it is a panoply of flashing, comet-like streaks, jagged streaks resembling lightning bolts, the while accompanied by staccato crashes, alarm bells, shattering bolts of thunder-like sound.

100   SHOOTING PAST THEM - AT HATCH

As Reef comes scrambling up into the Con.

           REEF
        (shouting)
What hit us???

          SIR IAN
        (drily)
The end of the world!

Wendover spreads his hands helplessly. Kent is still frowning at the view screen.

          KENT
It doesn't seem possible, but - could it be an electrical storm center - ?

          SIR IAN
        (incredulous)
Under _water_?

          KENT
High-intensity arcs will burn, submerged. And millions of volts...discharged in random directions...

          WENDOVER
        (to Dave)
Is there any way out of it?

          DAVE
Seems to be all around...

          WENDOVER
        (grimly)
What about down?

          DAVE
        (surprised)
I...don't know!

Wendover turns to Reef:

          WENDOVER
We're dead if we stay here, that's for sure.
        (bluntly)
Take her down! Maximum angle, maximum depth! Maybe even a little more!

          (CONTINUED)

100 (CONTINUED)

					REEF
			Aye, aye.

He moves to the helm, begins AD LIBBING directions to the helmsman. Wendover displays crossed fingers to Sir Ian, Kent and Dave.

101 SPECIAL EFFECT SHOT - TIGER SHARK

(This may also intercut earlier dialogue)

It seems to be buffeted by an underwater storm. The scene is lit by underwater lightning bolts, crashes like exploding skyrockets, the sub is tossed about like a chip. Finally, when it seems that nothing can survive the electrical barrage, we see the nose tilt down steeply, and the Shark glides deeper and deeper into the depths. CAMERA HOLDS as it goes below frame.

					DOWN WIPE TO:

102 DEEPER ANGLE - TILTING DOWN WITH SUB - SPECIAL EFFECTS SHOT

As it noses deeper and deeper into the depths, the bolts of lightning seem to follow it down, probing after it. But at last, the bolts are left behind, the turbulent waters are calm, the crashing noise subsides. Then we see that the sub is almost on the bottom. At last, it does touch and --

					DISSOLVE:

103
thru (OMITTED)
107

108 INT. WARD ROOM - NIGHT - GROUP SHOT - ABOUT TABLE - AT DINNER

Present are the Skipper, Sir Ian, Dr. Kent, Carl and Reef. They are just finishing the meal.

					KENT
				(almost as if be-
				ginning a lecture,
				he clears his throat)
			Sir Ian has evolved a theory. At
			first, I wasn't about to buy it.
				(continued)

					(CONTINUED)

108   (CONTINUED)

>   KENT (cont'd)
>   But, we have eliminated, one by
>   one, every other logical explana-
>   tion -

The others turn eagerly to Sir Ian.

>   SIR IAN
>   It is rather fantastic -

Sir Ian hesitates. Then, from beside his chair, he picks up a large, rolled chart. He unties the string binding it.

>   SIR IAN
>   Here is a chart of the Arctic
>   region. On it I have plotted
>   every instance of these strange
>   phenomena - sinkings, electrical
>   storms, our own experiences...

He unrolls the chart on the table top. Reef and Wendover exchange a perplexed look. Then they get up, come around, peer down over Sir Ian's shoulder at the chart. Sir Ian, with a pencil, gestures on the chart.

109   INSERT - CLOSEUP - THE CHART OF THE ARCTIC

And as Sir Ian's pencil moves, we see a circle of 'X's' about the North Pole, equidistant from it, each marked with a date, and, in print too fine to be read, the circumstances. As he points to one, in the Bering Straits...

>   SIR IAN O.S.
>   Here was where we encountered the
>   electrical storm...The Sturgeon
>   was lost just about this area.
>   Others...here, here, and here...

110   GROUP SHOT

As Sir Ian looks up from the chart, demands:

>   SIR IAN
>   Do you see it?

(CONTINUED)

110   (CONTINUED)

                    WENDOVER
          See what?

                    SIR IAN
          The pattern.
               (tapping the chart
                repeatedly)
          Each incident occurred almost
          precisely a thousand statute
          miles from the Pole. A line
          through the points of occurrence
          makes almost a complete circle...

111   INSERT - CLOSE SHOT - THE CHART

        As Sir Ian's pencil follows his remarks, tracing this
        concentric circle about the polar region.

                    SIR IAN O.S.
                  (continuing)
          ...about the North Pole.

112   GROUP SHOT

        Reef frowns, inquires bluntly:

                    REEF
          Which adds up to what, Sir Ian?

                    SIR IAN
               (significantly)
          I cannot accept the idea that
          these phenomena were either
          random, or natural.
               (a break)
          I believe they are motivated by...
          some sort of intelligence!

        The others react, Wendover and Reef exchange a look,
        then Wendover explodes angrily:

                    WENDOVER
          You mean somebody has been -

        But Sir Ian interrupts him firmly:

                    SIR IAN
          I did not mean to imply, neces-
          sarily, a 'human' intelligence.

                                            (CONTINUED)

112   (CONTINUED)

                    CARL
                (earnestly)
           Then - what on earth kind of in-
           telligence is it, Sir Ian?

                    SIR IAN
           Perhaps not 'on earth' at all.
           Perhaps it comes from beyond
           the earth!

113   REACTION SHOTS - MEMBERS OF THE GROUP - PANNING OVER
      FACES

      As they savor this alarming postulation.

114   TWO SHOT - REEF AND CARL

      Carl looks at him uncertainly. Reef asks grimly:

                    REEF
           Can anything be done about it?

115   THREE SHOT - KENT, WENDOVER AND SIR IAN

      Sir Ian looks thoughtfully at the chart.

                    SIR IAN
           I've been thinking about that.
                (tapping the chart)
           These appearances of...whatever
           we're dealing with...make almost
           a complete ring around the Pole.
           But there is what may be a signifi-
           cant gap, or break, in the ring...

116   INSERT - CLOSEUP - THE CHART

      Which centers, now, on the region in question, which
      Sir Ian's dialogue describes:

                    SIR IAN O.S.
           ...right here...the Queen Victoria
           Sea area, near Franz Joseph Land...

117   GROUP SHOT

As Sir Ian looks up from the chart, but Captain Wendover continues to study it absorbedly.

>   SIR IAN
>   (continuing)
>   ...above Murmansk, and Finland.
>
>   KENT
>   (looking at
>   Wendover)
>   Suppose our theorizing is correct?
>   Then this could be the next danger
>   point!
>
>   SIR IAN
>   What if the Tiger Shark were to
>   anticipate a bit? Perhaps be
>   lying there waiting - ?

Wendover frowns, intrigued by the possibility. Wendover bekcons Reef over to the chart:

>   WENDOVER
>   We'll chart a course straight
>   across the pole - to bring us
>   here -
>   (he looks up into
>   the tense faces)
>   - the Queen Victoria Sea!

Sir Ian and Kent exchange a look. Reef looks at Carl, who frowns tensely.

DISSOLVE TO:

118   (OMITTED)

REVISED 5-26-59   "ATOMIC SUBMARINE"   51-52

119   INSERT - ANIMATED MAP OF POLAR REGION

And now the progress line of the Tiger Shark's voyage moves directly across the Pole. As it reaches the Pole, a sign <u>pops in</u>: JUNE 1, 0730

> NARRATOR
> So - swiftly, implacably, the Tiger Shark moved across the Top of the World towards her rendezvous with...what?

DISSOLVE TO:

120   SPECIAL EFFECT SHOT - TIGER SHARK UNDER THE ICE

OMIT
121
122

123   INT. CONTROL ROOM - DAY - INSERT - CLOSE SHOT -
                                              POLAR CHART

As Dave's hands point out their position, course, and destination.

(CONTINUED)

REVISED 5-26-59   "ATOMIC SUBMARINE"   53-54

123 (CONTINUED)

                    DAVE O.S.
          We've been heading due south, 30
          degrees longitude. By my reckoning
          we're about ten angular seconds...

124 GROUP SHOT - DAVE REEF WENDOVER SIR IAN

     About Dave's navigator position.

                    DAVE
                    (continuing)
          ...short of the Arctic meridian, and
          that should be...

                    SIR IAN
                    (picking it up)
          ...the critical point - _if_ we're on
          the right track.

                    WENDOVER
          Prepare to surface. We'll run at
          flank speed.

OMIT
125-128

129 SPECIAL EFFECT SHOT - TIGER SHARK UNDERWATER

     It picks up speed, rises towards the surface.

                                        DISSOLVE TO:

130 STOCK SHOT - BOW OF SUB BREAKING SURFACE

OMIT
131

132 GROUP SHOT - INT. CONTROL ROOM - AT TV SCREEN - DAVE,
                    REEF, OPERATOR, WENDOVER, SIR IAN

     There is a shout from the operator at the TV screen.

                    OPERATOR
          Mr. Milburn - quick - look at
          this!

     They all move quickly to the TV screen.

REVISED 5-26-59 "ATOMIC SUBMARINE" 55.

133　　SPECIAL EFFECT SHOT - ICEBERG IN WATER - ON TV SCREEN

　　　　We see a giant iceberg in the water.

134　　REACTION SHOT - GROUP

135　　SPECIAL EFFECT SHOT - THEIR P.O.V. - THE ICEBERG -
　　　　　　　　　　　　　　　　　　　　　　　　　　　ON TV SCREEN

　　　　Now we see what appears to be a strange glow of
　　　　energy in the water beneath it. The iceberg seems
　　　　to creak and groan from internal pressures.

136　　CUTS TO COVER - THE CATACLYSM - SPECIAL EFFECT SHOT

　　　　As the ball of energy seems to melt, rend and then
　　　　literally explode the huge mass of ice. The iceberg
　　　　disintegrates and great masses of ice rush away from
　　　　the explosion center.

137　　SPECIAL EFFECT SHOTS - CLOSER CUTS, THE RUSHING ICE

56.

138   INT. CONTROL ROOM - AT TV SCREEN

As Reef yells:

>   REEF
>   Skipper! Those chunks of ice -
>   coming right at us!

The Skipper reacts, instantly yells:

>   WENDOVER
>   Dive! Dive!

139   (OMITTED)

140   INT. TIGER SHARK - STOCK SHOTS - ABOUT BOAT

During emergency dive procedure. THE DIVE ALARM is sounding.

141   REACTION SHOTS - PASSENGERS

Carl, Sir Ian and Dr. Kent.

142   SPECIAL EFFECT SHOT - TIGER SHARK

As it institutes emergency dive, begins to move beneath the waves. This INTERCUTS WITH:

143   SPECIAL EFFECT SHOT - LARGE CHUNK OF ICE

It rushes at express train speed directly toward Tiger Shark.

144   INT. CONTROL ROOM - DAY - FULL SHOT

The Captain, Reef, and Dave and the crewmen work desperately to get their sub into the safety of the depths. But now Dave, at the TV view screen, reacts in a frenzy to what he sees:

>   DAVE
>   Captain! Come here!

But the Captain is too busy.

145   SPECIAL EFFECT SHOT - UNDERWATER - ICE AND SUB

As the Tiger Shark has almost made it to safety, the great bulk of rushing ice lurches into frame, and just collides with the stern of the Tiger Shark. There is a great CLANGING SHOCK and the Tiger Shark staggers like a stricken fish, then quickly rights herself. But the screws slow down, then stop.

146   INT. CONTROL ROOM - DAY - FULL SHOT

Overlapping action above, as the scene LURCHES, and the men strive to maintain their balance. Dave is still oblivious to everything except what he sees on the screen.

     WENDOVER
    (snaps, to Reef)
Determine extent of damage, immediately.

     REEF
    (grabbing an
    intercom phone)
After torpedo room: Report!

     GRIFF'S VOICE
    (over intercom)
This is Griff, Captain. Moderate leak in overhead plates. Damage to main drive shaft housing. Forced to stop reactor engines.

     REEF
We're dead in the water!

     DAVE
    (insistently)
Skipper! You've got to see this! You too, Sir Ian!

Wendover and Sir Ian exchange a look, then move over behind Dave, look over his shoulder, react in astonishment.

     WENDOVER
Well, I'll be - !

     SIR IAN
    (wryly)
I'll be another!

58.

147   SPECIAL EFFECT SHOT - ON TELEVISION SCREEN

On the screen is a great, oval-shaped, glowing ellipse-saucer-shaped. It is perhaps three-hundred feet in diameter. On top is a great, blazing turret of light, remotely resembling a lighthouse beacon - seemingly the 'eye' of the thing. Beneath it are some sort of protuberances, perhaps a landing or settling gear. While they watch, the disc begins to recede from them.

148   THREE SHOT - WENDOVER, SIR IAN, DAVE

And then Reef joins them.

      REEF
What is it?

And then he catches sight of the thing on the viewscreen, frowns tensely.

149   SPECIAL EFFECT SHOT - THE TV SCREEN

And now the saucer grows smaller and smaller, until finally it is only a point of light.

150   GROUP SHOT - UP INTO FACES

      WENDOVER
    (snaps)
  Course and speed?

      DAVE
    (adjusting dials)
  Speed...about twenty-two knots.
  Course...due north!

      SIR IAN
    (a thoughtful murmur)
  Directly towards the Pole!

They look at him, trying to fathom his thoughts.

      DISSOLVE TO:

151   INT. CREW DINING ROOM - DAY - GROUP SHOT - ABOUT GRIFF, CHESTER, POWELL AND CARNEY

Griff, in his undershirt, covered with grease and dirt, has obviously been laboring mightily at the damage.

      (CONTINUED)

5-27-59 "ATOMIC SUBMARINE" 59.

151   (CONTINUED)

Powell and Carney are getting into full aqualung gear, including black rubber suits. Griff looks them over.

> GRIFF
> Okay - you two flounders look
> about set.
>   (he hefts the air tanks
>   on Powell's back and
>   admonishes)
> And remember - this ain't no swimming
> pool - we need a damage report!

> POWELL
>   (mutters)
> See what I mean about volunteering -

But before he can finish the sentence, Griff pulls the face mask down over his nose and mouth. Powell and Carney exit toward the stern.

152   INT. WARD ROOM - DAY - CLOSE SHOT - DRAWING OF SAUCER - ON TABLE TOP

With Sir Ian's hand, holding a pencil, completing the sketch.

> SIR IAN O.S.
> ...a pure oval shape, with this
> cyclops-like eye, or turret, on
> top. I'd estimate its diameter
> at 300 feet. No discernible ori-
> fices...

153   GROUP SHOT - ABOUT TABLE - TOWARD DOOR

This is a discussion group, or 'seminar' - and in the group are Sir Ian, Carl, Reef, Dave and Wendover. Sir Ian leans back, holding the pencil, while his sketch is passed around from one to the next. With a faintly amused expression, Sir Ian murmurs thoughtfully:

> SIR IAN
> 'The Eye of Cyclops..!'

> CARL
>   (looking up from the
>   drawing)
> What did you say, Sir Ian?

(CONTINUED)

153   (CONTINUED)

                    SIR IAN
          Just musing about our 'one-eyed
          adversary' and the legend of
          Homer.
              (to the group)
          'Cyclopes' were the Sons of
          Heaven, who forged the thunder-
          bolts thrown by Zeus.

                    WENDOVER
              (grimly)
          Our 'Cyclops' throws quite a
          thunderbolt, itself!

Now Dr. Kent appears in the doorway, carrying a well-filled briefcase, from which he has extracted a manila folder.

                    KENT
              (with satis-
               faction)
          I knew there was something
          familiar -

He puts down the briefcase, takes an 8 x 10 photograph from the manila folder, then lays the folder aside. He tosses the photograph on the table.

                    KENT
          Take a look.

They peer at it curiously, then someone lays Sir Ian's sketch alongside it.

154   INSERT - CLOSEUP - THE PHOTO AND SKETCH

And we see that the object in the photo - a 'flying saucer' - closely resembles the sketch.

                    KENT O.S.
          The picture was taken by an
          amateur astronomer, over
          New Mexico.

155   GROUP SHOT

As all examine the photos, astonished.

                                        (CONTINUED)

155   (CONTINUED)

                    KENT
          I've had it since I served
          on the Air Force Evaluation
          Board, for UFO reports.

As Sir Ian looks up inquiringly, Carl explains:

                    CARL
          Unidentified Flying Objects.

                    REEF
                (incredulously)
          Then...this is a 'flying
          saucer?'

                    KENT
          That was the popular designation.

                    CARL
                (curiously)
          But...weren't all the sightings
          in the sky - not under water?

Sir Ian picks up the photo, studies it as he reflects:

                    SIR IAN
          This would explain why there
          were never any reports of land-
          ings. It's possible that who-
          ever - or whatever - inhabits
          the craft is not a land creature,
          but a form of marine life.

                    DAVE
                (a wry smile)
          That would make our 'little green
          men' actually 'little green fish'???

                    REEF
                (shakes his head,
                marvelling)
          Undersea flying saucers!

156   SHOOTING PAST GROUP - TOWARD DOOR

       as Griff appears in it, dishevelled as before, but with
       a look of satisfaction. He makes a gesture of knocking,
       says:

                                                  (CONTINUED)

156 (CONTINUED)

>   GRIFF
> Excuse me, Skipper---
>
>   WENDOVER
> Yes, Griff?
>
>   GRIFF
> All internal repairs completed,
> and Frogmen report exterior
> damage minor.
>
>   REEF
>   (with eager
>   satisfaction)
> Then we can get under way?

As Griff nods, all look toward Wendover for orders.

>   WENDOVER
>   (snaps at Dave)
> You plotted the course of
> Cyclops?
>   (as Dave nods)
> Then that's _our_ course! Wherever
> _he_ goes, _we_ go.....until we get
> him!
>
>   SIR IAN
>   (an absent murmur)
> Or, perhaps, until he gets us?

A look passes among them; that possibility is by no means remote.

                                        DISSOLVE TO:

157 INSERT - ANIMATED MAP OF POLAR AREA

with the Tiger Shark course moving back and forth, up and around, the Pole.

>   NARRATOR
> So, the Tiger Shark began
> relentlessly stalking her
> space-enemy. Up to the Pole,
> back to the Arctic Circle...
> again, and again...a week...
> a fortnight, a month....

                                        DISSOLVE TO:

REVISED 5-26-59   "ATOMIC SUBMARINE"   63.

158   SPECIAL EFFECT SHOT - THE TIGER SHARK

moving implacably through undersea caverns, between
hidden mountains, under glaciers, etc.

(Omit semi-montage about Tiger Shark).

                                    DISSOLVE TO:

159   INSERT - ANIMATED MAP OF POLAR AREA

And now the lines for the voyage make up almost
a star-design about the Pole, up and back, to all
quarters.

Over these scenes:

            NARRATOR
        Never a glimpse of their enemy,
        but there were reports...new disasters,
        new ships and lives lost. Invariably,
        the Tiger Shark made for the scene,
        only to arrive after Cyclops had left.
        For all its desperation, the pursuit
        seemed fruitless.

160   SPECIAL EFFECT SHOT - TIGER SHARK CRUISING THROUGH ICE

            NARRATOR
        Then, on July 3, Dr. Kent and Sir
        Ian held an urgent discussion with
        Reef and the Skipper...

161   INT. WARD ROOM - NIGHT - CLOSE DOWN SHOT - CHART OF
                                                    VOYAGE

which appears like a great star - away from the Pole,
back to it - away - back, as in the animated chart
earlier. Now Kent's voice, desperately urgent, comes

                                    (CONTINUED)

161   (CONTINUED)

over, as his hand taps a pencil repeatedly directly on the Pole.

     KENT (o.s.)
  Why does Cyclops invariably
  return to the Pole between
  attacks - never two in
  succession. Always away...
  and back....away....and
  back....

162   GROUP SHOT - KENT, REEF, WENDOVER AND SIR IAN

about the chart.

     SIR IAN
  We've asked ourselves that -
  over and over - a thousand
  times.

     WENDOVER
    (irritably)
  But answers are what we need
  - not more questions!

     KENT
    (significantly)
  We think maybe, now, we have
  them!

Reef and Wendover react.

     KENT
  We took for granted his source
  of energy was nuclear. But
  suppose it isn't at all - what
  if it's magnetic?

     SIR IAN
  We harness energy on a small
  scale by cutting magnetic lines
  of force. Maybe Cyclops does
  it on a super scale....

     KENT
    (significantly
     again)
  The North Pole is the positive
  end of the biggest magnet of
  all - the Earth itself!

163 TWO SHOT - REEF AND WENDOVER

Wendover considers this gravely as Reef responds:

          REEF
What you're getting at: You
think our saucer-friend <u>has</u>
to return to the Pole, regularly
to....recharge his batteries?

164 TWO SHOT - SIR IAN AND KENT

          SIR IAN
That may be over-simplifying,
but---

He doesn't finish the sentence, obviously implying that
Reef's conclusion agrees with their own.

          KENT
Now: Our present tactics are
hopeless. But suppose we
could place ourselves <u>between</u>
Cyclops and the Pole....

165 GROUP SHOT

as Sir Ian picks up Kent's thought:

          SIR IAN
....in such a way as to prevent
his returning to it and, as you
put it....
    (a nod toward
     Reef)
...'recharging his batteries'?

          KENT
If we were lucky enough to catch
him with his power depleted....

          WENDOVER
    (triumphantly)
....we could polish him off with
an atomic fish!
    (claps Reef on
     the shoulder)
That's it, Reef! We'll wait until
the next report of trouble. Then
we'll lay on the bottom, right in
his path, and bushwack him!

(CONTINUED)

165   (CONTINUED)

>   SIR IAN
>   (frowns, puzzled)
>   'Bushwack?'
>
>   REEF
>   (a faint smile)
>   American tactical expression.

And as Reef and Wendover exchange a look, we...

                                             DISSOLVE TO:

166   SPECIAL EFFECT SHOT - TIGER SHARK

cruising at slow speed under the ice.

>   NARRATOR
>   So - a chance of tactics. Now
>   the Tiger Shark cruised almost
>   over the North Pole, waiting
>   for the radio report that would
>   put the plan into effect...
>   On July 13, at 1600 hours, it
>   came!

167   INT. WARD ROOM - DAY - MED. SHOT - REEF

drinking coffee. Behind him, now, we see Dave burst in excitedly from passage way.

>   DAVE
>   We got it, Reef!

Reef springs to his feet excitedly.

>   REEF
>   Cyclops?
>
>   DAVE
>   Sounds like it! Distress call,
>   from a small freighter, between
>   Ellesmere Island and Greenland.
>   One mayday, then...nothing.

As Reef moves toward the door, he demands:

>   REEF
>   Where's the Skipper?

                                             (CONTINUED)

167   (CONTINUED)

                    DAVE
              Already in the Con!

The two men exit. Now CAMERA ROLLS IN FOR CLOSEUP OF
CARL, who, standing in the door, has overheard the
conversation.

                                        DISSOLVE TO:

168   INT. CONTROL ROOM - NIGHT - GROUP SHOT - WENDOVER, DAVE,
       REEF, KENT AND SIR IAN

Dave is working over his navigation chart. The tension
in the Con is electric. Dave takes a compass, swings a
pair of arcs on the chart, looks up to announce:

                    DAVE
              We're here!

Wendover and the others cluster around.

                    WENDOVER
              You're sure?

Dave indicates on the chart.

169   INSERT - THE POLAR CHART

with a distinct line drawn from the reported sinking to
the Pole and another line...the course of the Tiger
Shark, just now intercepting it.

                    DAVE (o.s.)
              Here's where Cyclops knocked
              off the freighter. Here's the
              way he has to head for home...
              the Pole. And...
                    (indicates the
                     intersection)
              Here we are...right in his path!

170   GROUP SHOT

                    WENDOVER
                    (decisively)
              All right, then we're for it,
              right here. Sonar and TV, scan
              the bottom, find a nice spot for
              us to lie and wait for him --
              maybe a cave, or a valley.

                                        (CONTINUED)

REVISED 5-26-59   "ATOMIC SUBMARINE"   68-69-70

170   (CONTINUED)

                        WENDOVER (cont'd)
                    (to Reef)
                Soon as we're on the bottom, go
                through the boat, batten down
                whatever makes a noise, and turn off
                anything that hums or buzzes. I
                want absolute silence!

        They AD LIB further commands and movement about the
        con as we...

                                                DISSOLVE TO:

171   SPECIAL EFFECT SHOT - THE TIGER SHARK

        as she eases her way deep under the ice, sonar PINGS
        probing the way. At last, she eases down onto the
        bottom in a hollow, or undersea cave. The propellers
        are still, the ship lies silent, motionless, seemingly
        dead.

                                                DISSOLVE TO:

OMIT
172
173
174

175   SPECIAL EFFECT SHOT - TIGER SHARK ON BOTTOM

        There is no sign of life whatever.

                                                (CONTINUED)

71.

175   (CONTINUED)

                    NARRATOR
          Hour upon hour, the Tiger Shark
          lay in its deep-six ambush...
          The Arctic depths were as still
          and silent as an uninhabited
          world. Then, at 0600 hours....

                                        DISSOLVE TO:

176   INT. CONTROL ROOM - DAY - TRUCKING AND PANNING ABOUT
      THE CON

      We see Kent and Sir Ian, dozing in their chairs. Wendover
      himself is nodding. Now CAMERA MOVES to Dave, who yawns
      prodigiously, reaches for his coffeecup, finds to his dis-
      gust that it is empty. Then, almost absent-mindedly, he
      glances toward the gauges and view-plates. He reacts.

177   INSERT - CLOSE UP - METER

      which is labeled: RADIATION LEVEL. The needle flickers,
      makes a slight jump, then rises to a positive reading.

178   CLOSE SHOT - DAVE

      He reacts, all attention now. He turns dials to get a
      bearing on the source of radiation. Then he swings around
      in his chair to the television monitor, moves the dials to
      focus the TV camera in the direction of the radiation.

179   SPECIAL EFFECT SHOT - OPTICAL SHOT OF TV SCREEN

      And very faintly, in the extreme distance, we see a tiny
      speck of light growing slowly larger.

180   PAST DAVE - AT OTHERS

      as Dave calls in a sharp whisper:

                    DAVE
          Skipper! Dr. Kent!

      Instantly, the men come alert, move over behind him.
                    WENDOVER
          What is it?

                                        (CONTINUED)

180   (CONTINUED)

In answer, Dave points to the view screen. Both men react, exchange a look.

> KENT
> That's him! Has to be!

> DAVE
> (checking dials)
> Range, about twenty-two miles. Speed....I give it fourteen knots.

> KENT
> (checking instruments)
> His radiation level is very low!
> (to Wendover)
> That would confirm our theory - about having to return to the Pole!

> WENDOVER
> (grimly)
> It better be correct!
> (to Dave)
> Get me a setup on the TDC - range, about seven miles!

181   FULL SHOT - THE CONTROL ROOM

As Wendover moves to the intercom, Dave goes to work on the torpedo data computer. Sir Ian and Kent study the instruments.

> WENDOVER
> (into phone)
> Skipper to Exec: Arm atomic warheads! Load 1 and 2... Report to Con pronto!

Part of the above overlaps following:

182   INT. TORPEDO ROOM - DAY - GROUP SHOT - REEF, GRIFF AND DETAIL

As the VOICE comes over the intercom, Griff reacts, looks at Reef:

(CONTINUED)

182   (CONTINUED)

                    GRIFF
            Sounds like we mean business!

Reef doesn't deign to answer. He gestures to Griff:

                    REEF
            Griff, you arm No. 2. I'll
            handle No. 1.

Griff nods, moves over to one of the panel boards and starts manipulating it. Meantime, Reef is doing the same thing on another panel.

183   CUTS TO COVER - THIS ACTION
thru
183-C

184   SHOOTING OVER TORPEDO CONTROL PANELS - AT REEF, GRIFF AND DETAIL

As the arming is finished, and Reef moves from dials.

                    REEF
            Load One and Two. Then open
            outer doors!
                (grimly)
            And stand by for action!

Reef hurries to the far end of the torpedo room, and begins climbing the ladder. He glances back to see that Griff and another man are manipulating dials to open the inner tube doors.

                                        DISSOLVE TO:

185   SPECIAL EFFECT SHOT - EXT. OF TIGER SHARK - CLOSE ON TORPEDO TUBES

as we see the outer doors slowly lift, disclosing the torpedo warheads inside.

186   INT. CONTROL ROOM - DAY - FULL SHOT - PAST DAVE IN F.G.

as Dave sings out:

                                        (CONTINUED)

74.

186 (CONTINUED)

                    DAVE
          Range: Now fifteen miles!

Now Reef climbs up into the con, demands:

                    REEF
          You're sure it's Cyclops?

                    WENDOVER
                    (gesturing toward
                    TV screen)
          Take a look.

Reef comes over, stares, fascinated, down over Dave's shoulder.

187 SPECIAL EFFECT SHOT - OPTICAL SHOT - VIEW SCREEN

And now, in the TV screen, we can just make out the faint outlines of the approaching saucer - the oval shape, the glowing turret-eye. O.s., Dave now sings out:

                    DAVE (o.s.)
          Range...now 14.5 miles.

188 TWO SHOT - DAVE AND REEF

as they look down anxiously at the screen. Now there is a VOICE over the intercom:

                    GRIFF (o.s.)
                    (filter)
          Griff to Skipper. Tubes One
          and Two loaded. Outer doors
          open. Ready to fire.

                    WENDOVER (o.s.)
                    (obviously into
                    phone)
          Stand by!

                                        WIPE TO:

189 (OMITTED)

75.

190 SPECIAL EFFECT SHOT - THE CYCLOPS - MOVING TOWARD CAMERA

Through an undersea valley, the Cyclops moves silently, its glowing eye probing ahead for possible danger.

191 SPECIAL EFFECT SHOT - THE TIGER SHARK

still lying silently, in wait.

192 SPECIAL EFFECT SHOT - CYCLOPS - MOVING DIRECTLY TOWARD CAMERA

It is approaching very near, now.

193 INT. CONTROL ROOM - DAY - TRUCKING AND PANNING - OVER FACES

ENDING on Dave and Reef. Now Dave sings out:

           DAVE
    Range....ten miles!!

194 SPECIAL EFFECT SHOT - OVER TIGER SHARK - AT CYCLOPS

This is the first tie-in shot, showing the relative positions of the two craft. The Cyclops should still be a considerable distance away - merely a glowing spot in the water.

195 INT. TORPEDO ROOM - DAY - PANNING OVER TENSE FACES OF TORPEDO DETAIL - ENDING ON GRIFF

Griff stands near the firing buttons for tubes One and Two - clearly labeled. The tension is building.

196 INT. CONTROL ROOM - DAY - CLOSE SHOT - VIEW SCREEN - SPECIAL EFFECT SHOT

And on it, we see that Dave has adjusted cross-hairs for the Target Zero. The saucer moves across the view screen, toward the Target Zero.

           DAVE (o.s.)
    Range...eight miles....
    Seven and three-quarters.....

197   SPECIAL EFFECT SHOT - CYCLOPS

It looms huge and awesome IN CAMERA, now, sweeps by and above CAMERA and o.s. There is an awful RUSHING SOUND as it sweeps overhead.

198   INT. CONTROL ROOM - DAY - SHOOTING PAST DAVE AND REEF - AT OTHERS

as Dave sings out:

                    DAVE
         Zero minus ten....nine....

199   SPECIAL EFFECT SHOT - OPTICAL SHOT - VIEW SCREEN

The Cyclops approaches closer and closer to the 'x.'

                    DAVE (o.s.)
       ....eight...seven.....six....
       five....

200   INT. CONTROL ROOM - DAY - SHOOTING PAST DAVE AND REEF - AT OTHERS

                    DAVE
       ....four....three....two....

201   SPECIAL EFFECT SHOT - OPTICAL SHOT - VIEW SCREEN

And now the Cyclops moves directly into the cross of the 'x.'

                    DAVE (o.s.)
       ....one....Target.....

202   INT. CONTROL ROOM - DAY - SHOOTING PAST DAVE AND REEF - AT GROUP

                    DAVE
               (excitedly)
    Zero!

                    WENDOVER
             (barks into
             intercom)
    Fire Number One!

203   INT. TORPEDO ROOM - DAY - MED. SHOT - GRIFF AND OTHERS

as Griff moves swiftly, presses the firing lever, then barks into intercom:

        GRIFF
    Number One fired!

204   SPECIAL EFFECT SHOT - CLOSE ON TORPEDO TUBE

as the first torpedo bursts out and speeds away toward target.

205   INT. CONTROL ROOM - DAY - GROUP SHOT

        WENDOVER
        (into intercom)
    Fire Number Two!

206   INT. TORPEDO ROOM - DAY - MED. SHOT - GRIFF AND OTHERS

Griff fires Number Two, then reports:

        GRIFF
    Number Two fired!

207   SPECIAL EFFECT SHOT - CLOSE ON TORPEDO TUBE

as the second torpedo shoots from its tube after the first.

208   SPECIAL EFFECT SHOT - TYING TIGER SHARK AND CYCLOPS

And now we see the two torpedos, executing a great curving arc, 'homing' on their target. They are still a considerable distance from it.

209   SPECIAL EFFECT SHOT - CLOSE ON TWO TORPEDOS

as they WHOOSH BY CAMERA, speeding toward their target.

210   INT. CONTROL ROOM - DAY - TIGHT SHOT - ABOUT DAVE AND WENDOVER

Wendover checks his watch, demands of Reef:

(CONTINUED)

210   (CONTINUED)

                    WENDOVER
               What's the running time?

                      REEF
                   (checking TDC)
               Thirty-four seconds!

     All wait, tense, breathless, expectant.

211   REACTION SHOTS - ABOUT SUB

      (A) CONTROL ROOM
      (B) TORPEDO ROOM
      (C) CREW QUARTERS

     Carl, the crew, Griff and others, all silently counting
     the seconds.

212   SPECIAL EFFECT SHOT - THE SAUCER

     Now the luminous eye seems to turn to observe the approaching menace. There is a THROBBING BUZZ as of an energy discharge, and then the first torpedo comes in scene, seems to swerve to avoid the Cyclops, goes plunging on past it and o.s.

213   INT. CONTROL ROOM - DAY - SHOOTING PAST DAVE - AT VIEW PLATE - AT OTHERS

     as Dave, agony and disappointment in his tone, calls:

                      DAVE
               Number One...Missed!

     There is an AD LIB response of shock. Then Wendover complains to Reef:

                    WENDOVER
               How could it? We were dead on
               target, with a homing torpedo!

214   SPECIAL EFFECT SHOT - THE SAUCER - CLOSE

     Now, from some vent within the vehicle, a cloud of radiant, luminescent 'jelly' seems to stream out, enveloping it in a protective cloud. Just as the cloud is well-formed about the saucer, obscuring its outlines...

215   SPECIAL EFFECT SHOT - CLOSE ON SECOND TORPEDO

     It plunges through scene and off towards the saucer.

216   SPECIAL EFFECT SHOT - AT SAUCER

as the second torpedo burrows into the protective cloud, more and more slowly, probing vainly toward the still-visible 'eye.' Then...

217   SPECIAL EFFECT SHOT - CLOSE ON TORPEDO

as it buries itself in the mass of luminescent jelly. The propellers thrash madly, ineffectually. Then, gradually, they slow down, and the torpedo is completely surrounded by the mysterious mass.

218   INT. CONTROL ROOM - DAY - SPECIAL EFFECT SHOT - INSERT - THE TV SCREEN - OPTICAL SHOT

AND OVERLAPPING ACTION ABOVE, we see the torpedo slow down and stop, buried in the mass surrounding the saucer.

> DAVE (o.s.)
> Skipper - look at this!

219   TIGHT GROUP SHOT - LOW ANGLE - UP INTO FACES

as Reef, Wendover, Kent and Sir Ian cluster tightly about Dave. Carl enters from the hatch, joins them.

> DAVE
> (pointing)
> A mass of jelly-like stuff came out of the thing, and caught our torpedo!

> WENDOVER
> (exclaims)
> What???

Kent frowns, points.

> KENT
> It must function like a de-Gaussing field.
> (dubiously)
> We'll never get a torpedo through that!

Now Wendover's jaw sets grimly.

> WENDOVER
> Maybe not a torpedo...

They look at him as he moves o.s. to the intercom.

220   CLOSE SHOT - WENDOVER

as he barks into the intercom:

> WENDOVER
> This is the Captain: Blow bow tanks. Reactor Room, stand by: Soon as we're off the bottom, I want all ahead, flank speed, pronto!

221   FULL SHOT - THE CONTROL ROOM

as Dave asks alertly:

> DAVE
> What course, Skipper?

> WENDOVER
> (with grim purpose)
> Right at our one-eyed friend!

There are AD LIB surprised exclamations from all. Reef is incredulous:

> REEF
> Right _at_ him?

> WENDOVER
> That's what I said!

> REEF
> But - what can we accomplish?

> WENDOVER
> We can _ram_ him!

The others exchange quick, frightened looks. Dave is incredulous. Carl moves over to Wendover, admonishes quietly:

> CARL
> You've weighed the consequences, Captain - the lives involved?

Reef glares at him.

> WENDOVER
> Doctor -- I've weighed the lives Cyclops has taken, already...and _will_ take, in the future, unless _we_ can stop him, now!

(CONTINUED)

221 (CONTINUED)

>   CARL
>   We might find other means...
>
>   WENDOVER
>   What other means? If the Tiger
>   Shark can't destroy him, no power
>   on Earth can! Now brave yourselves!

Carl subsides, catches Reef's eye, looks away.

222 REACTION SHOTS - THE MEN

223 INSERTS - HANDS PULLING CONTROL LEVERS

These INTERCUT with faces, above.

224 SPECIAL EFFECT SHOT - THE TIGER SHARK - ON BOTTOM

Now it begins to rise slowly from its bed in the depths, Water pours from the ballast tanks. Then, with the boat floating free in the water...

225 SPECIAL EFFECT SHOT - CLOSE SHOT - SCREWS

as they begin to churn, picking up speed, then, finally, churn the water into a foamy wake.

226 SPECIAL EFFECT SHOT - THE TIGER SHARK

Like a great, predatory fish, it rises from the bottom, moving more and more swiftly. It makes a great climbing turn directly TOWARD CAMERA, then goes overhead and out, speeding toward the saucer.

227 INT. CONTROL ROOM - DAY - REACTION SHOTS - PRINCIPALS

They are all braced against the impending crash.

228 CLOSE SHOT - WENDOVER

as he speaks into the intercom.

>   WENDOVER
>   This is the Captain! All crew
>   members take collision stations!

229 (OMITTED)

230 INT. FORWARD TORPEDO ROOM - DAY - MED. FULL SHOT

as Griff AD LIBS orders for the men to lie in their bunks, brace themselves against structural members, etc.

231 SPECIAL EFFECT SHOT - TIGER SHARK

It has climbed to a level with the saucer, now levels off. It is picking up speed.

232 INT. CONTROL ROOM - DAY - CLOSE SHOT - DAVE

He adjusts the TV view screen, tenses for the shock. Reef appears just behind him. They exchange a grim look, then eye the screen, fascinated.

233 SPECIAL EFFECT SHOT - OPTICAL SHOT - THE TV SCREEN

Now we see the saucer looming up hugely, directly ahead.

234 CLOSE THREE SHOT - WENDOVER, KENT AND SIR IAN

as we hear Dave's voice:

> DAVE (o.s.)
> Stand by -- five seconds...four...three...two...

235 SPECIAL EFFECT SHOT - SAUCER AND TIGER SHARK

as they meet. The Tiger Shark plows into the protective jelly, which slows but cannot stop the juggernaut.

236 CLOSER CUTS - TIGER SHARK

plowing into the protective jelly.

237 FULL SHOT - THE CRASH

as the Tiger Shark, unstoppable, plows inexorably through the protective coating, slams against the saucer itself,

(CONTINUED)

237   (CONTINUED)

       then buries its bow deep within the Cyclops - like a har-
       poon driving into a huge creature of the depths. Perhaps
       a third of the Shark's length is driven deep into the
       saucer. Tremendous RENDING, TEARING NOISES accompany the
       crash, after which...complete, eerie silence.

238   CLOSER CUTS - THE CRASH

       As the bow rends the outer envelope of the saucer, the
       screws of the Tiger Shark churn powerfully against the
       restraining jelly...then a CLOSE SHOT of the Cyclops'
       'eye' shows the glow diminishing.

239   INT. CONTROL ROOM - DAY - SPECIAL EFFECT SHOT - OVER
       DAVE'S SHOULDER - AT TV SCREEN

       And we see the situation, that the nose of the Shark is
       buried deep within the saucer.

                           DAVE
                       (triumphantly)
                 We got him, Skipper - drove right
                 into him!

240   GROUP SHOT - ABOUT DAVE - UP INTO FACES

       as Wendover manages a grim, satisfied smile. Kent and
       Sir Ian eagerly check the view plate, and the gauges.

                           REEF
                 Speared him like a fish!

       Wendover moves to the intercom, announces:

                           WENDOVER
                 This is the Skipper! We did it,
                 men! Drove right through the
                 saucer's hide!

241   REACTION SHOTS - ABOUT THE SUB

       (A) CONTROL ROOM
       (B) TORPEDO ROOM
       (C) CREW'S QUARTERS

       as the men cheer.

242   INT. CONTROL ROOM - DAY - FULL SHOT

                    WENDOVER
                   (smiling)
          We'd better wiggle loose.
                   (speaks into
                   intercom)
          Reactor Room: I want all re-
          verse, full!

243   SPECIAL EFFECT SHOT - TIGER SHARK AND CYCLOPS

      Jammed together, they are sinking slowly in the water.

244   CLOSER SHOTS - THE PROPELLERS

      Overcoming the initial resistance of the jelly, they
      begin slowly turning.

245   FULL SHOT - TIGER SHARK AND CYCLOPS

      It is obvious, now, that they are headed for the
      bottom.

246   INT. CONTROL ROOM - DAY - FULL SHOT

      The room seems to vibrate as the mighty atomic reactor
      turbines exert full power on the propellers. Then Reef
      shakes his head, discouraged.

                    REEF
          We're stuck tight!

                    DAVE
                   (alarmed)
          Skipper! Look at the depth
          gauge!

      Wendover comes over, peers over Dave's shoulder.

85.

247   INSERT - CLOSE UP - DEPTH GAUGE

The dial moves rapidly. Now it is at 175 fathoms, rapidly moves to 180.

248   PAST DAVE AND WENDOVER - AT OTHERS

as Wendover, momentarily puzzled, remarks:

>   WENDOVER
>   A hundred and eighty fathoms!
>   We can't be sinking that
>   fast....
>
>   REEF
>   (coming over)
>   It's the screws, Skipper.
>   (gestures to
>   explain)
>   At our declination angle,
>   running in reverse, they're
>   pulling the Shark and Cyclops
>   right to the bottom.
>
>   WENDOVER
>   (frowns at gauge)
>   And we're at safe maximum
>   depth already....
>   (then barks
>   and order)
>   Stop engines!

Reef repeats the command into the intercom:

>   REEF
>   Stop engines!

249   SPECIAL EFFECT SHOT - CYCLOPS AND SHARK

sinking through the water, pulled lower and lower by the Shark's engines. Now the propellers stop. The two craft still continue sinking, but more slowly now.

                              SLOW DISSOLVE TO:

250   INSERT - WENDOVER'S HAND WRITING IN LOG

as the hand records: JULY 15, 10:00 HOURS. NOW LYING ON BOTTOM, LOCKED TO CYCLOPS, 200 FATHOMS.

                              (CONTINUED)

86.

250　(CONTINUED)

>   NARRATOR
>   Hours later, the two titantic
>   craft were still locked to-
>   gether in an apparent death
>   grip...
>
>   DISSOLVE TO:

251　SPECIAL EFFECT SHOT - TIGER SHARK AND CYCLOPS

lying on the ocean bottom, still with the Shark jammed into the saucer.

>   NARRATOR
>   (continuing)
>   ...on the bottom of the Arctic
>   Ocean, nearly twelve hundred
>   feet below the surface!
>
>   DISSOLVE TO:

252　INT. WARD ROOM - DAY - GROUP SHOT - ABOUT TABLE

Present are Wendover, Carl, Reef, Kent, Sir Ian and Dave. This is a grim, hopeless conclave. The silence, except for a faint trickle of water somewhere, is complete, eerie, ghastly. Faces are bathed in tense perspiration. Wendover shakes his head.

>   WENDOVER
>   If anyone has any more ideas...
>   I'll try anything, before just
>   lying here, waiting to die!

Now Reef explains an idea he has been toying with:

>   REEF
>   Suppose there's an atmosphere,
>   of some kind, inside Cyclops?
>
>   WENDOVER
>   (blankly)
>   What?
>
>   REEF
>   (to the group)
>   If we could get inside the saucer
>   - use our torches - maybe we could
>   cut the Shark loose?

                                              (CONTINUED)

252 (CONTINUED)

                    SIR IAN
That's all very fine, young man. But how would one go about <u>getting</u> inside Cyclops?

Reef takes a deep breath, throws a glance at Carl, then says:

                    REEF
Through the eye - with the Depth-Explorer!

Carl seizes this eagerly.

                    CARL
Yes - the Explorer was <u>built</u> to operate at even greater depths --

                    WENDOVER
                  (disturbed)
But suppose there isn't an atmosphere inside the saucer?

                    REEF
                  (bluntly)
Then the idea's no good. But we're no worse off than we are right now.

Dave picks this up eagerly.

                    DAVE
You've got to let us try, Skipper --

                    REEF
                  (startled)
'Us?'

                    DAVE
                  (ignoring him)
Reef and I can take the Explorer down, clamp it around the eye, and ---

                    CARL
                  (firmly)
No, you can't. But <u>I</u> can --
                  (to Reef)
I can deliver you to the eye. Then you --

                              (CONTINUED)

252 (CONTINUED - 2)

                REEF
            (sneeringly)
    Little out of your line, isn't
    it? You better stay aboard and
    make a speech -- maybe get 'em
    to ban flying saucers!

Carl bridles angrily.

                CARL
    That's enough, Holloway. I've
    told you before, wearing boards
    on your shoulders, and parading
    with a stiff spine doesn't auto-
    matically endow you with back-
    bone - !

                REEF
    - any more than being the son
    of Captain Neilsen does!

Wendover is watching this exchange with growing displeasure.

                CARL
    However our ideas disagree, as
    I've said before, I'm *not* a
    coward! And it happens you've
    got no choice: Either *I* take
    you down there, in the Lungfish,
    or you don't get there -

                REEF
            (bitterly)
    I'd sooner swim!

                WENDOVER
            (snaps)
    That's enough, Reef! Both of
    you!
            (to Reef)
    It so happens Dr. Neilsen's
    right. The odds are long
    enough, without making them
    longer.
            (he turns to Carl)
    Get the Explorer in the airlock,
    ready for launching.

                          (CONTINUED)

252   (CONTINUED - 3)

>   Carl nods. Throwing a final look at Reef, he goes to the passage way, climbs down. Wendover turns back to Reef, suggests:

>>   WENDOVER
>>   You better take Powell and
>>   Carney with you --

>>   DAVE
>>   The frogmen?

>>   WENDOVER
>>   With their underwater experience,
>>   they'll be invaluable. Take
>>   sidearms, and flare pistols --

>>   DAVE
>>   (puzzled)
>>   Sidearms? But the saucer's dead.

>>   WENDOVER
>>   (holding up crossed
>>   fingers)
>>   We hope!

>   Wendover holds out his hands, shakes both theirs. Reef turns to Dave.

>>   REEF
>>   Let's get ready.

>   They head for the passage way and exit. Wendover looks at Sir Ian and Kent, shakes his head solemnly.

>>   DISSOLVE TO:

253   INT. TORPEDO ROOM - DAY - FULL SHOT - AT AIRLOCK

We see the single hatch open, in which the Depth Explorer has been mounted. Carl, in a jumper and helmet, waits by the step with Powell and Carney, dressed in their rubber suits, with helmets and face plates. They carry breathing apparatus. Behind them, Dave and Reef appear, dressed similarly, carrying their equipment - portable torches, a bag of tools, sidearms, flare pistols, and... in Dave's case...a machine pistol (burp gun). Over this:

                    NARRATOR
          Preparations consumed only an
          hour. At 1100, everything was
          ready for this last, desperate
          attempt.

Now the four men join Carl at the airlock. Carl is tense, tight-lipped. Reef frowns, concerned.

                    REEF
          There's still time. You could
          show me how...?

Carl shakes his head firmly, gestures toward the hatch.

                    CARL
          Get in.

254   CUT TO COVER

the action of the five men climbing down hatch (into Explorer). When all are inside, Griff steps forward, closes the hatch. Then he closes the airlock, and goes to intercom.

255   INT. CONTROL ROOM - DAY - GROUP SHOT - WENDOVER, KENT, SIR IAN

And now Griff's voice comes over the intercom:

                              (CONTINUED)

255 (CONTINUED)

>   GRIFF (o.s.)
>   (filter)
>   Ready to open Airlock door,
>   Captain!

Wendover glances once at Kent and Sir Ian. Then he moves to the mike.

>   WENDOVER
>   (into mike)
>   Go ahead, Griff!

256 SPECIAL EFFECT SHOT - BELLY OF TIGER SHARK

Now we see the lock door slide open. A moment later, the Depth-Explorer moves out through the opening, like an animal being born. It hovers for a moment, just below the Shark. Then it maneuvers o.s. towards the Cyclops.

257 INT. DEPTH-EXPLORER - DAY - TIGHT - (AND WE MEAN TIGHT) GROUP SHOT

Carl operates the controls. The five men are wedged in shoulder to shoulder. Reef makes a gesture of direction. Carl nods, complies.

258 SPECIAL EFFECT SHOT - THE CYCLOPS

Now the Depth-Explorer moves into frame, drifts directly toward the great 'eye' - which still has a faint glow.

259 CLOSE SHOT - AT CYCLOPS' EYE - SPECIAL EFFECTS SHOT

The Depth-Explorer moves up with its hatch clamped magnetically, directly over the eye.

260 INT. DEPTH-EXPLORER

as Dave turns to Reef.

>   DAVE
>   Now what?

(CONTINUED)

REVISED 5-28-59   "ATOMIC SUBMARINE"   91.

260   (CONTINUED)

          REEF
     (looks at others, his glance
     lingering on Carl)
  Now what - shall we take
  a chance?

          CARL
     (solemnly)
  That's why we came.

Reef nods.

          REEF
  All right.
     (then)
  Better breathe oxygen, just
  in case.

The others all apply oxygen tubes to their mouths, go down hatch, Reef picking up a large tool like a wrecking bar.

260A   UNDER HATCH

Reef and Dave come down hatch into scene. We see the iris and Reef goes to work on it with the tool.

                              WIPE TO:

261   INSERT - CLOSE UP - FITTING OF EYE

as Reef's tools batter at it. Suddenly, it gives away.

262   SHOOTING AT EYE

as, suddenly, it SEEMS TO OPEN, LIKE A CAMERA IRIS, leaving a circular opening, big enough to crawl through.

262A   REACTION - DAVE & REEF

Now Reef sniffs at the atmosphere that pours in from the saucer. Surprised, enthused, he removes his oxygen tube, breathes deeply.

                              (CONTINUED)

REVISED 5-28-59   "ATOMIC SUBMARINE"

262A   (CONTINUED)

                            REEF
                Air! Pure air! Under high pressure!

                            DAVE
                That's a relief!

262B   INT. OF DEPTH EXPLORER

                            POWELL
                What happens now, sir?

262C   UNDER HATCH

        Reef thinks a moment, then decides.

                            REEF
                You all wait here. I'm going inside,
                take a look.

                            DAVE
                        (insistently)
                Not _alone_, you're not!

        The men ad lib (no)!

        Reef frowns at them, then grins gratefully, squeezes
        Dave's arm, and moves toward the open eye.

262D   INT. OF DEPTH EXPLORER

                            CARL
                Good luck, men!

262E   UNDER HATCH

        Reef smiles, begins crawling through the eye and
        into the saucer, followed by the others.

OMIT
263 to
266

267   INT. SHORT RAMP SECTION - DAY - SHOOTING TOWARDS
                                            OPENING ABOVE

        OVERLAPPING ACTION as the four men crawl down through
        the hole into this section of the ramp of the saucer.

OMIT
267A
267B

REVISED 5-26-59   "ATOMIC SUBMARINE"

267C   RAMP SECTION - TRUCKING SHOT - FOUR MEN - AGAINST BLACK

Reef gestures, leads the way down the ramp. Dave is at his elbow, the two frogmen just behind them. They light TORCHES or FLASHLIGHTS.

OMIT
267D
267E

267F   FOUR MEN - CHAMBER SECTION

They come down ramp section to chamber, stop, and look off screen.

268   FROM THEIR P.O.V. - TOWARD WOUND MADE BY TIGER SHARK

And we see the bow of the submarine extending into the chamber. But, strangely, there is not a drop of water, not a break in the surrounding wall.

268A   FOUR MEN

           DAVE
           (pointing)
How about that! The bow drove half through her, but she sealed herself right up.

           REEF
           (excitedly)
What's more important - there's our problem.
           (points)
The bow ram - the sawteeth are holding the Shark in the break. If we can cut the ram, the Shark can pull herself loose!

           DAVE
           (enthused)
I think you're right.

           REEF
           (to Powell)
Go back and tell Dr. Neilsen. Have him report to the Skipper.

                     (CONTINUED)

268   (CONTINUED)

        Powell nods, retreats. The others unsling their equipment.

                        REEF
                Now let's get to work.

        They light the torches, and advance on the protruding bow of the sub (o.s.).

269   INSERT - CLOSE UP - THE TORCHES

        as they begin biting into the metal of the submarine ram.

                                        WIPE TO:

260   INT. DEPTH-EXPLORER - DAY - CARL AND POWELL

        Carl has the radio mike in his hand and calls:

                        CARL
                Depth-Explorer to Tiger Shark.
                Do you read? Over.

271   INT. CONTROL ROOM - DAY - TIGHT THREE SHOT - WENDOVER, KENT AND SIR IAN

        The Skipper himself wears the headphones. He cries excitedly into the radio mike:

                        WENDOVER
                We read you! Go ahead, Doctor!
                        (then, as he
                        listens eagerly,
                        repeats)
                They're inside the saucer. It's
                filled with breathable air!

                        KENT
                Wonderful!

                        WENDOVER
                        (listening, then
                        enthusiastic)
                That's wonderful, Carl!
                        (to others)
                Reef thinks they can clear the Shark
                bow so we can pull ourself loose!

                                        (CONTINUED)

271   (CONTINUED)

> SIR IAN
> (ever the scientist)
> What is it like, inside Cyclops?
> This is a priceless opportunity
> for....

But Wendover ignores this, admonishes:

> WENDOVER
> Tell Reef: Be sure you're all
> clear before we make a move!
> Good!

He takes off the headphones, beams at the other men.

> WENDOVER
> Maybe we'll come out of this
> yet!

272   FULL SHOT - THE CON

And now Griff, operating the navigation equipment, frowns, perplexed, then calls:

> GRIFF
> Skipper - could you take a look
> here...?

> WENDOVER
> Something wrong?

> GRIFF
> The inertial navigation system.
> Must have been knocked out in
> the crash.

> WENDOVER
> Why do you say that?

> GRIFF
> We're dead in the water. But
> it indicates we're moving!

> WENDOVER
> What????

Sir Ian and Kent exchange a look, come over and join them.

> SIR IAN
> But that's impossible!

(CONTINUED)

REVISED 5-26-59   "ATOMIC SUBMARINE"

272   (CONTINUED)

Now Kent notices something. He points:

>   KENT
> The radiation level - from
> the saucer - it's rising!

>   SIR IAN
>   (suddenly fearful, to
>   Wendover)
> What direction does the system
> indicate?

>   WENDOVER
>   (suddenly grim)
> Due north. At five knots...no, six!

>   SIR IAN
>   (grave, thoughtful)
> Toward the Pole!

>   GRIFF
>   (demanding)
> But - that Cyclops is dead! We
> killed it...didn't we?
>   (as they look away)
> Didn't we?

                                    DISSOLVE TO:

273   SPECIAL EFFECT SHOT - TIGER SHARK AND CYCLOPS

with Depth-Explorer still clamped to the eye. Now we see, definitely, that the two craft, locked together, are indeed moving, slowly but perceptibly, along the ocean floor.

274   INT. CHAMBER SECTION OF SAUCER - DAY - CLOSEUP - FACES OF REEF, DAVE, POWELL, CARNEY

Weirdly lit in the glow of the torches.

274A
OMIT

REVISED 5-26-59   "ATOMIC SUBMARINE"
                                              97-A

OMIT
274B
274C

274D   CLOSE SHOT - REEF

       As he works, a weird SOUND OSCILLATION - varying
       wildly in pitch - sweeps over scene. Reef reacts,
       startled. The SOUND COMES AGAIN, and Reef turns,
       calls sharply:

                    REEF
                Dave?

274E   PAN SHOT - WITH DAVE

       As he detaches himself from the frogmen, moves
       into TWO SHOT with Reef.

                    DAVE
                Yeah?

                    REEF
                Listen!
                    (the SOUND comes again)
                Hear that?

       Dave has not reacted at all. He looks peculiarly
       at Reef.

                                        (CONTINUED)

REVISED 5-26-59   "ATOMIC SUBMARINE"   97-B

274E   (CONTINUED)

>   DAVE
>   I don't hear anything.
>   (he looks at Reef,
>   concerned)
>   Maybe you've been down here
>   too long. Why don't you go
>   back up and -
>
>   REEF
>   Strange you didn't hear it.

OMIT
274F

275   CLOSE SHOT - THE TORCHES

biting deeply into the steel of the ram. Now CAMERA TILTS DOWN SLOWLY, and as it is moving we...

                                        DOWN WIPE TO:

276   INT. GLOBE - DAY - SPECIAL EFFECTS SHOT

Though we see nothing of its construction at this point.

276A   INSERT - CLOSE SHOT - PROBING SPINES - TRICK SHOT
                                          (SPECIAL EFFECTS)

The black, catfish-or-sea urchin-like spines seem to rise from limp supineness. They stiffen, grope like fingers, move towards a series of grommet-like openings in the translucent wall of the sphere. Now a spine nears a grommet, slips into it, apparently making 'contact', for somewhere, a FAINT LIGHT comes on, and the scene becomes lighter. In a moment, another spine slips into another grommet-hole.

277   INT. CHAMBER SECTION - DAY - MED. SHOT - A LIGHT

To an accompanying tympany BEAT, a LIGHT SPOT, appears. A moment later, another drum beat, another LIGHT SPOT. (Note: This business may continue behind subsequent dialogue - more beats, more lights coming on)

278   CLOSE GROUP - THE WORKING PARTY - ABOUT RAM OF TIGER SHARK

As Reef continues working with the torch. Dave pushes up his goggles, reacts, surprised. He taps Reef on the shoulder.

                    DAVE
            Hey - you know somethin'? It's
            getting lighter in here!

                    REEF
                (a similar re-
                 action)
            You know - it is?

Now they give a sudden lurch. Dave looks down at his feet, then into Reef's face.

                    DAVE
            And if I didn't know better - I'd
            swear we were moving!

                    REEF
            Let's get back to work, and maybe
            we will be, soon.

279   INT. DEPTH-EXPLORER - DAY - CLOSE SHOT - CARL TALKING INTO MIKE

He looks about, worriedly.

                    CARL
                (into mike)
            ...I get an impression of move-
            ment, Captain. Is that possible?

                    VOICE OF WENDOVER
                (through phones)
            We have the same reaction, up
            here.

                                        (CONTINUED)

279   (CONTINUED)

                    CARL
                (very worried)
            But ---

280   INT. CONTROL ROOM - DAY - GROUP SHOT - AS BEFORE

      as the Skipper turns to the scientists.

                    WENDOVER
            Now they feel it...down below.

                    KENT
                (frowning at
                gauge)
            Radiation level...constantly
            rising...

                    SIR IAN
                (murmurs thought-
                fully)
            As we near the Pole...

                    KENT
                (sharply)
            There's got to be an explanation!

                    SIR IAN
                (mildly)
            There is.
                (as they study
                him)
            I believe our friend...Cyclops...
            is returning to life!

      A grim reaction, all around.

281   INT. GLOBE - DAY - MED. SHOT - TRICK SHOT - THE FINGERS
      (SPECIAL EFFECTS)

      as, now, the last of them contact their proper control
      points, and a complete circuit of lights FLASHES ON.
      The LIGHT INTENSITY rises.

282   INT. CHAMBER SECTION - DAY - GROUP SHOT - THE MEN

      working on the ram. Now, with a final cut with the
      torch, there is a CLANG, A RINGING SOUND, and then
      the ram drops free.

                                            (CONTINUED)

282   (CONTINUED)

>   REEF
>   (with satisfaction)
>   That does it! I think the Shark
>   can pull clear!

Now, we hear a weird, mechanical voice:

>   SAUCER-VOICE
>   Commander Holloway! Listen!

Reef reacts.

>   REEF
>   You hear that?

>   DAVE
>   (looking blank)
>   The sound again?

Now the voice repeats:

>   SAUCER-VOICE
>   Commander Holloway. Make no
>   resistance.

>   REEF
>   (nervously)
>   A voice, this time. It spoke
>   my name!

Reef draws his gun and Dave raises his machine gun.

283   (OMITTED)

284   MED. GROUP SHOT

And now the voice comes from another quarter:

>   SAUCER-VOICE
>   You will see that avails nothing!

Reef looks around, startled.

285   PAN SHOT - WITH POWELL

His nerve is going. He edges away from the group, then turns to bolt out of scene, heading for the Depth-Explorer. But just as he takes his first steps...

REVISED 5-26-59   "ATOMIC SUBMARINE"   101

286   PAN WITH POWELL

As he stumbles through the darkness.

286A   FLASH OF LIGHT

A flash of light comes down at Powell from somewhere.

287   CLOSEUP - POWELL

The light envelops him, and he cringes.

               POWELL
     Carney - help!

287A   THREE SHOT - CARNEY DAVE REEF

Reacting to Powell's cry.

               REEF
     Carney, see what's happened
     to Powell.

Carney moves o.s.

287B   CLOSEUP - POWELL - MAKEUP SHOT

We see the horrible effect of the light on his face.

287C   TRICK EFFECT - POWELL SHRIVELLED - PRODUCTION SHOT

Powell is shrivelled by the light. The last thing we see of him is...

287D   TRICK EFFECT - POWELL'S HANDS - SPECIAL EFFECTS SHOT

They disintegrate to jelly, and Powell is completely gone.

288   PANNING WITH CARNEY

As he reaches the spot where Powell was killed. He reacts, horrified.

288A   PANNING WITH CARNEY

As he moves away hurriedly.

288B   PANNING WITH CARNEY

As he turns, from the blackness, a burst of steam issues forth into his face.

288C   CLOSEUP - CARNEY

He screams as the steam envelops him and sinks out of scene.

REVISED 5-26-59　　　　"ATOMIC SUBMARINE"
　　　　　　　　　　　　　　　　　　　　　101-A

288-D　　TRICK SHOT - CARNEY - SPECIAL EFFECTS SHOT

　　　　As Carney's body disintegrates into the ground.

288-E　　TWO SHOT - DAVE REEF

　　　　Unaware of Powell and Carney's fate.

> DAVE
> Where do you think the voice you heard was coming from?
>
> REEF
> (points farther down the ramp)
> Somewhere down there?
>
> DAVE
> Wonder where Powell and Carney are?
>
> REEF
> We'll have to look for them later.

　　　　They move on.

289　　　THROUGH IRIS DOWN RAMP TO FLOOR - BLACK BACKING - DAY - PAN SHOT - DAVE AND REEF

　　　　They continue down ramp. Reef looks expectantly at Dave.

> REEF
> Well?
>
> DAVE
> I'm with you!

101-B

290 FLOOR - BLACK BACKING - DAY - UP SHOT - REEF AND DAVE

They come clambering down the ramp, reach the platform level. Then, awed, they look around them.

291 EST. SHOT ON FLOOR (PLATFORM) - CAVERNOUS INTERIOR - BACK AT TINY MEN ON PLATFORM - MATTE SHOT

We see a long, slender bridge, or catwalk, extending out into space, apparently reaching toward a great, opalescent sphere that seems to hang suspended on cushioning points, some sort of shock-absorbing system, in the very center of the saucer. A weird GLOW, seeming to become ever brighter, emanates from inside this sphere.

292 TWO SHOT - DAVE AND REEF

Awed, round-eyed, silent, they stare open-mouthed at the sight. But before they can make any comment...

SAUCER VOICE
Remove your weapons, Commander.
And come here - alone!

REEF
Come where?

Dave looks at him peculiarly.

DAVE
The voice again?

But Reef is too intent on the voice. Now he begins disarming as Dave looks incredulous.

DAVE
What're you doing?

293 MATTE SHOT - FROM THEIR P.O.V. - TOWARD GLOBE

Now, at the very tip of the spine-bridge, an IRIS OPENING appears in the side of the sphere.

SAUCER VOICE
(now seeming to come
from this opening)
To me - here!

102.

294   TWO SHOT - REEF AND DAVE

Reef has a distant look as he hands his weapons to Dave.

                    REEF
          Here - keep these.
                    (then)
          It wants me to come alone.

                    DAVE
                    (flaring)
          Oh it does???

Reef moves o.s. toward the bridge. Dave waits, very unwillingly.

295   INT. SECTION OF BRIDGE - LEADING TO SPHERE - DAY - REEF - ONTO BLACK

He inches his way tortuously across the slender support, toward the iris opening.

296   MATTE SHOT - BEHIND REEF - TOWARD SPHERE

He crawls cautiously towards the opening.

296A INT. PLATFORM - BLACK BACKING - DAY - CLOSE SHOT - DAVE

Angry, impatient, he sets Reef's weapons down. Then he clutches his submachine gun, watches Reef o.s.

297   INT. SPHERE - DAY - MED. SHOT - FROM INSIDE - IRIS OPENING

Now Reef appears, crawls cautiously up into the opening, then stands, looks inside. His eyes nearly start from his head as he takes in the incredible sight.

298   TRICK SHOT - FROM REEF'S P.O.V. - INTERIOR OF SPHERE - SPECIAL EFFECTS SHOT

His eyes range over the ceiling of the glove, then as he shifts his gaze to the bottom of the sphere, we see 'it' - a horrendous organism, like a giant sea urchin, the long, black, writhing spines now all in proper contact

(CONTINUED)

298   (CONTINUED)

with their grommet-sockets. And out of the center of the pulsating central 'body' rises a long stalk, and on the very tip of it a great, glowing 'eye.' The setup is like a monstrous rendering of the eye of a snail.

299   MATTE SHOT - UP PAST 'EYE' AT REEF IN IRIS

So he appears a tiny, miniature man compared to the cavernous size of the sphere. And now, apparently from the 'eye' itself, which seems to flicker and glow like an electron beam spectrometer, comes the saucer-voice again:

                SAUCER VOICE
          So, Commander Holloway - as
          you Earth inhabitants would
          express it - we meet 'face to
          face.'

300   CLOSE SHOT - REEF

As he says with sardonic inflection:

                REEF
          That's a face???

                SAUCER VOICE
          Point of view is everything.
          To us, your form of life is
          ugly as we appear to you.

                REEF
          Tell me something: Why can I
          hear you, when the others
          couldn't?

300A   FROM REEF'S P.O.V. - THE EYE

                SAUCER VOICE
          You do not 'hear' me! Our in-
          dividual brain frequencies are
          now attuned, and we exchange
          wave-thoughts.

                REEF O.S.
          You mean 'Extra Sensory Per-
          ception?'

                                         (CONTINUED)

300A (CONTINUED)

> SAUCER VOICE
> Whatever your 'earth-term' may
> be. The principal is ancient,
> and very simple.

300B CLOSE SHOT - REEF

Listening.

> SAUCER VOICE
> It is not necessary for you to
> speak. Your 'thought-response'
> will suffice.

(Note: From here on, in speech with the saucer, Reef's lips do not move - his responses, except to Dave, are all 'voice over')

300C INT. SECTION OF BRIDGE - DAY - DOWN SHOT - PANNING WITH DAVE

He cannot contain himself any longer, is now crawling out onto the bridge, toward Reef; cradling the sub-machine gun on his forearm as he goes.

300D INT. SPHERE - DAY - MATTE SHOT - UP PAST 'EYE' - AT REEF IN IRIS

The conversation continues:

> SAUCER VOICE
> My mission is to study various
> solar systems, and planets -
> select the most suitable for
> colonization -

> REEF
> - for horrors like yourself?

> SAUCER
> Of course. It may interest you
> to know I have visited hundreds
> of other worlds, and of all of
> them, your Earth seems most suit-
> able.

(CONTINUED)

300D (CONTINUED)

          REEF
         (drily)
Swell!

        SAUCER VOICE
         (sternly)
Your friend was to remain where he was!

300E CLOSE SHOT - REEF

He looks a bit bewildered:

          REEF
He did!

        SAUCER VOICE
I am afraid not. Therefore -

Now, to Reef's consternation, Dave suddenly appears beside him:

          REEF
      (to Dave, lip sync)
Dave - !

          DAVE
         (grimly)
What's goin' on in here, Lad?
What - ?

Then, Dave's mouth drops open, and he stares, incredulous.

300F MATTE SHOT - AS BEFORE - DAVE'S P.O.V. - THE CREATURE

        SAUCER VOICE
        (warningly)
Stand away from him, Commander!

300G TWO SHOT - DAVE AND REEF

As Dave, before Reef can stop him, steps forward belligerently, levels and submachine gun down at the creature.

          DAVE
       (menacingly)
So this is 'headquarters,' huh?
Well, you've sunk your last ship, you....

And he looses a burst with the sub-machine gun, so that we don't hear the appropriate name.

REVISED 5-26-59 "ATOMIC SUBMARINE"

105-A

300H SPECIAL EFFECT SHOT - DAVE - PRODUCTION SHOT

With a BOOM of tympany, a LIGHT STRIKES Dave, and suddenly he is melted, shrivelled to nothingness. The machine gun falls o.s.

300I CUT TO COVER - THIS ACTION

300J CLOSE SHOT - REEF

As he looks on, shocked, sobered, shaken. Then, in his thought-voice, he asks slowly:

> REEF
> Why not me? What am I - the closing act?
>
> SAUCER VOICE
> On the contrary. I want you - unharmed - perfect.
>
> REEF
> Why?
>
> SAUCER VOICE
> I have selected you, to return with me - along with several other specimens, for study. We will examine you and the others, discover desirable features to incorporate in our 'earth-colonizers.'

301 MATTE SHOT - REEF'S P.O.V. - THE ORGANISM

> REEF O.S.
> Then you just...'build them in?'
>
> SAUCER VOICE
> Of course. Evolution is much too slow a process.

(CONTINUED)

301 (CONTINUED)

> SAUCER VOICE
> On earth you build with inanimate material. We employ living tissue. This space vehicle, for example...

302 CUT TO COVER

303 MED. CLOSE SHOT - REEF

Awed, frightened, he looks about him at the construction of the chamber in which he is standing.

> SAUCER VOICE
> It is a living thing. When damaged - you would say 'wounded' - it immediately 'heals' itself.

> REEF
> (understanding)
> That's why no water leaked inside when we rammed you?

> SAUCER VOICE
> Of course. But it is time to begin the return voyage --

304 CLOSE SHOT - REEF'S HAND

And we see it creep up under his coat, grabbing the Very pistol.

305 MED. CLOSE SHOT - REEF

as he says grimly, threateningly:

> REEF
> To navigate, won't you have to... see your way?

> SAUCER VOICE
> Obviously.

> REEF
> That might be a little rough!

And Reef raises the Very pistol, fires.

107.

306 SPECIAL EFFECT SHOT - THE 'EYE' OF THE ORGANISM

as the flare strikes it and bursts. There is a SCREAM, an unearthly, shattering WAIL from the organism itself.

307 SPECIAL EFFECT SHOT - CLOSE ON 'EYE'

as the flare burns a hole in the iris, and the water, or whatever it contains, seems to drain from it, like a plastic bag when it is torn.

308 CLOSE SHOT - REEF

He reacts quickly, astonished at the effect of his shot. But then he wastes no time - turns and scrambles back out. SCREAMS OF PAIN from the creature follow him.

309 INT. SECTION OF BRIDGE - DAY - FAST PAN - WITH REEF

Heedless of the danger of falling, he scrambles madly back across the bridge. Beams of the death-dealing light just miss him as he goes, and SCREAMS from the wounded creature shatter the cavernous silence.

310 (OMITTED)

310A PANNING WITH REEF

He reaches the platform, races madly for the ramp. Beams of light again just miss him.

310B PANNING WITH REEF - UP RAMP

And suddenly, as he reaches the iris, he YELLS with pain, his foot caught in the iris.

REVISED 5-26-59   "ATOMIC SUBMARINE"
                                                    107-A-B

310-C   INSERT - CLOSEUP - REEF'S FOOT

            As he pulls his foot clear.

OMIT
310D
311

311-A   PANNING WITH REEF

            As he runs through the darkness.

311-B   PANNING WITH REEF

            As a beam of LIGHT just misses him.

311-C   CLOSEUP - STEAM

            As steam comes out of the darkness at him.

311-D   PANNING WITH REEF

            As he runs by, the steam just missing him.

311-E   CLOSE PAN - REEF

            As he races for the iris at the end of the ramp.

312   INT. DEPTH-EXPLORER - DAY - AT HATCH WINDOW - OVER
            CARL'S SHOULDER

            Carl reacts as the iris begins closing. Quickly, he
            grabs a crowbar, or other prop, wedges it into the
            iris, holding it open momentarily. A moment later,
            Reef literally hurls himself into the little sub,
            slams the hatch behind him, and exclaims:

                        REEF
                  Back to the Shark - right
                  now!

            Carl does not hesitate, begins working the controls.

                        CARL
                  What about Dave - and the
                  others?

312   (CONTINUED)

                    REEF
                  (grimly)
            'Fortunes of War!'

Carl frowns. Now Reef grasps the radio microphone, says quickly:

                    REEF
                  (into mike)
            This is Reef, Skipper -- in the
            Depth-Explorer. Don't wait for
            us - start engines, and pull loose!

313   INT. CONTROL ROOM - DAY - FULL SHOT - THE ROOM

as Wendover nods, responding to the radio message.

                    WENDOVER
            All right, Reef.

He turns to the intercom, orders:

                    WENDOVER
            Reactor Room! This is the Skipper!
            I want all reverse full-emergency
            power!

314   SPECIAL EFFECT SHOT - THE TIGER SHARK PROPELLERS

They begin to turn, slowly at first, then picking up speed.

315   SPECIAL EFFECT SHOT - SHARK AND DEPTH-EXPLORER

It moves away from the saucer, back up through the water to the belly of the Shark, at the airlock.

316   INT. LOWER CHAMBER OF SAUCER - DAY - SPECIAL EFFECT SHOT - CLOSE ON 'EYE'

And now we see, through a SERIES OF DISSOLVES that the eye is healing - restoring itself, like a balloon being blown up (maybe this would do it).

317   SPECIAL EFFECT SHOT - THE 'FINGERS'

Purposefully they probe into the 'circuit' apertures, and the power lights begin to glow radiantly.

109.

318 INT. FORWARD TORPEDO ROOM - DAY - FULL SHOT - AT AIRLOCK

As Griff superintends preparations to open the lock door, the men from the control room - Wendover, Kent and Sir Ian, hasten in. Now Griff cracks the hatch on the lock door, and in a moment, Reef staggers out, then helps Carl from the Explorer. Wendover frowns, glances inside:

                    WENDOVER
            What about --- ?

Reef only shakes his head. Faces are tense, then Reef declares bitterly:

                    REEF
            We didn't kill it, Skipper. And
            if it ever gets...back where it
            came from...the Earth is doomed,
            and everything and everybody on it!

319 SPECIAL EFFECT SHOT - TIGER SHARK AND SAUCER

And now, the mighty engines of the Shark succeed - the bow of the Shark pulls out of the hull of the saucer, and the two vehicles float freely in the water.

320 INT. FORWARD TORPEDO ROOM - DAY - GROUP SHOT

The scene JUMPS AND LURCHES. Then there is an exultant voice:

                    VOICE
                (over intercom)
            We've pulled loose, Skipper!
            We're free!

Wendover and Reef exchange an exultant look. Then they turn and run out toward the ladder to the con. Kent, Carl and Sir Ian follow more slowly.

321 INT. CONTROL ROOM - DAY - FULL SHOT - THE ROOM

As Wendover and Reef come scrambling up the ladder and through the hatch, the man at the helm indicates the TV screen. Wendover and Reef peer eagerly at it. Wendover smiles tightly.

110.

322 SPECIAL EFFECT SHOT - OPTICAL SHOT - THE TV SCREEN

And we see the saucer floating loose in the water. But, suddenly, with a tremendous burst of speed, the saucer moves away through the water, so rapidly as almost to become a blur.

          REEF (o.s.)
         (despairingly)
There it goes!

323 UP INTO FACES OF REEF AND WENDOVER

as Reef adjusts the dials of the screen, and Carl, Kent and Sir Ian appear behind them.

          REEF
Straight to the Pole - at almost fifty knots!

          WENDOVER
Nothing we can do, now.

          KENT
Excuse me, Captain - there may be one last, desperate chance - a one-in-a-thousand shot...

          WENDOVER
         (desperately)
Anything ---

          KENT
It's possible I could adapt one of the torpedo guidance systems to the ICBM - so it would 'home' on the saucer when he rises from the Pole.

          WENDOVER
What about time...?

                       (CONTINUED)

REVISED 5-26-59   "ATOMIC SUBMARINE"   110-A

323 (CONTINUED)

                    SIR IAN
              (a glance at Reef)
Cyclops will have to linger at
the Pole to recharge his power
banks.

                    WENDOVER
              (snaps)
All right - go to it.

                                   (CONTINUED)

111.

323   (CONTINUED)

                    WENDOVER (cont'd)
                (to Reef)
            Reef, you take over as navigator.
            Find us a pot-hole in the ice.

       And as they AD LIB orders and instructions, Kent and Sir
       Ian and Carl climb back down the hatch to go to work.

                                            DISSOLVE TO:

324   INT. FORWARD TORPEDO ROOM - DAY - CUTS TO COVER - WORK
      ON MISSILE - (STOCK IF AVAILABLE - OTHERWISE DISSOLVE TO
      325)

       with Carl, Kent, Griff and Sir Ian all at work, in-
       stalling complicated electronic equipment in the nose
       of the huge ICBM. Over this:

                    NARRATOR
            Adapt a complicated guidance
            system to a huge ballistic rocket
            - convert it to a water-to-air
            intercept missile? It was foolish,
            it was insane, it was fantastic -
            but it was their only hope - and
            the earth's only hope!

                                            WIPE TO:

325   FULL SHOT - THE GROUP

       as Kent steps back, wipes his hands on a piece of waste.

                    SIR IAN
            All ready?

                    KENT
                (dourly)
            As ready as we can be!
                (walking off)
            I'll report to the Skipper.

                                            DISSOLVE TO:

326   SPECIAL EFFECT SHOT - THE TIGER SHARK

       It is rising to the surface, under the ice. And now,
       as it nears the surface, a BEAM OF LIGHT, like a search-
       light, hits it, and the water becomes brighter.

327   INT. CONTROL ROOM - DAY - MED. CLOSE SHOT - WENDOVER AND REEF

as Reef, at the navigator's position, sings out:

>   REEF
> Right under our hole in the
> ice, Skipper.

328   SPECIAL EFFECT SHOT - DOWN ON ICE - SEEN ON TV SCREEN

We see a round, black hole of open water in the ice field.

329   INT. CONTROL ROOM - DAY - CLOSE SHOT - WENDOVER AND REEF

as Wendover glues his eye toward the screen.

>   WENDOVER
> What's the corrected bearing
> to the Magnetic Pole?
>
>   REEF
>   (checking)
> Minus three.

Wendover sets a knob on the screen, peers at it again.

330   SPECIAL EFFECT SHOT - OPTICAL SHOT - POV

All we see is fields of ice and snow. Finally the cross-hairs stop exactly at minus three.

331   MED. SHOT

as Wendover gestures toward the controls.

>   WENDOVER
> Take over here, Reef.

(CONTINUED)

113.

331 (CONTINUED)

Reef nods, looks at TV screen. Wendover moves to the intercom, barks:

              WENDOVER
       Prepare ICBM for firing!

Then he murmurs to Reef:

              WENDOVER
       Well, that's all we can do --
       until our space-friend decides
       to blast-off.

332   SPECIAL EFFECT SHOT - THE TIGER SHARK

And now, on the bow, we see the mighty ICBM lift from a recess on the deck, in front of the conning tower. It stands on end in its cradle, ready.

                              WIPE TO:

333   INT. CONTROL ROOM - DAY - MED. TWO SHOT - REEF AND WENDOVER

Reef's eyes on screen. Wendover waits tensely.
Now Reef reacts.

334   SPECIAL EFFECT SHOT - OPTICAL SHOT - THROUGH SCREEN - THE ICE

Suddenly, a phenomena like an undersea volcano rising. The ice rends and cracks, rises in a great bulge.

335   SPECIAL EFFECT SHOT - THE ICE

It breaks up, boils, tremendous rending, tearing NOISES. Then, from the depths of the water below, a familiar oval shape - smooth, glittering, beautiful - surmounted by the gleaming cyclops eye appears. The saucer rises from the water like a great porpoise, hovers just above the ice, then begins rising slowly into the air.

336   INT. CONTROL ROOM - DAY - REACTION SHOT - WENDOVER AND REEF

as Reef exclaims excitedly:

                              (CONTINUED)

336 (CONTINUED)

> REEF
> Skipper - I think - it *is*!
> It's Cyclops!

Wendover pushes him aside for a quick look himself. Then, he leaps for the intercom, barks:

> WENDOVER
> This is the Skipper! Fire!
> Fire!

337 SPECIAL EFFECT SHOT - THE TIGER SHARK

Now we see a discharge like compressed air below the ICBM. It floats up and away from the Shark, in a vertical position. Then, straight as an arrow, it heads for the surface.

338 SPECIAL EFFECT SHOT - THE HOLE IN THE ICE

Now, from the black water, the ICBM leaps into the air, like a suddenly released, air-filled ball. As it leaps above the surface, the mighty rocket engines ignite with a ROARING BLAST, and the ICBM leaps high into the air, roars up o.s.

339 SPECIAL EFFECT SHOT - WITH ICBM

It rises higher and higher, faster and faster, into the sky.

340 SPECIAL EFFECT SHOT - THE SAUCER

It, too, is moving faster and faster, on what should appear to be a converging course with the missile.

341 SPECIAL EFFECT SHOT - THE SKY

This is the 'money' shot - to make or break the picture. In one corner of the frame, the saucer rises swiftly. But as it moves to center frame, in from the opposite corner comes the ICBM, heading straight and true for the saucer. They meet.

The explosion is tremendous - a mighty, nuclear fireball, great chunks of debris hurled sizzling into space in all directions, a booming, pounding after-shock wave, then a great sweeping mushroom cloud. After this.....nothing but empty sky.

REVISED 5-26-59   "ATOMIC SUBMARINE"
                                                          115.

342   CUTS TO COVER - THE PHENOMENA ABOVE

343   INT. CONTROL ROOM - DAY - REACTION SHOT - PANNING
                                ALL THE PRINCIPALS

      The shock, the exultation, the relief, then the
      sagging easement of tension...it is beyond words.
      Wendover looks at Kent, with a look more eloquent
      than an hour speech. Sir Ian's eyes are misty with
      gratitude. Carl begins trembling with reaction, and
      Reef puts a comforting arm around him. Griff sags
      onto a stool, head down, just moving his head aimlessly
      from side to side. Reef and Wendover exchange a look
      of silent understanding.

                                         SLOW DISSOLVE TO:

344   EXT. OCEAN - NIGHT - LONG UP SHOT - THE NIGHT SKY
      (STOCK)

      on a moonless night, the stars glinting and sparkling
      like billions of distant diamonds.

345   SHOT - BOW OF SUBMARINE - SPECIAL EFFECTS SHOT

      as it swishes through the water on the homeward voyage.

                                              DISSOLVE:

345-A STOCK SHOT - NAVY YARD - NIGHT (as in 38A)

346   EXT. NAVY YARD - NIGHT - TWO SHOT - REEF AND CARL

      As they slowly walk away from the o.s. submarine towards
      the gate. Carl looks thoughtfully up at the sky as he
      stops for a moment.

                          CARL
                They're so remote - cold - beautiful,
                the stars. But now - I wonder -

                          REEF
                     (smiling fondly)
                Yes?

                          CARL
                     (whimsically)
                Which is the one - we have to worry
                about?

      Reef also looks up at the sky thoughtfully, shakes
      his head.

                                              (CONTINUED)

346 (CONTINUED)

>   REEF
>   Maybe - just 'maybe' - when their
>   ship doesn't return - they'll
>   decide not to come here, after all.
>
>   CARL
>   But if they do?
>
>   REEF
>   (soberly)
>   I don't know.
>
>   CARL
>   (a slight smile)
>   I wouldn't worry. So long as we
>   have boats like the Tiger Shark -
>   and people like you, the Skipper,
>   Dave, Kent, Sir Ian and my father -
>
>   REEF
>   (smiles)
>   And his 'egghead' son!
>   (he punches Carl's
>   arm jovially)
>   We'll give 'em a rough reception,
>   won't we?

They go out.

347 EXT. STARLIT SKY - NIGHT

SUPERIMPOSE:

>   END TITLE
>
>   FADE OUT:

T H E   E N D

Notes on the Script

By Tom Weaver

• The script cover, and page 1, both give the movie's title as *Atomic Submarine*. On-screen, it's preceded by a *The*. The cover includes the line "Gorham-Raylock Productions." Gorham is a smash-up of Alex **Gor**don and Orville H. **Ham**pton, so Raylock must be a melding of Jack **Ra**bin and Irving B**lock**.

• On page 1, the script says that the U.S.A.S. (United States Atom Sub) *Sturgeon* follows "the well-beaten Polar route." One wonders how you ascertain when water is "well-beaten."

• In the *Sturgeon* vs. saucer scene, the script calls for us to see the saucer more clearly than we do in the movie. Thanks to the script, I now know that the smoky wisps emanating from the *Sturgeon* were meant to convey that it was red-hot and melting. On paper, the atom sub pushes its way through the surface ice and becomes a fireball and then a mushroom cloud. In the movie, the shot of the surfacing sub dissolves into a shot of a small, smoky explosion and a few flying sparks.

The newspaper spinning toward the camera in the next shot is *The Capital Times* in the script, *Washington Journal* on-screen.

• During the Arctic Defense War Room meeting, Admiral Terhune reads aloud a partial list of recent polar phenomena. There's one more in the script than there is in the movie: "Complete disruption of communications with DEW line [Distant Early Warning Line] warning stations." I'd bet a bilge pump that when this script was perused by the government officials who scrutinized the scripts of movies involving the U.S. Navy, they asked for the elimination of that

Selmer Jackson plays an admiral in *Atomic Submarine*'s first reel, helping to plant the plot. Coincidentally or maybe not, he had just finished working in *The Gallant Hours* (1960), playing Admiral Chester Nimitz, a driving force behind the construction of America's first nuclear sub.

line; why put even the smallest ding in public faith in the DEW line? The DEW Line was a network of top-of-the-world radar stations designed to detect sinister Soviets in the sky; learn more about it in *The Deadly Mantis*' (1957) opening scene.

The dialogue at the bottom of script page 9 is also missing from the movie.

• Reef and Julie's make-out scene is interrupted by a knock at the hotel room door and a letter slipped under it, into the room, recalling him to duty. Reef's reaction in the movie is a couple of "Oh no"s. The script calls for him to "tragically" slap his forehead twice, to gaze regretfully at "this lovely, willing morsel" (Julie) and to end the scene by looking like he's almost crying.

Joi Lansing (on the couch) made a memorable incursion into *Atomic Submarine*'s mostly male cast, but she wasn't the only pretty in the picture: Jean Moorhead (on the right and in the *Amazing Colossal Man* photo below) was a 1955 Playboy Playmate and the star of the Ed Wood-scripted *The Violent Years* (1956).

 In the Crew Dining Room scene where Griff meets underwater demolition men Powell and Carney, the script gives Griff the extra line "I don't envy you swabbies, swimmin' in that North Pole ice water." As the scene wraps, notice that the frogmen's paperwork is in Carney's hands at the end of one shot and in his back pocket in the next.

The Ward Room scene where Reef tells Dave about Carl's relationship with his father ends with Dave asking, "Have you talked to Carl? Tried to get *his* side?" and Reef coming back at him with: "He's all front with no back. How can he have a *side*?!" In the script, Reef's retort is more direct: "'His' side? I've seen it, all right. A nice, bright yellow!"

In the movie, the *Tiger Shark* escapes the electric storm center by simply descending below it; we see the sub placidly planing downward through untroubled waters. The script calls for the sub to be storm-buffeted, in a shot lit by underwater lightning bolts, with crashes like exploding skyrockets. Even after it begins gliding into the depths, the waters are still turbulent and lightning bolts seem to follow it.

After a chunk of iceberg ice strikes the *Tiger Shark*, we get a shot of the Control Room very reminiscent of the yet-to-come *Voyage to the Bottom of the Sea* movie and teleseries, with Our Heroes lurching to and fro (and Commander Wendover flopping forward onto a table). And, again as in *Voyage*, they get a report on the full extent of the damage about 15 seconds later – less time than it would take for the Damage Control fellows to pick themselves up off the floor, much less inspect the sub stem to stern and prepare a comprehensive report.

The toy store quality flying saucer seen in the movie hardly lives up to its description in the script:

…a great, oval-shaped, glowing ellipse-saucer-shaped. It is perhaps three hundred feet in diameter. On top is a great, blazing turret of light, remotely resembling a lighthouse beacon – seemingly the "eye" of the thing.

👁 The *Tiger Shark* rams and pierces *Cyclops*, prompting Wendover to announce over the intercom to the crew, "We *did* it, boys. Drove right through the saucer's side." The script calls for shots of cheering men in the Control Room, Torpedo Room and Crew's Quarters.

👁 From the "I Didn't Need That Mental Image" Department: The script compares the *Lungfish* dropping down through the *Tiger Shark* keel escape hatch to "an animal being born."

👁 In the script, the *Lungfish*'s round base attaches to *Cyclops*' eye and the men inside open the hatch in the floor; now Reef batters Cyclops' surface with a tool like a wrecking bar, trying to bash through it. Suddenly the surface opens like a camera iris, creating a circular entryway.

👁 In the movie, the *Cyclops*' Chamber Section contains almost nothing but blackness; usually all we see are the men on lighted walkways and a ramp. This is as the script describes it, the only difference being that the men must make their own light: The two frogmen "light TORCHES or FLASHLIGHTS."

👁 In the movie, we don't see the Saucer Monster until Reef peers through the sphere opening and gets an eyeful. The script calls for us to get a tantalizing preview: The frogmen ply their blowtorches and Reef says he hears a voice (Reef to Dave: "Strange you don't hear it…"), and then the script calls for the camera to tilt down, there's a down wipe, and we see the following "TRICK SHOT (SPECIAL EFFECTS)":

The black, catfish-or-sea urchin-like spines seem to rise from limp supineness. They stiffen, grope like fingers, move towards a series of grommet-like openings in the translucent wall of the sphere. Now a spine nears a grommet, slips into it, apparently making "contact," for somewhere, a FAINT LIGHT comes on, and the scene becomes lighter. In a moment, another spine slips into another grommet-hole.

Frogmen Carney (Richard Tyler) and Powell (Ken Becker) are about to go for a swim in polar waters. Throughout the movie, the very tall, dark-haired Tyler and little blond Becker look like the Fred Flintstone and Barney of the submarine set.

The footage of the subs, saucer and Saucer Monster give *Atomic Submarine* an "Aurora Models vs. *Time with Beany*" vibe. *The Lungfish* is the only miniature that looks even slightly substantial.

The Atomic Submarine may not exactly get *good* in the homestretch, but at least it gets good'n'*weird*. Here Arthur Franz approaches the sphere within the saucer for his first look at the phallic Saucer Monster.

The last we see of Powell, after he gets caught in the lethal light, is a closeup of his outflung hand. In the script, the last we see of him is his hands (plural), just before they "disintegrate to Jelly, and Powell is completely gone."

In the next shot, spots of light begin to appear in other parts of the saucer.

In the movie, Carney finds Powell's burned body, hits the panic button and gets crushed by closing sliding doors. In the script, he hurriedly moves away from Powell's body and, out of the blackness, a burst of steam catches him in the face. "He screams as the steam envelops him and sinks out of scene." In a special effects shot, we were then to have seen his body as it "disintegrates into the ground."

In the movie, Dave sees the Saucer Monster and pumps six bullets into it. In the script, he lets loose with a submachine-gun.

In the script, Reef dots the Saucer Monster's eye with a flare, and then "[t]here is a SCREAM, an unearthly, shattering WAIL from the organism itself." As Reef runs, screams of pain follow him. In the movie, the Saucer Monster suffers in silence.

In the script, Reef – running from the Saucer Monster – contends not only with the deadly spots of light which get *thisclose* to zapping him, but also steam that comes out of the darkness and just misses him.

After the saucer is blown up, the script calls for the submariners' reaction to be "beyond words." Sir Ian's eyes get misty with gratitude, Carl is trembling (and Reef puts a comforting arm around him) and Griff drops onto a stool, head down. In the movie, Arthur Franz (Reef) and Bob Steele (Griff) seem to be trying to get this across, but the others don't play along. Brett Halsey (Carl) looks uninterested, and Tom Conway (Sir Ian) simply gives Victor Varconi a half-smile and a nod, like a guy who just watched his favorite baseball team win a game that put them just four games out of first place.

Not in the script: Reef, preparing to enter the *Lungfish*, kisses his "little black book" and says, "Girls: You go everywhere *I* go." This sets the table for the movie's leave-'em-laughing final line (also not in the script): Reef in the Bremerton Navy Yard, unsuccessfully searching his pockets and then half-growling, "You know, I think I lost my little black book on that lousy thing [the saucer]!" and shaking his fist at the sky.

Fun Facts

By Tom Weaver

There's a long, proud movie-TV tradition of submarines and monsters, and it's amusing to look back to early days of true-life history when the submarine *was* the monster: In 1914, Australia's first submarine, the AE1, was spotted by villagers on an island near the New Guinea island of New Britain and described by them as a "monster" or "devil fish."

In 1952, when the construction of the *Nautilus* was making news, low-budget producers Pine-Thomas announced that *High Voltage*, the story of an atom sub based on William Wister Haines' same-name novel, would be one of their next films for Paramount. At the same time, Columbia filed with the MPAA Title Registry Bureau the title *Atom Submarine* and assigned Robert Cohn, studio boss Harry Cohn's nephew, to produce. At the start of 1953, "In Hollywood" columnist Erskine Johnson reported that the abovementioned two movies, and a third, *Project X*, would battle it out to be the first on the screen with an atomic sub.

All these announcements led to nothing. In the meantime, the first movie to feature an atomic submarine in its storyline was probably *It Came from Beneath the Sea* (1955): The classic six-tentacle-giant-octopus adventure gives us (in a pre-credits sequence) narrated stock footage of the construction and launching of the *Nautilus*, and then opening and closing scenes set inside an atom sub captained by Kenneth Tobey. (The scenes were shot aboard a real sub, the *Hammerhead*—*not* atomic.) Because there *was* only one atom sub in the world (the *Nautilus*) in 1955, and because *It Came* viewers just saw the *Nautilus* in stock footage, presumably we're supposed to think Tobey's sub *is* the *Nautilus*. In the opener, Tobey and one of his men, Griff, talk about the advantages of an atom sub (Griff: "All [the men] do is eat and sleep. Press a button when there's some work to be done!"). When they're being chased by the octopus, Tobey issues the order, "Give those atoms a poke! Give me everything ya got!"

 Beginning in 1954, several years before Alex Gordon's movie was a twinkle in his eye, Allied Artists started announcing that they would produce a

Parts of *It Came from Beneath the Sea* take place on an atomic submarine but were shot on a "regular" sub. Its scripter obviously didn't know that would happen, because he has a lieutenant (Chuck Griffiths) say to the atom sub commander (Kenneth Tobey), "Roomy, gosh, this conning tower's just like a ballroom!" Ballroom? The conning tower is so tiny, the line should have been, "I'd stand a little closer, commander, but our clothes are in the way"!

movie titled *The Atomic Submarine*—but that proposed (and never made) picture was to have been based on a military historian's book on Admiral Hyman G. Rickover, "Father of the Nuclear Navy." In 1957, after AB-PT Pictures Corp. made *The Unearthly* and *Beginning of the End*, they included a movie called *Atomic Submarine* on their list of upcoming projects. Again, never made.

The Atomic Submarine begins the way Jules Verne's *Twenty Thousand Leagues Under the Sea* did: with the mysterious sinking of many ships at sea, and an expedition sent out to find and destroy whatever is responsible. In *Twenty Thousand*, the characters think it's a living creature but it turns out to be a sub; in *Atomic*, characters think it's a flying saucer but it (sorta) turns out to be a living creature.

Atomic Submarine gets props for being the first underwater flying saucer movie, but it did have an antecedent. In *Kronos* (1957), Earth is threatened by the outer space approach of an "asteroid" that looks like every movie and comic book flying saucer. It strobes with self-generated light and zigs and zags in the sky, and yet all the scientist characters persist in thinking it's an asteroid(!). It finally sets down in the Pacific. (Later in this loopy movie, when the boxy 100-foot-high gleaming-metal mechanical monster appears out of the ocean, a newspaper headline calls it a "GIANT SEA CREATURE"!) Other reminders of *The Atomic Submarine* in *Kronos*: a scene in which atomic missiles, launched from the ground, speed to catch up with the "asteroid," and a scene where scientist Jeff Morrow calls the "asteroid" an intelligent being, the same way *Atomic* characters talk about *Cyclops*. Like *Atomic*, *Kronos* had special effects by Jack Rabin, Irving Block and Louis DeWitt (and others), and it was based on a story by Block, so perhaps Block was responsible for some of the shared situations and dialogue.

Baby Boomer Monster Kids may think of *Atomic Submarine* while watching the animated *Jonny Quest* TV episode "The Robot Spy" (1964): What looks like a spaceship (but isn't) appears in the night sky near a military base, and briefly hides in the ocean from approaching interceptor jets. Inside the "spaceship" is a giant robot spider with a head with a large single eye, *à la* the Saucer Monster. "Robot Spy" also had an *Atomic Submarine*-type nail-biter finish with the "spaceship" making a getaway into the sky while Our Heroes race to deploy their destructive Para-Power Ray Gun before it gets out of range.

As Alex Gordon mentioned in our 2002 interview, agent Allen Connor, who ponied up some money toward *Atomic Submarine*, was previously an actor, busy in the 1920s and '30s. This book's readers might remember him for his serial appearances. In Chapter 10 of *Robinson Crusoe of Clipper Island* (1936), he's a baddie who slips a victim a poison cigarette and is more than willing to kill himself in order to kill hero Mala by crashing the biplane in which they're fighting. (We see the plane plunge into the water at chapter's end but, in one of Republic's most unforgivable cheats, at the next chapter's start we watch Mala pull it out of its deadly dive.) In *SOS Coast Guard* (1937), research chemist Connor's help is regularly sought by hero Ralph Byrd. The end of Chapter 10 finds Byrd and a kayoed Connor in the back of a burning truck that rolls off a high cliff into the ocean.

To the best of my knowledge, Gordon never mentioned Orville H. Hampton in connection with *Atomic Submarine* casting, but in his *Fangoria* interview, Hampton claimed that he was involved, "as well as consulting with the technicians on the underwater effects."

The two voice artists employed on *Atomic Submarine*, Pat Michaels (narrator) and John Hilliard (the Saucer Monster), were both newscasters. To provide the opening narration of his first sci-fi *Day the World Ended*, Gordon also used a newscaster, a soon-to-be biggie: Chet Huntley, co-anchor of NBC's *The Huntley-Brinkley Report*.

At the start of *Atomic Submarine*, the narrator makes it clear that it takes place in the future as he talks about "the late 1950s and early '60s" as though they were in the distant past, and calls the under-ice transpolar route "a vital highway for world travel and commerce" even though it was no such thing in 1959. But how far in the future? Apparently not far, since clothes and hair styles are strictly '50s, and the submarine and surface vessels we see in stock footage are of course all '50s or earlier. A number of online sources say the movie is set in 1968, but that's not specified in movie, script or pressbook, so who knows where that came from.

Truth be told, between the stock footage of old ships and the pile-up of geezers in the cast, a sense of yesteryear thoroughly permeates this "tale of tomorrow."

When this portrait was needed for the serial *Daughter of Don Q* (1946), its co-director Spencer Bennet was costumed, made-up by Bob Mark and photographed by Roman Freulich. Artist Lewis Physioc then used the photo as a reference and painted the portrait. (Photos courtesy Jack Mathis.)

Dick Foran Sued

LOS ANGELES— (AP) —Cowboy Actor Dick Foran has been sued for divorce by Susanne Rosser Foran, 28, his third wife. She is a former actress.

She alleged in her suit yesterday that Foran, 42, a former Princeton football player, forced her out of their Van Nuys home last Monday without allowing her to take her clothing or other belongings. She said he had threatened to disfigure her and take her life.

Mrs. Foran's Alimony Set at $100 A Month

Los Angeles, June 19 (AP)— Actress Susanne Rosser, who wanted $750-a-month temporary alimony from cowboy actor Dick Foran, had to settle today for $100 a month for the next five months.

Mrs. Foran charged that the actor had driven her out of their home and had hinted he might put arsenic in her food.

Cowboy-Actor Dick Foran Loses Fight With Officers

Damaged Lip and Guilty Plea on Drunk Charge Outcome of Argument

Cowboy-Actor Dick Foran, hero of many a screenland skirmish, yesterday found his usual role reversed in a real-life drama in which the fadeout showed him pleading guilty on a drunk charge.

The towering actor, 6 feet 3 inches in height, was placed under arrest after resisting questioning by Deputy Sheriffs Harry Zahn and Walter Schottmiller, who were attempting to investigate a report he had been in a fight outside of a Sunset Blvd. night club.

Foran, according to the officers, offered combat when they sought to interrogate him. There was a scuffle and during the melee the actor fell to the ground, hitting his lip against his car.

Arraigned later before Judge Cecil Holland of Beverly Hills Justice Court, Foran pleaded guilty and asked for probation. He was released on $250 bail. His hearing was set for Aug. 28.

Booked at Hollywood substation of the Sheriff's office, the actor gave his name as John Nicholas Foran of 1822 Camino Palmero Drive.

Dick Foran

Dick Foran (1910-79), a husky 6'3" redhead, was the amiable hero of many Westerns and even a few B-grade fright flicks (*The Mummy's Hand*, *Horror Island*), as fun and likable as horror heroes come. But newspapers sometimes told a different tale. Here's a representative sampling.

- The narrator and Commander Holloway's log provide viewers with the month and day of various events throughout the movie, from May 3 (the destruction of the *Sturgeon*) to July 15 (when the *Tiger Shark* rams the saucer), but never the year. Even the *Washington Journal* newspaper seen in the first reel lacks month-day-year in its masthead.

- Before the *Sturgeon* explodes on the ocean's surface 1000 miles from the North Pole, we see (on the miniature set) mountains in the distance. We see the same mountains (i.e., the same miniature set) when the saucer takes off from the North Pole. Yes, mountains at the North Pole.

When you think futuristic thrills and atomic adventure, you think Victor Varconi, Tom Conway, Bob Steele and Dick Foran. Well, you do if you're Alex Gordon. Any old actor who wasn't still in harness, Alex would put one back *on* him.

- *Atomic Submarine* was Jack Mulhall's last movie, after 300-plus, including Gordon's *The She-Creature*. His character, the Secretary of Defense, present at the Arctic Defense War Room confab, is every bit as dispensable as Navy Yard passersby Edmund Cobb and Frank Lackteen; I'd bet that Gordon had him written in just to provide a day's employment (or, more likely, an hour's employment) for screen vet Mulhall.

  Truth be told, a lot of *Atomic Submarine*'s characters are dispensable, as well as a number of the conversations. You could cut it down to 50 minutes and show it to a first-timer, and he would watch it without confusion and without suspecting that anything was missing.

- According to Dave, Reef is "the #1 howl in the entire sub wolf pack," and Reef wears no wedding ring in his scene with Julie. But later, aboard the *Tiger Shark*, he *does* have a ring on the third finger of his left hand. To whom aboard the sub is he signaling his unavailability?

- Near the start of *The Atomic Submarine*, there's a scene in which things are getting hot and heavy between Reef and his girl Julie when there's a knock at the apartment door and a summons for Reef to immediately return to duty. This is virtually a remake of an opening reel *Lost Continent* (1951) scene in which Air Force Major Cesar Romero is looking to get into Hillary Brooke's nookie jar, when the knock is heard at the apartment door and he must return to his base. *Atomic Submarine* scripter Orville H. Hampton worked as dialogue supervisor on *Lost Continent* and claims to have rewritten the script, so presumably he consciously duplicated the Cesar-Hillary scene for *Atomic*. In both movies, both heroes carry a little black book.

- Joi Lansing practiced for *Atomic*'s kissing-the-hero-on-the-eve-of-his-dangerous-mission scene by playing the same sort of scene (opposite Patrick Waltz) in the pre-credits sequence of *Queen of Outer Space* (1958).

- In the ward room scene where Wendover briefs his men about the *Tiger Shark*'s mission, notice on the table in front of Reef a copy of *Argosy*, the looooooong-running (1882-1978) pulp magazine. "I believe we were hoping to get some kind of a publicity plug in *Argosy*, some kind of mention or coverage," Alex Gordon told me.

- After Our Heroes spot the flying saucer, Dr. Kent comes up with a glossy 8x10 of an identical saucer, "taken by an amateur astronomer over New Mexico," and shows it to his colleagues in the *Tiger Shark* ward room. Funny that Kent should have thought that it'd be useful to pack and bring that photo along on a submarine heading for the North Pole, but it's a good thing he did.

Atomic Submarine scribe Orville H. Hampton made it clear what type actress he wanted in the role of Julie by describing her "lush female magnificence": "[C]ontoured and accoutered elegantly – with fine legs, long and sexy. Julie is drool-bait, especially for an undersea sailor who only comes up for air and 'so forth' every three months." Arthur Franz is ready for some of that "so forth."

Admiral William "Bull" Halsey, great uncle of *Atomic Submarine* star Brett Halsey. Brett's real name is Charles Hand, but when he was a Universal contractee, the studio's publicity department learned he was a relative of the admiral and made the change.

When the men of the *Tiger Shark* come to realize they're up against a flying saucer that hides underwater, Arthur Franz doesn't seem all that fazed. Well, if you'd already been aboard a flying saucer that hid under a *sand dune* (*Invaders from Mars*, 1953), you wouldn't be fazed either.

According to the movie's pressbook, Tom Conway was "induced to step out of retirement" for *The Atomic Submarine*. This must have come as news to Conway fans who had seen him several times on TV throughout 1959 (*Rawhide, Alfred Hitchcock Presents, Tightrope*); to the producers of the went-nowhere shot-on-video teleseries *Scene of the Crime* on which he guested; to theatergoers who saw him in the Pasadena Playhouse's *Bus Stop* with Mala Powers; to Conway's cast and crew mates on *12 to the Moon*, and especially to devotees of TV's *The Betty Hutton Show*, on which he was a regular. If Conway had been any *more* retired in 1959, he might have been unable to squeeze *Atomic Submarine* in!

It's funny to find Brett Halsey as a pouty peacenik, decrying soldiers and war throughout *Atomic Submarine*, when you know that in real life he was a nephew of World War II hero Admiral "Bull" Halsey. I asked him in a 2018 email if having the admiral in the upper branches of his family tree gave his career a boost, and he replied:

> The truth is it didn't have any influence, one way or another, except for once when I had a small part in a Western called *Gunman's Walk* [1958] starring Van Heflin and Tab Hunter. That film was especially enjoyable because I appeared in many scenes where my previous experience with roping and riding in our family business came in very handy.
>
> "Four Cowboys" were noted at the end of the cast list – no names, just four cowboys – and I was one of the four cowboys. My name wasn't even listed in the screen credits, but it was a good job because it ran for six or eight weeks of well-paid work. We were on location way out in the desert in Arizona and one day around

lunchtime, a Jeep carrying Admiral Halsey appeared out of nowhere and pulled up to a stop. Everyone went nuts: "What the hell is Admiral Halsey doing here?" Whisper, whisper, whisper. "He says he's come to have lunch with his nephew." Whisper, whisper. "Who's his nephew?" "Brett Halsey." "Who's Brett Halsey??" The producer wanted to set up a special lunch for the admiral but, no, no, he'd come to see me, and he got in the regular lunch line with me and the other cowboys — which made the studio brass more than a little uncomfortable. It didn't make my role in the film any bigger, but from that day forward, they all knew who *Brett Halsey* was.

Take a bow! At the North Pole, there's a Couldn't Be Closer Encounter of the Third Kind as the *Tiger Shark* lodges its nose in the alien ship.

As the *Tiger Shark* sits on the ocean bottom near the North Pole waiting for the saucer, Wendover orders "absolute silence" so that the saucer, currently en route to that spot, won't detect their presence. There's an hours-long whisper-quiet vigil until the saucer comes into view, at which point Wendover starts talking over the squawk box, orders the torpedo tubes loaded (which should have been done already), etc. In other words, Wendover orders that they needlessly sit in silence while the saucer is hundreds of miles away, and then when it finally gets within earshot, he creates quite a deluxe racket.

The *Tiger Shark* makes a diagonal dash at the saucer and rams it, and now sticks out of its underside at almost a 45-degree angle; it remains embedded in the saucer for a long stretch of footage. But inside the sub, all rooms are still horizontal. *Also*: After the sub rams the saucer, we see *and* hear the two vessels, locked together, hit the ocean bottom. But later, in order for the *Lungfish* to be lowered out of the *Tiger Shark*'s keel, they're *not* on the bottom any more.

The Saucer Monster, talking to Holloway about its ship, tells Holloway, "On Earth, you build with inanimate material. *We* employ living tissue. This space vehicle, for example. It is a living thing. When damaged – you would say 'wounded' – it immediately 'heals' itself."

This is the most bizarre element of *The Atomic Submarine*, partly because of the way it's completely bungled: *Long before* the Saucer Monster shares that incredible tidbit with Reef, the men of the *Tiger Shark* are already referring to *Cyclops* as a living thing. As the *Tiger Shark* prepares to start bird-dogging the *Cyclops*, Wendover says, "Wherever **he** goes, we go … until we get **him**!" and Sir Ian murmurs, "Or, perhaps, until **he** gets us?" What other movie flying saucer has ever been referred to as "he" rather than "it"? Even in real life, no one calls a UFO "he." Dr. Kent says, "We took for granted **his** source of energy was nuclear," and Reef, Sir Ian and Wendover join in the chorus of "him"s and "his"s. This continues for scene after scene; even characters who don't say these things accept them without demur. After *Tiger Shark* spears *Cyclops*, Wendover tells the group preparing to enter the saucer to bring side arms, and a puzzled Dave scoffs, "Side arms? The saucer's **dead**," as if they'd fatally speared a giant creature rather than a vessel. When the saucer starts moving toward the North Pole, an incredulous Griff says, "But – that *Cyclops* is dead! We killed it, didn't we?" Sir Ian explains the saucer's latest move with, "I believe our friend Cyclops is returning to life." Reef, getting back aboard the *Tiger Shark*, tells Wendover, "Skipper, we didn't kill it [by ramming it]."

Apparently screenwriter Hampton decided to make the saucer a living thing, but screwed up and had various characters referring to it as such even before the Saucer Monster spills that bean. And Rabin-Block-DeWitt screwed up by creating a strictly nuts-and-bolts spaceship model. The characters who've seen it and yet refer to it as if it were a living creature sound demented.

👁 The Saucer Monster reveals to Holloway that the saucer is a living thing, adding that it can be "damaged – *you* would say 'wounded.'" Ummm … no, Mr. Saucer Monster, we wouldn't. *We* would say "damaged," *you* would say "wounded."

👁 According to the Saucer Monster, the saucer can heal itself. And after Reef extinguishes its eye, the Saucer Monster heals *it*self. Is the Saucer Monster a *part* of the saucer? Is the Saucer Monster *the saucer*? I think that's the implication. In the pages of the script describing its "face-to-face" meeting with Reef, the alien is called "SAUCER VOICE," i.e., the voice of the saucer rather than the voice of a monster *in* the saucer. The *New York Post* reviewer bought it, writing that the *Tiger Shark*'s nemesis "looks like a flying saucer and TALKS."

👁 Does the Saucer Monster have cleaning people? After Reef shoots the space creature, his escape route should take him to the crushed body of Carney in the closing doors. Instead, he has a clear path to the *Lungfish*.

👁 The *Tiger Shark* crew members and scientists sound crazy as they persist in talking about the saucer as though it's a person, but the idea didn't start with this movie. Most Monster Kids know the name Kenneth Arnold, the bush pilot and businessman who told the world he spotted a formation of nine flying saucers while flying his own plane near Mount Rainier, Washington, in June 1947. Turns out that Arnold then spent a lot of time and money investigating the saucer phenomenon and came to some strange conclusions. In a 1952 interview conducted by Inez Robb, he said that he initially assumed that saucers were mechanical ships, but later became convinced that the so-called saucer is a "living force" of superior intelligence. Arnold: "[It is] a living, thinking creature" that inhabits the stratosphere or the troposphere.

👁 After the ballistic missile hits the saucer, we see stock footage of a ferocious ball of fire – supposedly the saucer – plummeting earthward. That's actually the first Atlas flight vehicle, Missile 4A, which took off on June 11, 1957, and almost immediately had engine trouble. A range safety officer pushed a button

"You Make Me Feel Like Franzing": Reef gets balletic when trying to avoid the Saucer Monster's deadly light.

that set off an on-board explosion. It was all captured in spectacular color footage, viewable on YouTube. One of the other movies that used it as stock footage was *Lightning Bolt* (1966).

Alex Gordon must have been happy with Spencer Bennet's direction (or perhaps just his speed): On July 7, 1959, a few weeks after *Atomic Submarine* wrapped, *Variety* reported that Gordon had signed the director to a non-exclusive pact "calling for him to direct six pix during the next 18 months." Bennet directed *no* movies for Gordon during the next 18 months; Gordon did try to get Columbia to let Bennet direct *The Underwater City* (1962), but the studio turned thumbs down. In a letter Bennet wrote to *Boxoffice* magazine (published in their January 1, 1962, issue), he reminisced:

> There comes a time in life when one starts thinking of calling it quits in the business world. For yours truly, this coming January will record 50 years of service in the motion picture industry. The records will show that I started in 1912 at the Edison Studio in Fordham, N.Y. Believe me, I have seen a lot come and go in our business.
>
> The last picture I directed was *Atomic Submarine* for Allied Artists in June 1959. You see, I have been submerged for over two years, and the prospects of surfacing at this time is very doubtful, particularly when one reaches the age of 69. Thank God I am in good health. Play handball every day—have been for the past 35 years. At least I am enjoying my retirement.
>
> …The time has come for me to step aside and let the younger guys take over. General MacArthur said, "Old soldiers just fade away" and I say that directors, actors, etc., just "dissolve out."

Bennet did direct Gordon's last two movies (which were also Bennet's last two movies), the Westerns *The Bounty Killer* and *Requiem for a Gunfighter*, in 1964.

What can you say about an underwater movie whose cast never got within miles of any body of water? *Atomic Submarine*'s scenes with actors were all shot at Allied Artists, either on a stage or just

Behind the scenes on Alex's *The Bounty Killer* (1965): A gun-wieldin', wheelchair-ridin' "Broncho Billy" Anderson in front of Alex, Buster Crabbe, Richard Arlen, Dan Duryea, set visitor Richard Gordon, Fuzzy Knight and the movie's producer Pat B. Rooney.

outside (the Bremerton Navy Yard scenes). You don't even see water in the "underwater" effects footage. In the whole movie, the only water we see is in the stock footage. Oh, and in a shot where Bob Steele's face shines like it's a little sweaty.

One of *Atomic Submarine*'s selling points was that it was "the very FIRST [movie] about the nuclear operated undersea craft." But it was preceded by *It Came from Beneath the Sea* and also *On the Beach* (1959), and I'd bet at least a few more.

With an idea of putting "*Gunsmoke* in space," Jack Rabin approached NBC with some sketches and pitched a new TV series, *Outpost in Space*. Early in 1959, a pilot was shot at MGM starring Robert Fuller and featuring sets from *Forbidden Planet* (1956) and *North by Northwest* (1959) – and the *Atomic Submarine* flying saucer.

The Atomic Submarine was retitled for German release, but even the new title offered no hint of its sci-fi-monster content: *Auf U-17 ist die Hölle los*, which translates to the rather exciting title *On U-17 All Hell Breaks Loose*(!).

Atomic Submarine's above-the-line cost (story, cast, director, etc.) was approximately $23,500, below the line almost $105,000. Total: approximately $128,500. "General studio overhead," $9420, raised the grand total to just short of $138,000. By the end of 1960, it made $146,081.75 domestically. As of 1968, the domestic was at $184,237.63; total collections (including TV), $316,546.64.

Of course *Voyage to the Bottom of the Sea* offered up several episodes which, in one way or another, called to mind *The Atomic Submarine*. Just a sampling: *Seaview* searches for a spaceship in the ocean in "The Sky Is Falling" (1964). "The Condemned" (1965) features a monster that looks a bit like the Saucer Monster – and Arthur Franz heads the guest cast. In "Flaming Ice" (1968), the *Seaview* goes under the polar cap and discovers an air-filled grotto and hostile, white-skinned, blue-lipped Frost Men (hailing from an ice planet). As in *Atomic Submarine*'s climax, the aliens are in their saucer heading back into space when the *Seaview* blasts them to bits. Michael Pate plays the aptly named alien Gelid (a synonym for *cold*).

Just one week later, *Voyage* again echoed *Atomic Submarine* with "Attack!" A flying saucer destroys a fleet of ships, which is just their curtain-raising act: They've set up a base 800 feet below sea level and it's filled with flying saucers waiting to destroy every major city on Earth. In addition to a ship-destroying flying saucer and saucers on the ocean floor, "Attack!" features a cell set that's nothing but blackness, à la *Cyclops*. (Also, in a steal from 1951's *The Day the Earth Stood Still*, Skip Homeier plays a Klaatu-like alien peacenik.)

When discussing *The Atomic Submarine*, Alex Gordon would sometimes mention a Charles Band movie that "stole the whole thing" (*Atomic*'s storyline) but never mentioned the title, maybe because he didn't remember it. Seems to me the movie has to be the made-in-Spain *Endless Descent* (1990), which I once watched as part of my job as *Fangoria* magazine's video reviewer "Dr. Cyclops." I wouldn't go nearly so far

Going by the Internet, many *Atomic Submarine* fans feel sure that Kang and Kodos, space aliens regularly featured in "Treehouse of Horror" episodes of TV's *The Simpsons*, were based on the Saucer Monster. Kang and Kodos' creators claim their inspiration was an EC comic book cover. Let's see that comic book cover, fellas.

as to say that *Endless Descent* "stole the whole thing" but, unprompted by Gordon, I did mention *Atomic Submarine* in my *Fango* #107 review. Here's part of it:

> The nuclear sub *Siren I* has been lost somewhere on the ocean floor, and now *Siren II*, manned (and womanned) by a multinational crew, is scouring the seabed for the missing ship. 20,000 clichés under the sea and endless dissent later, they find an air-filled suboceanic world of nasty bug-like critters and a deadly Green Slime-ish algae.... *Endless Descent* is yet another in the long line of *Leviathan-DeepStar Six*-etc. takeoffs..., but at least you can marvel at the bad acting and the kind of toilet-tank miniature sets that take all the "special" out of special FX. A computer screen gives a diver's occupation as *driver*. People shout out what depth they're at while readouts shown in closeup give a different figure. A diver is dispatched at a point miles below the surface in a regular skin diver's outfit [divers shouldn't go deeper than 130 *feet*], and 4000 feet shy of his destination. And so on. The '50s-era plot, harking back to oldies-but-goodies like *The Atomic Submarine* and *Mutiny in Outer Space*, is so predictable that you can announce what's going to happen next every step of the way....

👁 *The Atomic Submarine* was shot at Allied Artists, formerly Monogram, formerly (etc., etc.), all the way back to 1912. In 1978, the place was declared a Los Angeles Historic-Cultural Monument. Now it's the Church of Scientology's Scientology Media Productions and, according to *LA Weekly*, offers "soundstages with 'robotically controlled cameras,' a scenery shop, screening rooms, a visual-effects center and even a television broadcast studio, with the rumored goal of, eventually, creating a 24-hour Scientology cable station."

Fortunes of war!

👁 Math question: If approximately $138,000 (the budget of *Atomic Submarine*) had the same buying power in 1959 as $561,804 in 1989, how could *The Abyss* (1989) cost *$45 million* and come out 100 times worse?

Alex Gordon's "In-Depth" Interviews

Interviews by Tom Weaver

This appendix is comprised of two interviews I did with producer Alex Gordon, starting with the *Atomic Submarine* chat we had in 2002. At that time, I knew less than I do now about *Atomic Submarine* and the chronology of the events that led up to it, so I was unable to steer Gordon right when he got a few things wrong. For instance, he told me that *Submarine Seahawk* was a finished product by the time he began planning *Atomic Submarine*; that's incorrect, he hadn't yet *made Seahawk* when he announced *Atomic*. Timeline-wise, give what's in the Production History more credence than what's in this interview.

After *The Atomic Submarine*, Gordon's next movie was *The Underwater City*, made for Columbia in 1961 and released the following year. Since it's another Gordon-Orville H. Hampton underwater sci-fi adventure, I thought it was enough of a "shirt-tail relative" to *Atomic Submarine* that readers of this book might be interested in my 2003 interview with Alex on that subject. It begins after the end of the *Atomic* interview.

Alex Gordon on *The Atomic Submarine*

According to 1958 press clippings, the journey of the Nautilus *inspired you to make your movie.*

That had something to do with it, yes, it *was* based on the idea of something like the *Nautilus*. But actually I had made a submarine picture before, *Submarine Seahawk* [1958] with John Bentley, the British actor, at American International, written by Orville Hampton. And I was always interested in submarines and old submarine pictures like *Hell Below* [1933] with Walter Huston, *Devil's Playground* [1937] with Richard Dix, *Submarine D-1* [1937] with Pat O'Brien and others like that. Hampton and I thought it might be an interesting idea to try a submarine picture. Also, we knew we could buy stock footage and we wouldn't have to actually go *out* on a submarine, but instead just build a submarine set on the soundstage. That would make it easier budget-wise to make a submarine picture. When we made *Submarine Seahawk*, it was possible through my brother Dick [movie producer Richard Gordon], and Dick's connection with Seven Arts, to obtain stock footage from the Warner Brothers pictures *Destination Tokyo* and *Air Force* [1943], spectacular footage. It was rather funny: In their review of *Submarine Seahawk*, *The Los Angeles Times* said, "Particularly impressive is the inclusion of the authentic footage of the Battle of the Coral Sea, making *Submarine Seahawk* look much bigger than it actually is." But of course [*laughs*], even in the Warner Brothers pictures, it wasn't authentic footage, it was special effects!

Anyway, after *Submarine Seahawk* I thought, "Well, that seemed to come out pretty well. Let's try another submarine picture." Orville Hampton and I had formed a company called Gorham Productions—Gordon and Hampton—and we thought we would do two projects, one a submarine picture, the other a picture called *The Beetle*. At just about that time, after *Submarine Seahawk*, I severed my connections with American International. I wasn't getting any money on my percentages on my AIP pictures, and I realized it would just go on like that.

You once wrote that Atomic Submarine *was suggested by [special effects men] Jack Rabin and Irving Block.*

I forget now how I first met Rabin and Block—I think they came to *me*, because I was identified with some special effects pictures. They said they had an idea of a combination of a submarine picture and a horror picture. So we were discussing it, and they said that they would come in for a very good price and do a lot of special effects on deferment and so on. There were some script rewrites, and then when the script was done and we all sort of liked the way it came out, I took it over to Allied Artists, to Allied's president Steve Broidy. He said that he liked the idea of the picture, if we could make it for a *price*. "Let's budget the picture and see how we come out," Broidy said, "and then see if we can work out a deal."

Did you do the budgeting?

No, I got my regular production manager Bart Carré to make a budget for the picture, and he came out at $135-137,000, depending on the cast. [In a different, later interview, Gordon said that Allied Artists made the budget for the picture.] So 135,000, if you can believe that. Now stars getting 20 and 25 million dollars, and here's a whole picture that's supposed to be made in eight days for $135,000.

I went back to Allied Artists and they said that they would put up 60 percent of the budget, and then recoup it in first position. And we would have to come up with the balance of 40 percent, and be in second position. That was their regular deal for independents on my level. Also, we would have to supply a completion bond. A completion bond is a person who was worth the money that, if the picture ran into trouble and ran out of money, this person would put up the money to complete the picture.

So the picture was budgeted for eight days of production, plus however long it would take to do the special effects. The special effects costs were limited to between $25,000-27,000. Oh, and Allied Artists said we would have to use part of the regular crew that they had on salary year-round for their various pictures, so we would need to use Edward Morey, Jr., who was production manager on virtually all Allied Artists pictures.

Instead of Bart Carré, who was usually production manager on your movies.

Bart Carré was still tied up with American International Pictures, so he couldn't have done it anyway. Bart said, "Look, I can't go over to Allied Artists with you because I'm doing more AIP pictures. Use Clark Pavlow." The crew was a combination of a few Allied Artists people but mostly "our" people [Gordon regulars] like Harry Reif the set decorator, who was on all my pictures, and Judy Hart the script supervisor, who was the daughter of Edward L. Cahn and was script supervisor on the pictures that Cahn did at American International. And I selected [director of photography] Gilbert Warrenton—Bart Carré had suggested him, and I immediately was thrilled to have him.

Bart Carré on the set of *The She-Creature*. When New York's Museum of Modern Art did their AIP retrospective (July 26-August 28, 1979), the commemorative booklet sang Carré's praises: "[He] had worked on Douglas Fairbanks' *The Mark of Zorro* in 1920 and as a production supervisor over the next 35 years learned how to make every dollar spent look like ten on the screen."

Warrenton later photographed Master of the World *[1961] for director William Witney, who complained to me that he was "so god-damn slow."*

Incredible! Somebody should have told Witney that Warrenton turned out *our* picture, with all the effects and the lighting and all that, in eight days.

Before we get even further ahead of ourselves—how did you go about raising your end of the money?

Henry Schrage, who had co-produced a couple of Bert I. Gordon's pictures, had recently broken up with Bert Gordon. He agreed to put up some of the money that we needed for our 40 percent of the budget, and in return for that, he became a co-producer. He wanted a better credit than he had on Bert Gordon pictures. Schrage put up $19,000 but we actually needed more than that, we needed ...

Forty percent of 135,000—whatever the heck that is!

[*Laughs*] Yeah, that's right. Through connections with Dick, I flew to New York to try and get a man named

Peter Gettinger, a well-known finance man for independent movies, to put up some of the money and a completion bond. And would you believe that the day I flew, I got complete laryngitis! When Dick took me in there to talk to Gettinger, I could hardly talk! I was croaking—it was very embarrassing! And Gettinger told me, "Look, you made a *lousy* deal with Allied Artists. I'm not going to put up any money *or* a completion bond."

I'd heard that a man by the name of Theodore Ticktin had put up a completion bond for one or two pictures, so I went to see him and he was a *very* nice man. Now *there* was a person you could really talk to—*and* a very good financing man. He was actually a builder here [in California], building and buying real estate and so on. He was interested and we got on very well with him, and he (I guess) thought I had an honest face [*laughs*].

There's a lot of peering at screens and dials in the movie's first half as the *Tiger Shark* tracks its quarry. Terror does not ensue in the second half, but mild amusement puts in an appearance. Pictured: Paul Dubov, Brett Halsey, Victor Varconi.

Anyway, to make a long story short, he agreed to put up a completion bond for us. That was, of course, a great break. Then I got a couple of friends of mine to put up a little money—one was an agent, Allen Connor, and another one was a personal friend, a businessman. The agent put up $5000, the other $7500 to help us with some of the 40 percent on our end.

Allen Connor the actor?

Yes, in the 1930s, he was in some Republic pictures. Then he became an agent with the Wallace Middleton Agency.

What did your total budget come to?

$137,931. The above-the-line, the story, cast, director and everything, came to $23,554. Below-the-line, $104,957. So a total of $128,511. So we had to have the figure between the 128,511 and 137,931 as deferments. Naturally my producer's fee, my $5000, was deferred, and Rabin-Block was the other deferment.

Then the rest of the money came from Allied Artists.

Right. Allied Artists was interested in a lot of small independent pictures, pictures which were exploitable, and where they only needed to put up 60 percent of the money and had first position. They figured they would certainly make *that* back, even if the *producer* didn't get any money! Those who were in second position were often left empty-handed.

Being in second position—that's when it got "iffy"!

That's when it got very iffy! As I mentioned, I was told by certain people that I didn't make a very good deal with them. But I had no real clout at the time. Steve Broidy was a very tough person to deal with. He was considered a great humanitarian and he was on all the boards of all the benevolent societies and motion picture charities…but sitting across a desk from him, he would talk very loud at you (and he had a voice like a bullfrog) and was very pushy, like a steamroller pushing over you if you carne up with any thoughts. He was one of these "booming" people, it seemed he couldn't just speak in a normal voice. A lot of big movie executives were like that—I guess they were trying to intimidate you. And, frankly, I was a bit intimidated by him! Also, it didn't work that I reminded him that I was the one responsible for bringing Monogram's "Rough Riders" Westerns from 1941-42 to England. Originally they weren't going to be shown over there because of the "Bacon or Bogart" situation.

You're going to have to explain that one!

Due to World War II, there was at that time a restriction on importing American pictures. In Parliament, someone had said, "Look, what do you prefer, bacon or Humphrey Bogart? We've got to limit the number of pictures that can come in. We need the convoys for food and weapons and things—we can't use that much shipping space importing movies!" So I wrote Pathé Pictures [the British distributor of Monogram Pictures], I bombarded them, urging them to bring in the Rough Riders. I said Buck Jones, Tim McCoy and Raymond Hatton, the stars of the Rough Riders series, were still big names in England, and promised to help to promote them through my Westerners Club [a fan club devoted to Western stars]. And finally they *did*, they brought in *Arizona Bound* and *The Gunman from Bodie* [both 1941], the first two, and then they brought in *Forbidden Trails* [1941], *Down Texas Way*, *Ghost Town Law* and *Below the Border* [all 1942]. Those Rough Riders pictures were shown in England, and Monogram made quite a bit of money out of it ... but when I brought it up, Broidy brushed that aside. He wasn't the type that you could talk to about something like that. He was just business. And his second-in-command, his "hatchet man," George Burrows, was even tougher. Burrows was the financial man.

Were you able to make it in eight days, as planned?
Eight days. And then Rabin and Block had several weeks for their special effects.

Where was the picture shot?
Entirely at Allied Artists' studios at the corner of Sunset and Hollywood Boulevard. They had a series of bungalows and one soundstage, so that's where we were shooting it. It was all shot on the one soundstage.

Were you pleased with the set-up at Allied Artists and the sets and all?
The submarine set was marvelous. That was the set decorators and Warrenton with his lenses and lighting. In fact, when my wife Ruth came on the set, she said, "That set is so small ... how can you get anybody *in* that set?" And Warrenton said, "Come here and look through the camera." When she looked through the camera, it was like you were in a real submarine. It was the same with *Submarine Seahawk*.

Representing the interior of the flying saucer with just a black set and a narrow walkway ... did you think this "worked"?
I thought that black set and narrow walkway worked very well. When I first saw it, I didn't think for a moment that it was impressive, but once it had the

"How come I can't get any music on this thing??": Arthur Franz poses as a stout-hearted submariner of the atomic future.

lighting and everything, everybody agreed that it was very effective.

I'm assuming it was done that way because there wasn't much money going around.
Yes, it was. But even with no money, [the set designers] still wanted to give it whatever they could—inventive lighting and so on.

You mentioned your wife Ruth a moment ago. You gave her an "Assistant to Producer" credit on the picture.
She was actually the dialogue coach, because Victor Varconi, who had a strong Hungarian accent, found it very difficult to speak the lines that he was given. It never even occurred to me when we first had the script, but there *were* a lot of technical explanations, a lot of technical verbiage from Varconi, when they're all sitting there, talking about things. And he had a lot of trouble with the pronunciation and memorizing those lines. Ruth said, "Why don't you let me take him aside and coach him, go over the lines with him? That might help him." (She had done this before, she had worked in a little theater group for quite a while.) And it did help Varconi; at least people in Peoria and Muleshoe, Texas, and Paducah could understand what Victor was trying

to say! Then, when a couple of the others said, "Can I read lines with you too?," I said, "Let her get some kind of a credit." So that's how she got in on that.

And the rest of the actors? Any problems from any of them?
Well, Arthur Franz was a strange man. He was "up" on his dialogue, he never kept you waiting, and he said all his lines and everything, hardly ever fluffed. But he wanted to come and see the rushes—and even bring his *kids* to see the rushes! I said, "I'm sorry, Arthur. Allied Artists does not allow actors to see rushes"—I made it appear that it was all Allied. If Allied *had* allowed it, I would have *maybe* given way, I don't know, because he was so emphatic about it. But I didn't like the idea of actors seeing rushes either, because they may want to do something over again, so on and so forth. I couldn't have that on that kind of a picture so I said, "I'm sorry" and blamed it on Allied Artists' policy. He was upset about that, and he went and sat in a corner of the set and sulked. He would do all his stuff very professionally, but then if I wanted to sort of approach him on something, sometimes he'd shun me and sit down all alone on the stairs, waiting for his next shot. It wasn't easy to have little conversations with him, like with the others. So he was not too friendly, but I thought he came off well in the picture. Brett Halsey was a very sweet man, very nice. He was always with the girls, but he was a nice guy and worked very hard and knew his lines. Bob Steele, of course, was like "family," and we had a great time.

Dick Foran was an absolute delight. I was talking to him about all his Westerns and serials and all that. Real nice guy. He rather underplayed his part in the picture; he could have given it, I think, a little more emphasis. But that's all right. After principal photography was completed on the eighth day on time and schedule, we had a little party on the soundstage for the cast and crew, and I decided to pull a surprise on Dick. I had in my record collection a 78 RPM record of Foran singing "The Prairie Is My Home" [from one of his 1930s Warner Brothers Westerns] and "Mexicali Rose." I bought it in England as a kid and brought it with me when I came to America after the War. As everyone was having drinks and buffet meals, I put on the record over the loudspeaker, waiting for Foran's reaction.

Dick was talking with some people and suddenly stopped in mid-sentence. With a look of utter surprise, he exploded, "My God, that's *me* singing!" When both sides had been played, he rushed up to me and said, "Where on Earth did you get that record? I've never *heard* it before!" It seems that, around the same time Dick recorded "Mexicali Rose," it was also recorded by Gene Autry, and

Old habits die hard: Decades after his B-Western heyday, Dick Foran brings a six-shooter along on an atom sub search for deep-sea dangers.

Autry's became a gold record for him immediately. The Gene Autry version was such a big hit that the record company shelved the Dick Foran one, except in England. It was a fun moment that has stayed in my memory.

To me, Tom Conway looks a lot older here than he does in his other pictures for you. Was that due to his drinking?
I don't really remember that Tom Conway looked so much older, but if he did, it was due to his illness, because this wasn't too long after *Runaway Daughters* ... and he was having other health problems too. He didn't really have a drinking problem. Perhaps he did drink a little too much at times, but never on the set when we were working. But sometimes, when we were at his house, he was inclined to take that extra drink. Whether that had anything to do with his illnesses or not, I don't know, but anyway, he wasn't too well. But he was definitely "with it," he knew all his lines and didn't fluff.

Did you get along well with Rabin and Block?
I got along with them *until* I saw the so-called "monster." They made a miniature figure of the one-eyed alien, a puppet like **Señor W**ences might have [*laughs*], about a foot and a half high—about the size of

the figure that was used in *King Kong* [1933]. They never showed it to me, I never saw it until after they shot it. I kept asking, I wanted to see it, and they (probably realizing what my reaction would be) refused to show it to me. So I was mad as hell. And then when I finally saw it on the screen, in rushes, I was fit to be tied. [In a different, later interview, Gordon said that he did get to see the puppet before it was photographed.] I said it was so awful and it looked so cheap that I didn't want a monster in the picture. So we went to Steve Broidy—Rabin and Block and Hampton and I. I don't think we actually took the puppet with us, I think we just took the few feet of footage that they had shot. I said to Broidy, "This is going to look very, very bad. It's not a good special effect. I don't think we ought to show the monster, I think we ought to just suggest it." And Broidy said, "No, we gotta have a monster. *Gotta* have a monster." I said, "Well, wait 'til you see it. I won't be on the lot that day!"

Tom Conway, Arthur Franz, Dick Foran and Victor Varconi danced 'til they dropped at the *Atomic Submarine* wrap party.

So I had to agree to do it. And, actually, I *will* say this for Rabin and Block: When it was photographed for the picture, the way the cameraman did it, it doesn't look at all bad and I was satisfied. Especially with the sound effects, and the diffused alien voice, and the set and all. Amazingly to me, the audience at the preview enjoyed it thoroughly. There was no jeering or anything like that, they *bought* it. So I changed my mind, I now think it was adequate. But at the time, of course, I was very, very upset and disappointed.

When you told Broidy it was very, very bad, were Rabin and Block within earshot?

Oh, yes, they were sitting right there [*laughs*]! I told him I thought it was a lousy monster!

Did Gilbert Warrenton also photograph Rabin and Block's effects footage?

No, Rabin and Block did all that in their lab.

Rabin and Block get a co-producing credit.

They didn't co-produce the picture *except* if you want to say that their special effects made it a "co-production" venture. You might say they deserved their credit because they did produce the special effects.

How about your other co-producer, Henry Schrage? Was he involved in the making of the movie?

Schrage was strictly a money man. He had nothing to do with the actual production of the picture, but he wanted a credit. And Hampton also had nothing to do with the picture at all except the script. "Gorham Productions," Gordon and Hampton, was formed to make films, but it was dissolved after we did *The Underwater City* [1962] at Columbia Studios because Hampton got a deal working for Edward Small, making a whole bunch of pictures there. So Hampton and I had to dissolve the company.

And Allied Artists was pleased with it when you screened it for them?

Yes. One of their executives, Ben Schwalb, said, "It's a good little picture…," indicating that it was all right for Allied Artists.

Jack Rabin told an interviewer that Atomic Submarine *was "a horrible picture."*

I'm surprised, because he later came to us wanting to do another project.

Whose idea was the "Electro-Sonic" music? How well did you think that worked?

The composer Alexander Laszlo was recommended to us by Bart Carré, and [Laszlo] had the idea for the Electro-Sonic music score. He gave us a sample of it and we liked the idea, so we worked with him. I think it worked all right. I like "full" music scores, I'm not crazy about [electronic] music, but I thought it came through all right for this picture.

Did Atomic Submarine *have a preview, the way so many of your AIP pictures did? What was the audience reaction?*

It was previewed in Seattle. It was on a single bill there, in a first-run theater for Allied Artists. I wasn't present because I didn't know they were going to do it. I probably couldn't have gotten up to Seattle anyway. But it was very good, the reaction.

You can't really tell from the poster of Atomic Submarine, *and you definitely can't tell from the trailer, that it's sci-fi. Was Allied Artists trying to sell it as a "straight" submarine action movie?*

I never thought about it, but I suppose the poster *doesn't* really indicate that it's sci-fi. If you look at the lobby cards, however, there is an indication that there is some terror there. There's not a big emphasis on it, they don't show the one-eyed creature and all that. But I don't think they were trying to sell it as a straightforward submarine picture.

The trailer promises "adventures beneath the waves" and that kind of stuff. No indication of the flying saucer, the monster, nothing.

Well, you're probably right then, maybe Allied Artists *did* try to sell it as a straightforward submarine picture.

Was it profitable for Allied Artists and you?

It was *not* profitable for us, although everybody got their money back. At first we weren't getting any money, of course, because Allied Artists was getting their 60 percent back first. After they had recouped their 60 percent and it came to our 40 percent, they began falling further and further behind in their reports to us. I had to keep calling about the reports, which were supposed to be quarterly. And there was no money. Sometimes they'd send us (like) $300 when they were supposed to send (like) $3000. This was going on and on, and I kept calling and calling and calling, and there'd be no reply. Their lawyer was Steve Broidy's future son-in-law Jack Sattinger, and I had the most *terrible* time with him. He was a Jack Carson look-alike and a Jack Carson "type," and I had a love-hate relationship with him. I *liked* the guy personally, and whenever we were face to face he was very nice. But he never returned my phone calls. Whenever he said we would have a contract, or this

Alex with *every* movie fan's favorite home appliance.

piece of paper, or that piece of paper, or that he would call me back, he never would. I sat by my phone literally all day—I didn't have an office, I was working out of my home at the time, and I was really in very bad shape there, my nerves were really on edge because this was a touch-and-go situation and I had people "on the hook" and that kind of thing. I went through a year or more of just terrible times. And later I realized that Allied Artists had money problems. They were pulling all kinds of [shenanigans] in order to try and get their house in order financially—but then they went broke, went into bankruptcy, and actually went out of business.

Finally, through our lawyer, I got a report of what they owed us, and it was something like $8400. We were entitled to that, that was part of our return, but with them in bankruptcy, we had to get a judgment against them. That took another I-don't-remember-*how*-many months. Finally we got a judgment against them and they were forced to pay it, but our lawyer took half of it.

But everybody who put up any cash on the picture eventually got paid back in full. Schrage was paid first, all the others got their money back too, Rabin and Block got their deferment, everybody got paid fully. I was last with my producer's fee, and *that* went to paying

Alex Gordon—already the producer of the subsea action movies *Submarine Seahawk* and *The Atomic Submarine*—"threepeated" with *The Underwater City*.

some [other outstanding debts], so I never really got any money out of the picture. When Dick arranged for a VHS home video deal on the picture, we got some money, but that also went towards paying what we still were "out" on expenses, personally. So when you ask, "Was it profitable for Allied Artists?," it was profitable for Allied Artists. But not for me and my co-producers!

Did The Abyss *[1989] remind you a bit of the plot of* Atomic Submarine?

As soon as I saw that, I thought, "That's a direct steal from *The Atomic Submarine*." And there was another picture, made by Charles Band, where they used a one-eyed creature that was a direct steal.

Rate your horror-science fiction pictures, in order of preference.

I'd say probably *Day the World Ended* ... *The She-Creature* ... *The Atomic Submarine* ... then *Voodoo Woman*. The script of *Atomic Submarine*, of course, isn't the greatest, and some of the lines are a little ... [*trails off, laughs*]. But I think the acting, for the most part, is okay. No great shakes, but it's competent. And there are so many diverse characters—Tom Conway is so different from Victor Varconi, and Varconi from Dick Foran, and so on. Arthur Franz, I think, is okay, and also Brett Halsey. But I'm not complaining. Thinking of all the grief we had to get it on the screen, I think it's adequate in its category.

Alex Gordon on *The Underwater City*

Introduction: The road to scientific progress is fraught with unexpected perils—particularly when it leads off-shore and to the floor of the ocean, as in *The Underwater City*. This SF entry depicts the building of a futuristic manned complex 30 fathoms under the sea, with William Lundigan as the head construction engineer, Julie Adams as a physician and Carl Benton Reid as the project head. A forward-looking subsea adventure, it was made in color and "FantaScope" and features an array of impressive low-budget effects, miniatures and ingenious dry-for-wet sets.

Unfortunately for producer Alex Gordon, the road from script to screen to distribution was also fraught with a number of perils and pitfalls, from casting disputes to ongoing set battles with the film's alcoholic star—the whole frustrating experience eventually culminating in a lawsuit by Gordon's Neptune Productions against Hollywood giant Columbia Pictures! Gordon dredges up the dramatic story...

The idea for *The Underwater City* started with my wife Ruth Gordon, or "Ruth Alexander" as she called herself professionally. In an issue of *American Weekly*, she saw an article about scientists looking into the possibility of a farm type of community on the floor of the ocean. The idea was to build structures on land, tow them out to sea and lower them to the bottom, where the inhabitants would harvest the sea (fish, plant life and other edibles) to provide food for the ever-increasing number of hungry people in the world. Ruth said it might make a good movie—she was *always* finding things in the papers and coming up with ideas. We had already done *The Atomic Submarine* [1959], which dealt with bottom-of-the-ocean activity, so we thought, "Well, maybe this might be a good one to follow up with, if we can get a deal somewhere."

I went to my then-partner Orville H. Hampton, who had already written *Jet Attack* and *Submarine Seahawk* [both 1958] for me at American International, and had written *The Atomic Submarine*. He thought it was an *excellent* idea, and agreed to do an outline on speculation. At the time, my agent was Lester Salkow—he handled Vincent Price and other well-known names. When Hampton's outline was written, I gave it to Salkow and he said he'd take it to Columbia, to Irving Briskin, head of second-level productions. Salkow had an "in" with Columbia, because of Vincent Price—Salkow had made the deal for Price to be in Columbia's *The Tingler* [1959] and other films.

An appointment was made and Orville Hampton, Salkow, Salkow's "second in command" Maury Calder and I had what I thought was a very nice meeting. Briskin called himself the King of the Bs because he was in charge of the second level unit there—the Westerns and the second features. Making some small talk, I threw out all kinds of things that I knew about the early days of Columbia Pictures, because I knew that Briskin had been there since the early '30s. Later on in life, I realized that those things don't really *mean* anything to these people. They don't care about the past, just their position within the company and what they're doing *now*.

Once we got down to business, we talked budget and schedule and so on. Briskin was sounding us out and trying to figure, very roughly, what kind of budget category the picture would fall into. Finally Briskin offered two options. If I would let Columbia producer Charles Schneer produce *The Underwater City* under his banner (I would be associate producer), they would give it a budget of $650,000. If I insisted on producing it myself, then we would get a much smaller budget, 350,000. I said, "I have made about 18 pictures, American International and Allied Artists and so on, and so I certainly would like to be the producer on this." Briskin said okay. When the question of black-and-white or color came up, there was an immediate mutual agreement that it *had* to be in color, especially as there was going to be bottom-of-the-ocean activity in it.

Hampton and I formed a company called Neptune Productions to make this picture with Columbia. My salary as producer was $5000. Initially Hampton wanted to be co-producer, but I had to say, "Look, I've got solo producer credits on all my pictures. I don't mind if you're associate producer, as you were on *The Atomic Submarine*, but I don't feel I should split co-producer credit with you." He went along with that (although, ultimately, he didn't take a producer credit at all, and in fact put his pen name "Owen Harris" on the picture). He began writing the script, and when he was done, which didn't take very long, Columbia did budget the picture at $350,000. A budget of $350,000 meant that we had six days of principal photography, and then a few weeks of special effects. When they asked who I would get to do the special effects, the miniatures of the underwater city and so on, I suggested Howard Anderson and his company, because Howard had a very good reputation for such work. And, to lay it out and oversee it, Howard Lydecker, one of the top special effects men in the business. Columbia approved that.

For director, I suggested Edward L. Cahn, who had directed several of my films at AIP. Columbia agreed to Eddie, so Hampton and I went to see him at Edward Small Productions, located on the Sam Goldwyn lot. Eddie said he'd *love* to do it with us, but he had an exclusive deal for about a dozen B pictures at Edward Small and he really didn't have the time to do an outside picture. I next pitched Spencer Bennet to Columbia and they nixed him. Bennet had done many Westerns and serials, and they felt he was too identified with B product. At that point, I suggested Frank McDonald. I knew McDonald personally, he'd directed a lot of Gene Autry's Westerns—not only features but also TV episodes. He was a very nice guy and very efficient, and I knew we would have no problem with him. (And I knew he would give me no trouble on casting [*laughs*]!) We met with him and he said he'd be very pleased to do it, and Columbia approved him.

When it came to the casting session, I had to go through Max Arnow, who had been the casting director at Columbia for many years. I suggested Richard Denning, whom I had worked with on *Day the World Ended*, *Girls in Prison* and *The Oklahoma Woman* [all 1956] and who I knew would be very reliable. But Arnow rejected the idea, even though Denning had worked for Columbia not only in leads but then later in second leads, supporting people like George Montgomery and so on. By that time, they'd figured he'd done too many cheapies, and Arnow wanted somebody a little "stronger" for the lead. He soon began sending actors 'round to see me, and one of them was Glenn Corbett. Columbia had Corbett under contract and they were willing to go with him in the lead because they were trying to "build" him. I thought he was capable of doing a good job, but I had to tell him, "This is my first picture for Columbia and I really *do* need a more identifiable 'name.' I'm not trying to insult you, and I'm sure that you'll go far." He said he understood perfectly.

After I turned down Corbett, and a couple of others who Arnow suggested, Arnow started throwing around crazy names like Joel McCrea and George Hamilton and a few others in that bracket. It made absolutely no sense—I even said to him, "We can't *possibly* afford

Mission accomplished: The establishment of Amphibia City is celebrated on the sea floor—which will soon open up and swallow it!

these kind of names on a budget of $350,000. We've got to get somebody who's $10,000 *tops*." (Actually, I'm sure Arnow had no intention of actually trying to get those people—I think he was just grandstanding a little bit.) Finally, at a meeting, Irving Briskin said, "Well, how 'bout William Lundigan? Lundigan did that TV series *Men into Space* and he's identified with science fiction." I didn't know Lundigan personally, but I'd always thought he was all right on the screen—nothing special, but "all right"—and certainly a "medium" type of name. I said, "Okay, why don't Hampton and I have lunch with Lundigan and his agent, and see if he would be interested?" So we did, we met for lunch at the Nickodell, a hangout for the movie crowd on Melrose, just around the corner from Paramount. And, yes, Lundigan was interested and said that he would do it. I'm pretty sure his salary was less than 10,000, but then, it *was* a six-day picture.

Next it came to casting the girl. I don't know if Nancy Kovack was Max Arnow's girlfriend or not, but it seemed she was around all the time, and he had her come in. She was very nice, but I said, "She's not a *name*. Yes, she's played supporting roles in a couple of Columbia pictures, but I really think that, even though this is a low-budget picture, we need *some* sort of a name that is recognizable." *I* wanted Audrey Dalton, but she was at this time too expensive. Finally somebody mentioned Julie Adams, and as soon as they did, I said, "Oh, *yes*! If we can get her for the price, I would be *delighted* with Julie Adams." They had her come in, and she was *very*, very nice. I remember discussing with her the six pictures she did simultaneously for Ron Ormond [in 1949], six Westerns with James Ellison and Russell Hayden in which, acting under the name Betty Adams, she was the leading lady. They shot six pictures all at the same time with the identical cast! Anyway, Julie Adams agreed to do *The Underwater City*.

Now it came to casting the older scientist, and I offered it to Basil Rathbone. I didn't know him personally but I thought he would be a good choice for that role. And I got a *very, very* nice letter from Basil Rathbone, which I still have, in which he thanked me profusely for thinking of him, and said he would love to do it, but then went on to say that he was just taking off on a one-man lecture tour of colleges that would take him out of the area for three months or longer. We now began kicking other names around, and one agent said, "How 'bout Raymond Massey?" I said [*with disbelief*], "Why, you don't think Raymond Massey is going to do a *six-day picture*?" The agent said, "He's back East right now and he isn't doing *any*thing. As long as you stop for half an hour at four o'clock every afternoon and serve him tea—he's an English gentleman and likes to have his tea—he'll do it. $7500 a week." I said, "My *God*, just $7500 for *Raymond Massey*? Certainly!"—I *jumped* at it!

As for the rest of the cast, Roy Roberts [as businessman Tim Graham] was sort of a mutual agreement—I didn't care too much one way or the other. Chet Douglas [as frogman Marlow] was a young guy who used to come around *constantly* to audition. Paul Dubov [geophysical engineer Burnett], of course, was one of my "regulars." Karen Norris [Phyllis the dietitian] I didn't really know but I didn't object when they suggested her. Edward Mallory [Lt. Wally Steele] was unfamiliar to me, but he looked all right. Kathie Browne [as Steele's newlywed wife] was very sweet. She later married Darren McGavin. And, of course, I also wanted my "regular oldtimers" Edmund Cobb and Frank Lackteen in the picture, and there was no problem from Columbia about that.

Now I had my interview with the man who used to say, "You have nothing to fear but Fier himself!": Jack Fier, the production manager at Columbia. He was a tough-talking oldtimer, a John Ford type, loud and intimidating. I'd heard horror stories about him, so in order to perhaps mollify him a little bit, perhaps ingratiate myself with him, the first time I met him, I brought in a bunch of pressbooks from Mascot serials (I knew that he had in the early '30s worked on the Mascot serials). I wanted him to know that I knew his background, that I knew he had worked on those serials and he had produced the Tim McCoy films at Columbia and I said I knew Tim McCoy and so on. That sort of softened him—but only temporarily! He didn't really fall for all that, but at least he *acknowledged* it! A short time later, just a couple of days before shooting was scheduled to start, Fier had the whole crew in to give them a pep talk—like Gen. Patton would do before the Battle of the Bulge! It was right at Columbia, in one of the meeting rooms, and I would say there were about 30 of us there altogether, crew members and so on. He told everybody that they'd better shape up if they ever wanted to work at Columbia again; "If you think that the Army was rough, you haven't seen *any*thing yet!"; he said that what *he* says *goes*, never mind about listening to anybody else; and, of course, "You have nothing to fear but Fier himself!"—which he said sort of jokingly. He was a tough hombre, but I guess he knew his stuff. I felt like I was back in the Army with my sergeant major!

A day or two before the picture was due to start, we had our first problem: Raymond Massey was on his way out to Hollywood from New York when suddenly there were weather problems and the plane had to be diverted to Boston. All of a sudden, it was going to take an extra day for him to get out here. Irving Briskin announced that he certainly wasn't going to shoot around Massey or change anything, and so we would have to get somebody else to play the part. And then he pushed in Carl Benton Reid. Reid was a very good actor, certainly nothing wrong with him, very nice guy--but there's a vast difference between having Raymond Massey in a picture, and Carl Benton Reid!

The second problem came on the first day of shooting. I got there a couple of hours ahead of time, and as the morning progressed, we realized we couldn't find William Lundigan—that he wasn't there! An hour later I finally found him in his dressing room, just sitting there, completely unprepared, and he had the most tremendous hangover. He hadn't read the script, he didn't know any lines, he didn't know *any*thing. He said, "I'm not feeling well this morning...I don't know whether I can do this..." I said, "Listen, you *gotta* come out..." I was absolutely *frantic*, because this was the first day of shooting—what was I going to *do*? I don't remember if I called Frank McDonald in or not, I *may* have; I know I wasn't alone in pushing him out there onto the set. Of course he still didn't know his lines, and McDonald had to feed him his lines.

And so it went throughout the picture: Lundigan was always late coming on set and always, when he stepped into the scene, he wasn't ready with his lines. He blamed it all on, "I don't know what's wrong with me...I must have the flu..." but it was obvious he'd been drinking. We lost hour after hour when he couldn't do his stuff. It was an absolute disaster.

For scenes of the actors walking on the ocean floor, we shot on Columbia's Stage 33. It was a large soundstage, perfectly dry of course, but "dressed" to look like the bottom of the ocean. The set was impressive-looking in person, because it covered most of the stage. The camera shot through a large fish tank in which we had some very small fish swimming; to heighten the effect, there was a continuously revolving paddle in the tank, stirring the water in order to create a bit of a ripple effect. Lights were reflected off huge tinfoil flats, suspended from the stage ceiling and rolled slightly. This bathed the entire set in what looked like reflected rays of the sun, so familiar underwater. To complete the illusion, we also had the actors walking in slow motion. Between the set dressing and the tank and the fish and the reflected light and the slow-motion actors, we actually did achieve the effect that they were on the bottom of the ocean. Incidentally, some of the diving equipment that the actors wore, and a few other things on the underwater set, were supplied by Jon Hall, who by this time had retired from acting—he was now developing underwater camera equipment and renting out stock footage and so forth.

Again, however, there was trouble. I believe we began shooting these ocean floor scenes on the third day—and Lundigan refused to get into his diving outfit. As usual, he said he just wasn't up to it, he kept saying he wasn't feeling well. He even refused to come out of his dressing room. So I called for a double. And then Lundigan had the effrontery to call the Screen Actors Guild and have a representative come out to Columbia and threaten to *fine* us, because there was another actor there in his part when he, Lundigan, could and should be doing it! It was ridiculous! I told the Guild guy, "*You* get him out there. *We* can't get him out of his dressing room, he doesn't know his lines—how the hell can we shoot with him in this condition?"

Dry-for-wet sets were used in *Underwater City* scenes set in Davy Jones' Locker, including the "aquaculturalists" leaving their mini-sub and pilfering potables from a sunken ship.

"He'll be all right, he'll be all right," the Guild guy said. "You've got to use the actor if he's able to play the part..." So on the other days of shooting on the ocean floor set, we had to use Lundigan, even though it took forever to get that outfit on him. (At least when he was in that diving outfit, he didn't have any dialogue.) I don't know if the Screen Actors Guild actually did make Columbia pay a fine, but they *said* they would. I'm sure Columbia was probably very well "in" with SAG and probably worked it out some way, and it wouldn't have been a large fine in any case. But it caused a problem on the set.

There was an additional problem on the ocean floor set. The actors' air tanks produced helium-filled bubbles that rose up into the air, and the effect was marvelous. The problem, the thing that nobody anticipated was that they would then come back *down* again! We had bubbles coming out of these tanks, and it looked very realistic, but then as the scene continued, suddenly you saw the bubbles dropping down again, and everybody was saying, "What the hell is *that*?" We had to put men up in the rafters of the soundstage with fans to blow the bubbles away before they could come back down into the scene. That took us a little while to solve, but it turned out all right.

We shot some exteriors at the Columbia Ranch-- that was where Eddie Cobb and Frank Lackteen were going to shoot their scenes. But that morning, when I went to pick up Frank Lackteen at his little one-room place in Hollywood and drive him to the Columbia Ranch, he was in bed, shivering, and he said he was sick and that he couldn't do it. I realized that there wasn't really anything wrong with him, that it was stage fright— he just felt he couldn't do it. He said, "I'm really ill, I'm in such a bad way. I don't even have my rent...", which was $125. I said, "Frank, let me take care of that," and I wrote him a check for $125. Then I said, "Obviously you *need* the 250 that we can pay you, so get in the car. I'll drive you there, you don't have to work, you certainly don't have any lines, you don't have to even step in front of the *camera* if you don't want to. I can 'cover' that. But you've got to come to the lot, you've got to sign in. Then I can pay you the 250 bucks for a day's work. If you don't come out there at *all*, then you can't get paid." That was the way I persuaded him, and he came along with me. And once he was out there, he was okay. But at first he wasn't going to do it, he was suffering from such stage fright. It was a strange situation!

But even stranger was the fact that we had a second assistant director who, all he did was report to the front office. Jack Fier never came on the set but he had this second assistant director reporting to him every hour whether we were behind schedule or if there was a problem and this and that and so on. That was very, very awkward, a tough situation to *be* in. It was like a police state, everybody was watching us all the time! But before everything started going downhill, with Lundigan and with this second assistant director and all, I *loved* being at Columbia. Every day I looked out of the window of my office, overlooking the Columbia lot, and it was amazing to me: "Here I am in an office at Columbia, producing a picture!" And, another nice experience: The Three Stooges were shooting on the set next to us, so it gave me an opportunity to meet Moe Howard. Larry Fine I just sort of said hello to—he was always off to Vegas, gambling and so on. But Moe I talked to almost every day. Actually, *he* came on *our* set and he wanted to know what we were doing. I was absolutely dumbfounded: Here I'm standing, talking to somebody who *looks* like Moe, and yet he *talks* like the most creative kind of producer-writer-all-around-filmmaker. Obviously I knew that he wasn't going to be like he was in his movies, but I also didn't expect *this*. If you closed your eyes, you'd think you were talking to any one of the Hollywood big shots. It was very, very impressive, the way he knew the business inside out. He was a remarkable person.

Instead of going six days, *Underwater City* went seven, a day over schedule, which everybody was very unhappy about. It was Lundigan who caused the delay—nobody else held us up in any way. Well, we *did* have that little problem with the bubbles, but we solved that very quickly. So that alone would not have caused it, it was strictly Lundigan. With him refusing to come out of his dressing room and never knowing his lines, we just kept getting behind and behind and behind; I remember Frank McDonald going out of his mind. Lundigan was responsible, completely responsible, for the delay and the extra day. It was nothing but a hassle with him.

Now it was time for the special effects guys to start shooting the effects footage. We'd made a deal with Howard Anderson and Co. to do the special effects *under* Howard Lydecker's supervision. Lydecker was absolutely great. He did the special effects on most Republic pictures, everything from *S.O.S. Tidal Wave* [1939] to serials and Westerns, he and his brother Theodore. Howard had the whole layout, every shot storyboarded—there was a completely detailed storyboard, down to the tiniest thing, in his office at Columbia, which was next to mine. He knew exactly what he was going to do all along the way.

I don't remember how long the post-production special effects took—maybe about six weeks. Not awfully long, but certainly longer than the principal photography on the picture! The destruction of the underwater city and the scenes of the octopus and the giant eel, those were shot by Howard Anderson in a tank in Santa Monica. The octopus and the eel, they didn't hurt each other in their fight scene, they just sort of swam against each other and so on, but neither one was hurt. (The octopus stuff was not all that exciting, but at least it was *there*!) I wasn't there for the shooting of any of that, but I *was* on the set every minute at the studio and at the Columbia Ranch.

Ronald Stein did the music score for *The Underwater City*—I remember I had to put up a little bit of a fight for him, but I'm glad I did. Briskin said, "Look, we've got George Duning here at Columbia, he's our music director. Why not use *him*?" I said, "It would be very expensive to do it the way Duning would do it, with a big orchestra and 'scoring to picture' and so on. Ronnie Stein does it with*out* 'scoring to picture.' He looks at the movie on a Moviola and he times every sequence where he will write music, and then he goes away and he does it all. He doesn't have to 'score to picture.'" I won Briskin over that way, I said, "We just don't have the budget," and he gave in. [The definition of "scoring to picture": The orchestra performs while the scene for which that piece of music was written is projected on a screen behind them.]

Briskin insisted, though, that we use a studio orchestra; Ronnie couldn't go down to Mexico or anywhere else on *The Underwater City*, Columbia being a signatory to the guilds and all that. So Ronnie Stein conducted the studio orchestra.

When we finally got to the end of the picture, I thought it wasn't bad. Briskin looked at the rough cut and made some comments, I forget now what they were, but nothing disparaging. He thought it was all right for a co-feature. Columbia was going to put it out with *The Three Stooges Meet Hercules* [1962]--*Hercules* was supposed to be the companion picture, because it was in black-and-white, and *Underwater City* was supposed to be the top of the bill. Or at least equal-billed. Anyway, we had *Underwater City* all done and Irving Briskin approved it, and now it was supposed to be shown to Sam Briskin, Irving's brother, who was head of production on a higher level there.

The screening for Sam Briskin was an absolute disaster. Irving was not present, it was just Sam and me in the Columbia executive screening room. He blew his top: "We can't release the picture this way! It doesn't have enough action, it doesn't have *this*, it doesn't have *that*. It needs all *kinds* of things." And he told me, "Put together about ten minutes of stock shots from other pictures, real disaster footage and creatures and all that sort of thing, and we'll put that on at the front of the picture, or work it in *some*where with some narration

Alex with the posters of his two undersea sci-fi adventures, *The Atomic Submarine* and *The Underwater City*.

over it. Maybe *then* we can release the picture." When I came away from that encounter, of course, I could hardly *walk*! Here Irving had *approved* it, and Sam said it was unreleasable!

It took me about a week to scour every stock shot library in town. I borrowed everything from Cecil B. DeMille's *Reap the Wild Wind* [1942] on down, and I got a *terrific* ten-minute reel of action and ships being crushed and just *every*thing—it was absolutely great. And Sam Briskin told me, "Well, we'll let you know about this…"

That was on a Friday. And the following Monday, I found out that *The Underwater City* was already *playing*, I forget where, *some*where on the West Coast—and *in black-and-white*! Here I'd been working on this reel of action for a week or longer, of course getting all color footage, and then I come to find out it's already playing and it's playing in black-and-white! (And I had a *contract* that specified that it would be in color.) It had opened somewhere solo, and then went out as the second feature to *The Three Stooges Meet Hercules* instead of the other way around!

I went to see it in a theater and sure enough it was in black-and-white. It looked completely washed-out in black-and-white because (naturally) the underwater stuff had been shot as though for color, and timed for color. When you see *that* in black-and-white, it's just like running off a black-and-white print of a color picture. In the bottom-of-the-ocean scenes, you couldn't see the bubbles, you couldn't see *any*thing distinctly—there was no real contrast. Hampton went by himself and saw it too. That's when we decided we would sue. The picture's box office potential had obviously been damaged, you could tell that from the bookings that it got. The bookings it *didn't* get, I should say!

I got in touch with my lawyer Irwin Spiegel, and we tried to get Columbia to give us an explanation. Well, they said, they didn't want to spend the money on color prints, this and that, so on and so forth. Anyway, the end result was that we had to sue them—I wasn't going to stand for *this*. So Neptune Productions sued Columbia, and the thing dragged on for about five years. Then Spiegel lost interest because he was working on spec, and eventually the statute of limitations simply ran out. By then, of course, I'd started getting reports on the picture, and we were deeper in the hole every time a report came in. Finally Columbia just stopped sending reports

altogether, they told us it really wasn't worth it because no money was coming in on it. So that's how that situation ended.

Needless to say, Columbia didn't pick up my option. I had a six-picture deal, but they cancelled that. So I was *out* of Columbia, and that was the end of the saga of *The Underwater City*. I was glad that eventually it began playing on TV in color, and if it ever comes out on home video, I hope it will be in color. Naturally I want my stuff to be seen in the best possible light.

It's not one of my favorites amongst my movies, it's way down on the list. Hampton, Salkow and I hoped for much more, and we hoped we might get a multiple picture deal out of it. We thought this might help us get into a slightly higher bracket. With all the problems that we had, and the end results, it was a very disappointing experience. But we had embarked on it with the best of intentions—I still remember how *very* excited my wife Ruth was when she saw the article about the underwater farm community. Which is a notion that keeps popping up, it's never a dead issue for long. It comes up from time to time and then it's dormant, and then it comes up *again*. In fact, just last week [May 2002] it was on the radio—somebody in the House or Senate brought it up, they were talking about trying to figure out how they could farm the ocean floor, to alleviate world hunger. It's definitely an ongoing thing in the various think tanks, but I guess they haven't yet figured out how to do it properly, and "at a price." We've always thought that this is one idea that should certainly be followed up and investigated.

"Here Comes Mr. Gordon"

By Karen Latham Everson

The first word that comes to mind when I think about my friend Alex Gordon is "enthusiastic." If Alex liked something, he *loved* it. His favorite word was "terrific": "Thanks for the *terrific* letter," "Your card was *terrific*," "That was a *terrific* movie," "What a *terrific* meal." You get the idea.

Alex loved movies. He loved movie stars: his longtime friend and employer, Gene Autry; his favorite non-singing Western star, Buck Jones; the German film star, Zarah Leander; actress Helen Gilbert; and his all-time-favorite female star, Ginger Rogers, whom he affectionately dubbed "Miss R."

Once Alex was aware of a friend's favorites, he never forgot those, either. He sent me birthday cards with the Three Stooges, alerted me when a Van Johnson movie was showing, made tapes for me of films I wanted to see or those he thought I needed to see.

I met Alex a few weeks after I married Bill Everson. It was 1988, and Bill and Alex had been friends for almost 50 years, since the time they were boys in England. Bill first got to know Alex and his brother Richard through their fan club and magazine, *The Westerner*. Bill was a member-subscriber, wrote voluminous Letters to the Editors, and won quite a few of the contests the Gordons sponsored. Because of the high quality of the magazine, which at one point had 5000 subscribers, Bill assumed that Alex and Dick were grown men. Because of Bill's tremendous knowledge of movies present and past, and his ability as a writer, the Gordon brothers

Presumably Alex Gordon could have cameo-ed in every one of his movies, but he did it just once, in *The Lawless Rider*, made in 1952: That's Alex in the white hat on the right.

assumed *he* was a grown man. Imagine everyone's surprise when Bill met them at their London home during World War II and found out they were teenagers, just a few years older than he was.

Alex and Dick were the sons of German émigrés. Both their parents loved movies, so Alex and his brother began going to the cinema at a young age. The first movie Alex remembered seeing was *Redskin* (1929), when he was six years old. One of his favorite questions to ask a new acquaintance was, "What was the first movie you saw?" followed quickly by, "Who is your favorite movie star?"

Alex kept up his magazine-publishing and moviegoing while he was at a boarding school in Dorset. He would proudly tell the story of sneaking out of school to see *Trader Horn* (1931). He was caught as he was sneaking back into the dormitory, and his punishment was "six strokes of the cane" by the headmaster. He always said that the movie was more than worth the punishment!

By the time the Battle of Britain began in 1940, Alex was out of school and back in London. But the air raids and threat of falling bombs didn't stop him (or Dick, or Bill) from going to see the movies he felt he needed to see. Alex told stories about more than once having to walk home from the movies through the blackout, because buses weren't running; or having to leave the cinema during a film to relocate to a shelter.

Slightly before this time, the Gordons had changed the name of their organization from the Westerners

A shot of Alex Gordon, Richard Gordon and William K. Everson, taken in 1950 at Richard's first office, the General Motors Building at 57th and Broadway in New York City.

Club to the Gene Autry Friendship Club. And in 1939, Alex met his idol when Autry did a personal appearance tour of the U.K. Alex didn't know it at the time, but this meeting would eventually lead to a lifelong association with Autry.

Alex was in the British Army from 1942 until 1946, in the 11th Armored Division. He got in trouble with the Army censors when he attempted to mail out the final issue of his magazine. He was told that it would be impossible because there was not enough staff available to read through 5000 copies of the publication in search of content that might be useful to the enemy. Alex argued that the censors needed only to read *one* copy, since each copy was identical. For this he was put on charges, for insubordination! Thanks to volunteers, however, the last issue did get to subscribers on time.

When he was mustered out of the Army, a year after the war ended, he returned to London and got his first film job, as a publicist for Renown Pictures. A year after that, he was persuaded by his brother Dick to move to the United States. In New York, where Dick started his own company Gordon Films, Alex became an assistant booker for the Walter Reade Theater chain. He and Dick also wrote articles for British film magazines, based on interviews they were able to do with some of their favorite actors – people like Bela Lugosi, Boris Karloff, Johnny Mack Brown, Buster Crabbe and others who lived in or visited New York City. The Gordons became friends with many of these people. One of my very favorite photos is of Alex, Dick and Bill (who moved to the States in 1950) having dinner at a fancy New York restaurant with Bela Lugosi and his wife Lillian. The three boyhood friends look like they can't believe their luck at being there with the Lugosis.

Alex (left) with his friend and longtime employer Gene Autry. The two jaspers on the right are unidentified.

During this period, Alex met up with Gene Autry again, at the Madison Square Garden Rodeo. This time Gene asked Alex to join his organization, as an advance man for his coast-to-coast appearances. Alex jumped at the opportunity – especially because Autry offered him $125 a week, plus expenses. This was $85 more per week than he was making at Walter Reade.

In 1952, Alex moved out to Hollywood, where he eventually began writing film scripts and, of course, trying to get them produced. He ended up on the ground floor of James H. Nicholson and Samuel Z. Arkoff's

American International Pictures. He produced such films for AIP as *Day the World Ended*, *The She-Creature* and *Girls in Prison*.

He loved to cast his pictures with names from the silent and early sound films, bringing in such actors as Mae Marsh, Franklyn Farnum, Chester Morris, Richard Arlen, Tim McCoy, Anna Sten, Raymond Hatton, Bob Steele, Johnny Mack Brown, Buster Crabbe and Helen Gilbert, the girl of Alex's boyhood dreams. Arkoff didn't always approve of Alex's casting or the way he would spend money for limousines and other extras to make these older actors feel appreciated. Arkoff said more than once, "Alex goes down to the actors' graveyard and digs these people up!"

In his early writing and producing days, Alex met another young aspiring filmmaker: Ed Wood. They were roommates for a while, to keep expenses down. Alex introduced Wood to Bela Lugosi (no, it didn't happen the way it was shown in the 1994 movie *Ed Wood*). The original story and script for Wood's *Bride of the Monster* [1956] was written by Alex. As he later told the story, Alex maintained his friendship and shared living space with Wood until one day coming home and finding Wood in full drag – makeup and clothing. Alex could put up with a lot where movies were concerned, but this was too much for him!

Fun with Fuzzys: Once Richard and Alex relocated to the U.S., they got to meet many of their B-Western favorites, including Al "Fuzzy" St. John and Fuzzy Knight.

Alex was something of a ladies' man in those days – certainly not a Lothario, but he never lacked for dates. In the mid-1950s he met an air hostess with Scandinavian Airlines, Ruth Mary Succop. She was a native Californian, a strikingly beautiful brunette. And she loved movies! They hit it off right away. Unfortunately for Alex, however, Ruth's taste in movies ran toward the sophisticated end of the spectrum. She loved foreign films and lush Hollywood romances. She didn't see any of the low-budget films Alex had produced until after they were engaged, when Alex took her to a double feature of *Shake, Rattle and Rock* and *Voodoo Woman*. After the screening, Ruth gave him his ring back. She ended the evening by asking him, "Why don't you make *nice* movies, like *The Red Shoes*?"

Alex was completely devastated. He phoned the people he was closest to and told them the sad story. Bill felt very bad for his friend, but brother Dick was able to ride to the rescue – like Jones, McCoy and Hatton in one of the Rough Riders films the three friends loved so much. Dick flew to California and took Ruth to lunch, where he explained to her the difference between AIP and MGM and just how the movie business works. Ruth finally came around, she and Alex were married, and they remained together for more than 45 years.

Alex cast "the girl of his boyhood dreams," actress Helen Gilbert, in one of his movies, *Girls in Prison* (1956), and stands arm-in-arm with her in this behind-the-scenes shot. Left to right, Gordon, Gilbert, the movie's star Richard Denning and Gilbert's sister Mari Finley.

They were a devoted couple. With Ruth, Alex became totally Americanized. He became a citizen, cared deeply about American politics, learned to drive, lost his British accent and (thanks to Gene Autry's ownership of the California Angels) became a baseball fan. They lived in a small apartment near the La Brea Tar Pits.

Ruth and Alex were partners in every sense of the word. She even adapted her thinking enough to co-write three of his films (under the *nom de screen* Ruth Alexander): *The Underwater City*, *Requiem for a Gunfighter* and *The Bounty Killer*. They spoke with the same cadence. They finished one another's sentences. They cared for Ruth's disabled sister. They drank the same kind of Scotch, and ate the same hearty food. Ruth called him "Ag," his initials, but pronounced as a word.

They never indulged in public displays of affection, but their love was evident in every other way. And as she accepted Dick and Bill as part of her family, Ruth also welcomed me, just as Alex did.

Alex made his last movies in 1964, the aforementioned *Bounty Killer* and *Requiem for a Gunfighter*. Then he switched directions. He accepted a job at 20th Century-Fox, in the newly created position of Head of Film Preservation. Even though he was told that many of the company's pre-1935 films no longer existed, he doggedly went through the vaults and found a number of "lost" films by John Ford, F.W. Murnau, Erich von Stroheim, Rowland V. Lee, William K. Howard and D.W. Griffith. Thanks to Alex's tenacity, his friend Bill Everson received a special dispensation to obtain prints *and* permission to incorporate these films into his teaching in New York City and his lecture series around the world; and movie fans can now sit in their living rooms and watch the films with little effort at all.

Alex's enthusiasm for this job was both a blessing and a curse. The powers that be soon tired of him spending so much time looking for films in which they saw no commercial value. Bill said that, after a while, Alex had to "bribe the little old ladies" who were gatekeepers of the Fox film vaults, with candy and flowers, so that he could continue to dig. And on one of Bill's visits to Hollywood, Alex apparently kept the ladies charmed while Bill did a bit of digging on his own. Alex could charm anyone.

But he also could get his way without using charm. Once in the early '90s, Cinefest (a yearly gathering of collectors and fans that Alex, Dick and Bill never missed) bussed festival-goers from Syracuse to Rochester's George Eastman House for a day of screening rare 35mm films. A western Alex was anxious to see came on. Soon the audience was grumbling, because the silent print had only flash titles. The projectionist stopped the film, and some suggested that it be abandoned and the next movie on the bill be started. Alex was not going to let this happen. He stood up, faced the crowd looking angrier and more determined than I'd ever seen him, and said, "Oh, come on! We all have seen hundreds of Westerns. You *know* you'll be able to follow the story. What's the problem?" Then he motioned to the projectionist, who started the film back up. And Alex was right; we may have missed a few nuances in the plot, but nothing that couldn't be covered by our knowledge of the Western genre and archetypes.

Neither his charm nor his bulldog tenacity, however, could save Alex's job at 20th Century-Fox. His enthusiasm and rule-bending (generally because he wanted the films to be seen by others) caused him to be fired.

In 1978, he returned to work for the Gene Autry organization, as Gene's personal film historian and archivist. He got Gene's films out on video (many of them restored to full length after having been cut for television), and was also in charge of clearing rights when people wanted to use Gene's music. Alex saw his job as an almost-sacred duty. He did not want Autry's name or music used in any questionable way. He was so upset when "Back in the Saddle Again" was used as a raunchy joke in *Semi-Tough* [1977] that he redoubled his efforts to find out exactly how Autry's recordings would be used in each and every case before granting permission. Gene Autry died in 1998, but Alex was with the Autry organization until his own death in 2003, keeping Gene's legacy alive for generations of movie fans. Alex said in a 1995 conversation that working for Autry was "a very satisfying end to my existence."

Alex always looked younger than his age. Even after heart bypass surgery and treatment for cancer, he had the same boyish face and personality. This was partly due to good genes, but also due to that enthusiastic approach to everything. When he, Dick and Bill were together talking, the years fell away and you could imagine that they were young boys again. I never failed to know immediately when Bill was on the phone with Alex; during those conversations, Bill always laughed more and had a different, lighter tone to his voice.

I've always regretted not being able to visit Alex at the end of his life, but the end came quickly and unexpectedly. The cancer had come back, and I knew he

Alex Gordon, his wife Ruth and brother Richard on the set of one of the Rod Cameron Westerns that Alex made at Paramount in 1964.

As the decades passed, Alex and Richard stayed young by meeting and socializing with generations of new fans. Sharing a meal in this shot, left to right, are Alex, Jim Condon, Mike Dobbs, Richard and Ray Cabana.

wasn't well; but I was in the middle of moving, and every time I would ask, I was told that he was doing all right, and not to worry. Maybe if I'd seen Alex in the hospital, he would have seemed different. Maybe that's why he didn't want visitors. But somehow I think he would have managed to summon enough energy to talk about *The Phantom Empire*, or one of the Rough Riders movies, or a romantic comedy with "Miss R." And he'd tell me how *terrific* it all was.

ALEX GORDON'S "REGULAR OLDTIMERS": EDMUND COBB AND FRANK LACKTEEN

By Scott Gallinghouse

EDITOR'S NOTE: Producer Alex Gordon was particularly devoted to veteran actors Edmund Cobb and Frank Lackteen and he cast them every time he could; he went to extraordinary lengths to get them into *Atomic Submarine* as extras (Alex tells the tale on pages 23 and 24). Alex, now watching their silent movies *with* them in that Big Screening Room in the Sky, wouldn't consider this book complete without a special nod to these two players. Researcher Scott Gallinghouse has gone above and beyond and furnished the following comprehensive write-ups.

According to a 1961 newspaper article, Alex Gordon began looking upon Edmund Cobb as a hero in the early 1930s when Alex saw the Cobb-starring Western *Four Square Steve*. Decades later, when Alex produced his first picture *Apache Woman* (1955), Cobb was one of the first actors he signed.

Edmund Cobb

Edmund Cobb was a notable screen presence for more than 50 years. His appearances on film stretched from 1912 to 1966. Throughout those years, and over 650 roles, he proved to be a reliable pro who contributed to the quality of each film in which he appeared.

Edmund Fessenden Cobb was born in Albuquerque, New Mexico, on June 23, 1892. His parents, William Henry Cobb and Eddie/Edwinna Ross, owned the Cobb Studio, a photography studio in Albuquerque. Cobb had three siblings: Susan R. Cobb (1894-1897); Daphne M. Cobb (1898-1928); and Wilfred B. Cobb (1901-1982).

The 1900 Census lists Edmund Cobb, age seven, residing with his parents and two sisters in Albuquerque; Cobb is described as "at school." According to publicity items, "As a mere boy Cobb became a cowpuncher, and while so engaged he learned all the tricks of the trade..." This same article also reported that Cobb "first heard the call of the stage from a small stock company."

This assertion is supported by a brief biography for Cobb published in the 1919 Motion Picture Studio Directory. After noting Cobb's 1892 birth, the summary states: "stage career, stk." However, an early incident almost derailed Cobb's professional career before it began. Shortly after his fourteenth birthday, Cobb was involved in the first of several brushes with death. *The Albuquerque Journal* (August 5, 1906) ran the following item under the headline A QUART OF WHISKEY SAVED EDMUND COBB:

Edmund Cobb, son of the well-known photographer, is now able to be up and around, after a two weeks siege with a rattlesnake bite. It came very near being a serious proposition with Edmund, but it is believed the worst is safely over.

The young man unearthed a big rattler at a ranch down near the stockyards and went after it with a stick. After he had, as he thought, killed the venomous reptile, he was preparing to cut off its rattles as a memento when the snake turned like lightning and sank its fangs into his finger. With unusual presence of mind the boy tied a string tightly around his finger below the wound, ran to the house, got a big bottle of whiskey and drank down a quart of the liquor almost without stopping. He was at once driven to town and placed under a doctor's care and thanks to the timely aid of the "booze" will recover. The scar is almost healed although still slightly painful.

Within a few years, Cobb faced his next hurdle: the premature death of his father on March 6, 1909. *The Albuquerque Journal* (March 7, 1909) reported:

William H. Cobb, for 30 years a resident of Albuquerque, passed away yesterday afternoon at 2 o'clock at his ranch three miles south of this city at the age of 49 years. His death removes one of the pioneers of the city; long a familiar figure in Albuquerque. Mr. Cobb, who was born in New York City in 1861, arrived in Albuquerque in 1879, being one of the party of engineers who surveyed the line of the Atchison, Topeka & Santa Fe into Albuquerque. He was a graduate of Harvard University.

Mr. Cobb was in the photograph business here for 19 years, being for years one of the most successful photographers in the southwest and who also served for 11 years in the Albuquerque volunteer fire department. He married Etta [*sic*] Ross, sister of Pitt Ross, the civil engineer, and daughter of the late United States Senator Ross of this city. Besides his wife the deceased leaves four children, Susan R., Daphne, Edmund F. and Wilfred Cobb, and a sister, Miss E.F. Cobb. His father, E.P. Cobb, is still living in New York at an advanced age.

Heart failure was the cause of Mr. Cobb's death. During recent years he had followed his favorite hobby as a naturalist and taxidermist at his studio and shop on West Gold Avenue.

The funeral will take place at the home south of the city Monday, March 8, at 2:30 p.m. Interment in the family burying ground, with Rev. Fletcher Cook in charge of the services.

The Albuquerque Journal reported on the funeral in the March 9, 1909 issue:

The funeral of the late William H. Cobb, whose death occurred Saturday afternoon, was held at the Cobb homestead, four miles south of the city, yesterday afternoon. A large number of friends attended the services, which were conducted by Rev. Fletcher Cook, rector of St. John's Episcopal Church. The remains were laid to rest in the family burial ground in a spot selected by Mr. Cobb before his death.

The 1910 Federal Census for San Jose, Mexico, includes an enumeration for the widowed photographer Eddie Ross Cobb and her four children. Their residence is described as "East of R.R. Track." Although Edmund's occupation is listed as "none," it appears from later publicity that he was a member of the Buffalo Bill Wild West Show around this time, in addition to his membership in the unnamed theatrical stock company. (This association with the Wild West Show would lead to a career opportunity for Edmund several years afterward.)

In 1912, Cobb stepped before motion picture cameras for the first time in the D.W. Griffith short subject *A Pueblo Legend*, filmed on location in New Mexico. Other shorts filmed in New Mexico followed; when Cobb relocated to Colorado, he began appearing in Western shorts for Pikes Peak Films. Cobb met actress Helen Marie Hayes and they married on October 26, 1914, in Colorado Springs.

Soon after, while working in the short subject *The Heart of a Man*, Cobb had yet another close call. *The Colorado Springs Gazette* reported:

Falling from the second story of a burning building at Austin Bluffs yesterday afternoon in the fire scene in *The Heart of a Man*, Edmund F. Cobb, leading man of the Pikes Peak Films company, narrowly escaped death. He fell inside the building which was blazing fiercely and was rescued a few minutes later by members of the company.

After recovering, Cobb finished the scene and the fall was used as an added thrill in the picture.

Cobb's injuries consisted of severe burns on the face and on his right arm. His hair on the right side of his head was badly singed and his right ear was burned. He was attended by Dr. O.R. Gillott.

A very young Edmund Cobb.

his safety and Jackson Carlisle and Dick Sterling entered the building to find Cobb unconscious from smoke. He had fallen about eight feet into a mass of burning embers. Cobb was dragged from the building and recovered a short time later, finishing the scene. The action was changed to meet the emergency and Cobb, instead of making his exit from the upper window, broke open the door and walked out in regular fashion. Before the fire was started, the building was sprinkled with oil to make it burn rapidly and smoke pots were placed inside. Cobb's escape from death is considered miraculous.

According to members of the company, Cobb will be able to work again in three or four days.

The building in which the accident occurred was constructed especially for the fire scene in the story. In this scene, some claim jumpers, failing to jump the claim of the heroine, set fire to her cabin. The hero rode to her rescue, entered the house and helped her down a rope from a window on the second story. There was a platform inside the building on which the pair stood when the rescue was effected. Cobb succeeded in letting the heroine, Miss Josephine West, down the rope in safety but when he himself attempted to follow her to safety, his spur caught on the window sill and he fell back into the building.

Those on the outside thought that Cobb made the fall to give an extra thrill to the picture, and that he was safe on the platform. The camera man kept turning the crank expecting Cobb to reappear. After a moment, however, fear was entertained for

Shortly thereafter, an old friend of Cobb's made good on a promise that offered Cobb an unusual opportunity in the nascent film industry:

A friendship which began years ago between Edmund F. Cobb, juvenile leading man of the Pikes Peak Films company, and Al Jacoby, now general manager of the Acme Moving Picture Producing Company of Pleasantville, N.J., has resulted in Cobb receiving a large block of stock in the Acme company, as well as the producing managership of a branch of the organization.

When Jacoby and Cobb were members of the Buffalo Bill Wild West show several years ago, they shared alike in the fortunes and misfortunes that came. Cobb befriended Jacoby frequently when the latter needed money, and Jacoby's appreciation is shown by a letter which Cobb has just received, telling him that he had been made [one] of the directors of the Acme company, as well as receiving a large block of stock.

"When Jacoby and I belonged to the same company, we promised each other that whatever fortune either one of us would have in the future would be shared alike by both of us," said Cobb yesterday. Al has been lucky and it seems that he has not forgotten to keep his word.'

"The Acme Corporation is to have three companies producing pictures. I will be managing director of the western company, which will produce western features exclusively. In all probability, Colorado Springs will be headquarters for the company.

"I am convinced that Colorado Springs and the Pikes Peak region, is the best region in the world for the production of motion pictures. The western branch of the Acme Company will start operations next summer and probably we will locate here."

Despite Cobb's hopes, it appears that this venture into production failed. There is no evidence that any westerns were produced by Edmund Cobb under the banner of the Acme Moving Picture Producing Company. (Indeed, while Acme announced ambitious plans to construct "one of the finest equipped photoplay studios in the country" in Absecon, New Jersey, around May or June of 1915, and touted capitalization for the New Jersey-based corporation at $100,000, the Annual Report of the New Jersey State Board of Taxes and Assessment for 1916 tells a different story altogether. The report lists the capital stock for the company at a mere $4663. Further, there is no indication that the company paid New Jersey corporate taxes after 1916, suggesting a swift demise for the fledgling studio.)

It also appears that Cobb lost his enthusiasm for the Pikes Peak Films after his brush with death during filming of *The Heart of a Man*; the actor is only credited with one more film for the company, a short subject entitled *The Cost*. Cobb's attachment to the Colorado-based company may have also waned as a result of a series of mishaps on later productions. During filming of a scene for the company's *The Greater Barrier* in mid-December 1914, lead actor George Gebhart "narrowly escaped being crushed to death ... when his horse stumbled and fell on him during the filming of a 'wild chase' scene."

This accident occurred mere days after Otis Thayer, Pikes Peak's managing director, had returned from New York, where he had "secured a contract for a two-reel western drama to be produced by the ... company every week"! Within two weeks, *The Colorado Springs Gazette* was reporting that actor Lawrence Jossenberger was accidentally shot in the groin while filming a running fight between bandits and a mail coach driver for *The White Trail*. According to contemporary newspaper accounts, a live bullet had been mixed with blank cartridges by accident. This accident followed closely on the heels of prior injuries to Jossenberger: During the filming of a previous short for Pike's Peak, he sustained a broken arm and rib when a cliff crumbled under him, dashing him down 40 feet, whereupon the horse he had been riding fell on top of him. Ossenberger lost a leg as a result of the *White Trail* incident.

Whatever Edmund Cobb's feelings about the Pike's Peak Photoplay Company may have been, they became inconsequential shortly thereafter. After 13 films, the company failed when its distributor, United Films Services, declared bankruptcy in early 1915, owing the Pike's Peak Photoplay Company almost $10,000. By that time, however, Cobb, perhaps sensing impending disaster, had signed a contract with Essanay Studios, a film production company based in Chicago. By September 1915, newspapers were carrying the following item as part of the syndicated "In the Photoplay World" column:

> Edmund F. Cobb, although one of the newer Essanay players, rapidly is gaining a place as one of the most popular. He is only 23 years old, but has been an actor since 16, playing first in stock and later with Lubin, working under Romaine Fielding. He has been with Essanay since April. He has played the lead in such Essanay productions as *The Quitter, The Return of Gentleman Joe, Mind Over Motor* and *His Crucible*, and had important parts also in *The Man Trail, Jane of the Soil* and *The Circular Path*.

This item provides a great deal of information. It suggests that Cobb embarked on his acting career around 1908, and supports later claims that he began acting in a theatrical stock company. The article also serves to illustrate the breakneck pace at which studios churned out films, particularly short subjects. Using the named short subjects as a guide (in conjunction with the listing of Cobb's credits on the Internet Movie Database), we can see that Cobb completed at least nine films at Essanay between April and September of 1915! Finally, Cobb's association with the Chicago-based Essanay Studios serves to explain the site of the birth of his only child. Within a week of the appearances of this newspaper item, Cobb's wife Helen gave birth to their daughter Eddie Marie Cobb in Chicago on September 26, 1915. However, if one is to believe another item in an "In the Photoplay World" column a month later, Edmund and Helen delayed christening their baby girl for a time:

> Congratulations are now in order for Bryant Washburn and Edmund F. Cobb, Essanay leading men, who in the last few weeks have become proud possessors of bouncing babies. ...Cobb's is a girl, for which a name has not yet been chosen. Mrs. Washburn is known as Mabel Forrest, an Essanay actress. Mrs. Cobb is also an actress.

By the end of 1915, Cobb had completed another half-dozen Essanay shorts. His hometown newspaper, *The Albuquerque Journal*, carried a short article on a showing of one of his films at the local theater:

> Edmund F. Cobb, of this city, who is now working with one of the feature companies of the Essanay Motion Picture company in Chicago,

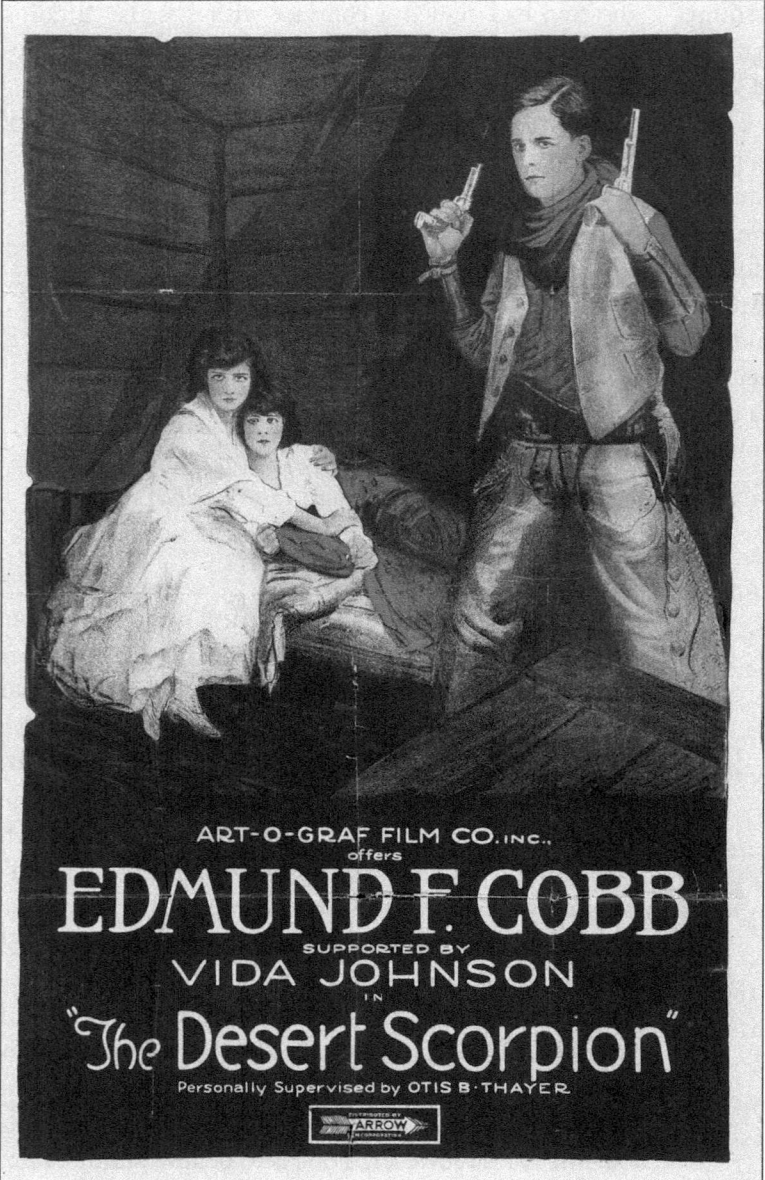

The poster for one of Cobb's made-in-Colorado adventure films.

has probably risen more rapidly In his chosen vocation than any of the younger stars on the screen today. Starting with one of the smaller companies a few months ago, his ability was soon noticed by the higher-ups in the Essanay organization and he was very promptly called into Chicago and put in one of the feature companies.

Mr. Cobb is possessed of youth, good looks and furthermore knows how to wear clothes. One of the best of Mr. Cobb's recent pictures, *The Papered Door,* in which he is the co-star with Ruth Stonehouse, will be shown at the B theater today.

Despite Cobb's association with Essanay Studios, evidence suggests that the actor may have forsworn motion pictures if only briefly. Cobb's World War I Registration card shows that he registered for the draft in Albuquerque. Cobb also listed his occupation as a self-employed farmer. He claimed an exemption from military service, at least in part because he had a wife and child dependent on him for support. He also claimed that he was affected with heart trouble.

Cobb's return to New Mexico was short-lived. The 1919 Motion Picture Studio Directory included a brief biography of the actor within its listing of "ACTORS-HEAVIES":

> COBB, Edmund Fessenden, also leads: b. Albuquerque, N.M. 1892; stage career, stk.; screen career, Frontier, Warners-Lariat, Lubin, Essanay (*The Stranger Case of Mary Page, Twin Fates, Money to Burn*). Hght. 6, 1; wght. 165; dark complexion, brown hair, brown eyes; rides, swims. Ad., Essanay, Chicago.

Around this time, Cobb left the relative security of Essanay Studios to return to Denver. Cobb's old friend Otis Thayer had become managing director of a new motion picture producing company based there, the Art-O-Graf Film Company, and Thayer immediately sought the services of Cobb as the company's leading man. The fledgling studio made a bid to disprove the "critics who said motion pictures could not be made in Colorado" (perhaps referring to the failure of the Pike's Peak Company) by producing several pictures in 1919. The company touted its accomplishments in the January 1, 1920, *Denver Rocky Mountain News*:

> During the year just past Art-O-Graf produced three pictures which reviewers have pronounced as real successes. The first, *Miss Arizona,* has been shown thruout the country and was favorably received. The other two productions, *Wolves of the Street* and *The Desert Scorpion*, are now in the course of distribution – the Arrow Film Company and the Supreme Photoplay Corporation having signed long contracts to place them before the movie public.
>
> Every scene in all three of these pictures was "shot" in Colorado. We believe that the scenic

beauties of these photoplays cannot be equaled any other place in creation. We have decided that Colorado is the best place in all the world to make pictures and in this great commonwealth we are going to guide our destinies during the year of 1920...

In again wishing our friends and neighbors all the good things which the new year may hold, we desire to call your attention to the fact that Edmund F. Cobb, our leading man, referred to by reviewers as "America's fasting rising film star," and Otis B. Thayer, our veteran managing director, have renewed their 1920 contracts.

Columnist Katherine Anne Porter described a visit to the Art-O-Graf plant in the context of the initial enthusiasm the principals felt for the venture:

That Denver will be another Los Angeles some day is the prediction of those connected with the new enterprise. And indeed, the beginning is auspicious. The [Art-O-Graf] building is a low, rambling affair, somewhat in the Spanish mission style. Inside, beyond the offices, there are fitted up long studios flooded with natural sunlight. In this the actors work in a flesh greasepaint. There is no need for the devastating mercury light here – that unnatural glow which turns blue eyes purple and red lips blue, causing the actors to look like newly buried plague victims arisen for a stroll.

Here are the tiny cubby holes of scenes, interior settings all in a row. Edward [sic] Cobb, serious-eyed young leading man, once of Essanay, stood talking to a pale pretty blonde girl. You'd be serious too, if you possessed one-half the enemies that person has in the picture now. We went into the projection room and saw a few disjointed feet of the film "run off" for inspection.

The scenes were made in Steamboat Springs. The little village is there to stay, and the Colorado mountains loom in the background with a realism not to be achieved by any scene maker in screenland. The leading woman, Vida Johnson, has been playing in a New York company, but she started life in Oklahoma, and learned to ride before she walked, in a way Oklahoma children have.

Meno Welsh, ingénue from Metro, is the small, pathetic, prayerful person who loves the Western hero, but doesn't get 'im. Never. The dashing Vida claims him in the last scene, a touching fadeout in the usual clinch! The play is alive with villains who can't let well enough alone, but they are all vanquished at last. Serves them right.

Denver Rocky Mountain News columnist Helen Easton expanded on the Art-O-Graf company's ambitious plans in a lengthy report on the filming of one of the company's productions in 1919:

One morning last spring, before the townspeople of Steamboat Springs had rubbed the sleep from their weary eyes, a veritable caravan of movie actors and picture props had stolen into their city and almost overnight had built a summer canvas studio for an experiment on the advisability of choosing Colorado as the center of a large motion picture industry in the western drama.

Nothing less than a city patterned after Universal City in California will satisfy the managers, who, in time, hope to absorb the film studio in Englewood as an addition to their studios in Routt County where the outdoor scenes of the pictures will be made. Colorado is selected to lead in Western dramas. Directors and managers heretofore formed the largest possibilities for Western pictures in this state...

It is all there. None of your paper mache cataracts or painted sunsets, but in full glory of Colorado's dangerous and rugged grandeur he can direct his scene with the inspiration of the realistic. The realistic, the meat of movie life. The movie actor who does not boast of the time when he lost two front teeth in a hand-to-hand reel combat or broke his leg in three places when he jumped from a skyscraper is yet to be found. Movie press agents are prone to append the actuality of the movement of the action in the fourth episode as a prescription of faith, for the lowly movie fan who takes his Western movie thrills with a grain of doubt.

Consequently, when Edmund Cobb, the leading man of the Art-O-Graf company swung across Fish cataract on a hastily improvised cable, bridging a drop of 200 feet, which overlooked a cataract, and later actually sent the villain reeling from a blow in the jaw, Routt County settlers were filled with amazement.

The horsemanship of Charley Tipton, the world champion bronco buster from Cheyenne, and the daredeviltry of Mack McCormick, an idol of Cheyenne frontier days, won the admiration of

Cobb with Mary Beth Milford in the short *Bashful Whirlwind* (1925).

the whole county, and in less than two weeks the entire countryside entertained its newly arrived friends at a regular all-night mountain dance and offered its possessions, ranches and all to the disposal of the movie operators.

The camera was fed swiftly. In three weeks the first picture was finished and work on *The Last of the Open Range*, a thriller of the feud between the sheep and cattle men, was begun on the Jim McWilliams ranch, where 1000 head of long-horned cattle were run into a stampede and 2000 head of sheep marooned during a storm near Hahn's peak, where much of the action takes place.

Here the movie-actor worshiper is doomed to a disappointing flop. Contrary to the popular idea that movie men exist in luxury and ease, the Art-O-Graf company lived on sardines for three whole days. Who can believe it? It happened thus; Hahn's peak was climbed one morning before sunrise. Chocolates and sardines – a happy ration – were carried by the players, who were to receive more substantial foodstuffs upon their arrival at the top.

But the company did not meet their wagon load of supplies until they retraced their steps down the mountain three days later.

…The company is not confined to the Western hair-raiser alone. Three commercial pictures have been filmed for the coal and oil industries in Routt County and another commercial movie to be used as a weekly has shot some of the largest lumber camps and hay ranches in Colorado.

At present the company is working on a 30-reel serial, one of infinite surprises and suspension. Snow scenes and shooting scrapes, kidnaping maneuvers and lots of love and western bar scenes will figure in regular wooly drama, the press agent says.

One of the most gigantic productions to be filmed next spring is *The Meeker Massacre*, that bloody conflict between the early defenseless pioneer and the western Indian who resented the usurpation of the right to his happy hunting ground. Actual local settings will be used and the famous red race track will be built for the picture. Every detail in history will be regarded. Seventy-five Ute Indians and their fat-painted squaws, with 300 soldiers from Utah, will take part in the picture.

Moving picture directors in looking over the field years ago thought no impediment stood in the way of Colorado's success. Before the selection of the California site as a moving picture rendezvous, Eastern picture men, some of the most prominent at that time, preferred Colorado to the Western coast and it was a mere flip of fortune – the whim of a big financial backer, that won for Universal City the biggest movie in the states.

Her presence in the West will not hinder the industry here. California does not begin to have the natural setting for western drama nor the percentage of sunlighted days to the years that Colorado has.

It is clear that Edmund Cobb's commitment to the success of the Art-O-Gaf enterprise was total. According to the 1920 federal census, Cobb and his wife Helen had taken up residence in Denver. More revealing is the fact that their four-year old daughter Eddie Marie was enumerated as living with Helen's parents, Charles and Martha Hayes, in Chattanooga, Tennessee. Obviously, the Cobbs intended to focus solely on their occupations, listed, respectively, as "Actor—Motion Pictures" and "Actress—Motion Pictures."

For a time, the Art-O-Graf company seemed to thrive in its Colorado environs; Cobb appeared in more than a half-dozen feature-length films for Art-O-Graf between 1920 and 1923, including two films with wife Helen, *Riders of the Range* and *A Rodeo Mixup*. However, lawsuits, funding and distribution issues appear to have doomed the venture by the early 1920s. In a seeming attempt to hedge his bets with Art-O-Graf, Cobb committed to star in films to be produced by the Superior Foto Play Company,

another project undertaken by Otis B. Thayer. Cobb's involvement with the "Superior Foto Play Co." is highlighted in the brief biography provided for the actor in the 1921 Motion Picture Studio Directory. Yet information concerning the Superior Foto Play Company is sketchy. It is unclear how closely aligned this venture may have been with Art-O-Graf, given Thayer's close involvement with both. Newspaper advertisements began appearing in Colorado newspapers early in 1921 in which Thayer is listed as president of the fledgling company. These advertisements were very similar in tone and content to earlier Art-O-Graf postings. In the midst of stock offerings to interested investors, the advertisements represented that the company was "employing several score people in the production of 12 Western drama features and 53 comedies," all to be distributed by Arrow Corporation in New York. Again, it seems that Thayer's reach exceeded his grasp, and that Superior Foto Play Company was doomed to an early death. Items in newspapers from the period mention only one Superior Foto Play Company production, a film known as either *The White Riders of the Range* (in one item) or *The White Riders*. One Colorado newspaper identifies the film as "the first picture to be made by the Superior Foto Play company"; the item goes on to mention that it was given a preview showing at a local theater, during which it was noted that "the photography was poor in spots, some of the 'long shots' of the cattle country and of a herd in the middle distance, being so dark that it was difficult to distinguish even the figures in the immediate foreground." The second article, referring to the film as *The White Riders*, identifies Edmund F. Cobb as the star, Courtney Ryley Cooper as the writer, and the Superior Foto Play Company as the producer. Yet this film sounds like Cobb's 1923 film *Riders of the Range*, which all sources list as being produced by Art-O-Graf!

Whatever the explanation, there appears to be no mention of the Superior Foto Play Company producing further films, nor did Otis Thayer realize his dream of making Colorado the "Mecca of the Movies." This sobering reality forced Edmund Cobb to re-locate to California to continue his screen career. Soon, a columnist was reporting that he "will star in a series of stories of the Northwest Royal Mounted to be made for Universal."

Cobb did in fact begin a long association with Universal Pictures; he also appeared in Ashton Dearholt productions plus films for the Arrow Company around 1923. The actor became so popular during this period that press agents were able to publicize him by no more than the nickname "Two-fisted Ed" and still draw patrons to theaters.

Cobb continued to appear in a combination of shorts, serials and features through the mid-1920s. Offscreen, his marriage was crumbling. According to Cobb's family, he and Helen divorced some time between 1925 and 1927, when daughter Eddie was 10 or 12. Around the same time, Cobb solidified his relationship with Universal with appearances in a number of Western short subjects known as Mustang two-reelers. Interspersed among these shorts were roles in the Universal serials *Fighting with Buffalo Bill* (1926) and *A Final Reckoning* (1928).

Notice that the horse gets better billing than Cobb. I bet Cobb noticed!

A half-dozen features mixed with nearly two dozen short subjects carried Cobb into the sound era. The coming of talkies worked a significant change in his career: With a few notable exceptions, his career as a leading man was over. The 1930s saw the actor assigned increasingly to villainous or supporting roles. Away from Universal, Cobb performed the role of Prince Kuwa in the 1931 serial *The Sign of the Wolf*, one of the very few independently produced serials that attempted to challenge the predominance of Universal and Mascot in the chapterplay arena during the early to mid-1930s.

The 1930 Federal Census indicates that Cobb had custody of his daughter at the time. Edmund F. Cobb and 14-year old Eddie were enumerated as residing in a rental property at 1612 North Alexandria Avenue in Los Angeles. Ex-wife Helen re-married in January 1930, but whatever happiness she experienced was short-lived. According to family members, Helen died of tuberculosis in 1932.

Cobb continued to make numerous onscreen appearances throughout the 1930s, although many of his roles were uncredited bits. A bright spot was his marriage to Vivian Marie Winter in Los Angeles on July 24, 1934. As if to signal his good fortune, Cobb was cast in one of Universal's best sound-era serials, *The Red Rider* (1934). He appeared to great advantage as cowboy Johnny Snow, sidekick to star Buck Jones. The year 1934 also saw Cobb's last attempts at lead roles, but both *Racketeer Round-up* and *The Rawhide Terror* (released in 1935) were at best forgettable low-budget independent productions.

By the mid-1930s, Cobb's career began benefitting from two events: the birth of Republic Studios, and the

Tom Tyler gets tough with Cobb in *Tracy Rides* (1934).

Right to left, Cobb, Dick Foran, Glenn Strange and Frank Faylen in *The Cherokee Strip* (1937).

rise of the "series" film. When Cobb gravitated away from Universal after his role as Nicolai in *Ace Drummond* (1936), he found ample employment at Republic, particularly with the studio's serial division. At the same time, the success of Gene Autry in a series of films commencing in 1934, coupled with the low-budget Hopalong Cassidy series, introduced the notion of producing Westerns with a continuing set of characters from film to film.

Cobb had a change-of-pace role as a *nice* rustler, allowed to ride off into the sunset with stolen cattle, in 1935's *Arizona Bad Man*. Right to left in still: Cobb, Reb Randall, Lois January and Tommy Bupp.

In Republic's first serial *Darkest Africa* (1936), baddies Cobb, Lucien Prival and Wheeler Oakman oversee their slaves mining for diamonds. All three pay with their lives, but not before hero Clyde Beatty gets in a lick at Cobb.

Not only were these films a valuable training ground for promising newcomers, the productions also provided a reliable haven for veterans like Edmund Cobb. He was able to support himself and his family with his work in series films at Universal, Columbia, Republic and Warner Bros. throughout the 1930s. During his career, Cobb found roles in the Gene Autry series, the Three Mesquiteers films, several Dick Foran westerns, and numerous films with Johnny Mack Brown, Buck Jones, Tom Mix, Roy Rogers and Ken Maynard.

By 1940, Cobb's career path in films was largely set: uncredited bits and small parts in motion pictures at the major studios, interspersed with larger roles in serials and entries in "series" Westerns. However, the sheer volume of his appearances on film apparently served to keep the actor solvent; Cobb averaged around two dozen film appearances each year from 1938 through the end of World War II. During that period, Cobb and his wife resided in a rented house at 11150 La Maida in North Hollywood.

The end of the war brought with it a slight reduction in Cobb's film work, although he still managed to work in more than a dozen films each year from 1946 through 1950. The rapid expansion of the television medium beginning in the late 1940s offered Cobb an entirely new arena for work – one which the actor was quick to exploit. Cobb landed roles in such series as *The Range Rider*, *Adventures of Superman*, *The Lone Ranger*, *The Gene Autry Show*, *Adventures of Wild Bill Hickok* and *The Cisco Kid* in the early to mid-1950s, while he still found work in Westerns and serials on the big screen.

From 1955 through 1960, Cobb's appearances in motion pictures tapered off in favor of television work in fare such as *Highway Patrol*, *Circus Boy*, *Fury*, *Sky King*, *Sergeant Preston of the Yukon*, *Dragnet*, *Lassie* and others. Heart problems started to limit his work thereafter, although he made a few uncredited appearances in film and TV before a brief role as a driver in the "Morella" segment of AIP's *Tales of Terror* (1962). After appearing in Alex Gordon's Westerns *Requiem for a Gunfighter* and *The Bounty Killer* (both 1965) and producer A.C. Lyles' *Johnny Reno* (1966), Cobb retired from performing.

Cobb's daughter Eddie Marie died in Spokane, Washington, on September 1, 1970. His second wife Vivian died on July 26, 1974, at the Motion Picture and Television Hospital in Woodland Hills, California. Edmund Cobb followed his wife three weeks later. He died of bronchopneumonia at the Motion Picture and Television Hospital on August 15, 1974.

Frank Lackteen

Frank Lackteen's basilisk eyes will cause shudders of apprehension...

—publicity for the Pathe serial *The Fire Detective* (1929) in *The San Diego Union*, February 17, 1929

Frank Lackteen parlayed his gaunt, cadaverous looks and spare frame into a 50-year career in motion pictures and television. His strikingly different, exotic appearance made him a natural as a villain, and he appeared in scores of films as everything from an Indian chief to an Oriental. As an actor, Lackteen achieved his greatest notoriety in silent films. Major roles became harder to come by with the passing of the silent era, but his heavily accented speech often provided an added dimension to his portrayals in sound films.

Lackteen often portrayed men of mystery in his film career; ironically, there is a good deal of mystery surrounding *his* origins and early life. Based upon available records, we can now say with some assurance that

a. Frank Lackteen's birth name was Mohammed Hassan Lackteen;

b. His parents were Hassan ("Sam") Lackteen and Ishe ("Miriam") Akroush;

c. Lackteen had two older brothers, Mahmoud ("Michael") Lackteen (July 23, 1884-June 26, 1947) and Abdulla ("Tom") Lackteen (November 5, 1892-August 10, 1945).

Little else of Lackteen's beginnings can be reported with certainty – particularly in light of questionable claims regarding Lackteen's origins that have appeared in print over the years. For example, a number of sources state that his parents were Russian immigrants. Frank and his brothers never made such a claim in official documents. But available documentation as to the nativity of Lackteen's parents *adds* to the confusion. In various documents, "Sam" and "Miriam" are either identified as Persian, Syrian or Turkish.

This uncertainty extends beyond the origins of Lackteen's parents. Frank also seemed unsure about where and when he was born. At various times, he claimed in official documents that his date of birth was May 10, 1893, August 29, 1895, and August 29, 1897. A brief biography of the actor from the 1930s provided August 29, 1894, as Lackteen's birthday.

There is also a great deal of disagreement among available sources regarding the site of Lackteen's birth. He himself wavered between listing Syria and Turkey as his birthplace in a number of official papers, often being somewhat more specific in describing his birthplace as "Kubber-ilias" (or phonetic variations on that location such as "Kubalias"). In later years, both Lackteen and his brothers settled on "Beyrouth" as the place of their births; oddly, they usually selected the French spelling of Beirut, the capital of Lebanon, in official documentation. It appears that "Kubber-ilias" is more properly known as Qabb Ilyas, a municipality in eastern Lebanon, about 28 miles from Beirut. This still doesn't answer for certain where Lackteen was born, but it seems to be in what is now Lebanon.

Although little is known of Lackteen's early life, the slight biographical materials available on the actor assert that he began his education in a "Protestant American school in Kubber-ilias." (Presumably, that would place the start of Lackteen's schooling around the turn of the twentieth century. Was it anticipation of coming events that led Lackteen's family to put him in an American school?)

Apparently, plans were in place for the Lackteen family to relocate to America. We can state with some confidence that Frank's older brothers, "Tom" and "Michael," immigrated to the U.S. in late 1900, while younger brother Frank and father "Sam" followed four years later. There is no indication that Frank's mother immigrated to the U.S. Official papers do indicate that the family may have made its way to America in stages. In an early document in which Frank declared his intention to become a U.S. citizen, he claimed that he had immigrated to the U.S. from Marseilles, France. In his later Petition for Naturalization, Lackteen declared that his last foreign residence before emigrating was "Kingston, Jamaica, West Indies." This later claim perhaps lends credence to the assertion in the 1930s bio materials that Lackteen visited Spain, Puerto Rico and Jamaica, then came to the United States to live.

A 1928 newspaper item provides some additional details. Very likely drawn from publicity materials, this item includes the claim that Lackteen's father "came to America when Frank was a small child and settled in Lawrence, Mass., where he conducted business as a rug importer." This article goes on to state that the young Frank Lackteen was educated in Lawrence and, between the hours in school, was taught the art of rug-making and his native language. This assertion finds support in the actor's 1930s mini-biography, which maintains that Lackteen continued his education for "five years in Lawrence, Mass."

Some time around 1909, Frank apparently moved

from Lawrence, along with his father and older brothers, to nearby Springfield, Massachusetts. Springfield's 1909 City Directory contains a listing for Frank's older brother Thomas, employed as both a "barber" and a "boot-black" at 202 Main Street; he is listed as a boarder at 187 Main Street. The 1910 Springfield Directory not only shows Thomas boarding at 425 State Street, but also lists Frank's father Hassan at that address, along with older brother Michael. The 1910 Federal Census confirms that Frank was residing with his father and two older brothers on State Street. The census also reports that Frank was employed as a cutter at a Springfield cotton mill, perhaps substantiating an assertion in a 1927 newspaper item that Frank originally intended to enter the "woolen business."

The family's stay in Springfield was a temporary one; the 1911 Springfield Directory reflects that Frank's father Hassan/Sam went back to Lawrence, a move confirmed by the 1911 Lawrence City Directory. It is unknown whether Frank returned to Lawrence with his father or remained in Springfield with his brothers. In either case, none of the family stayed in Springfield much longer. Michael journeyed to Europe on business in early 1911 and returned to New York from Le Havre on April 23, 1911, but he was not listed in Springfield city directories thereafter. Similarly, Thomas was no longer listed in the Springfield directories after 1912.

Surviving official papers make it clear that Sam, Tom and Frank Lackteen next moved to Highland Park, Michigan. According to a 1916 ship manifest, Michael lived in Montreal, Canada, for a short time. Michael's stay in Montreal was certainly fortunate for Frank Lackteen's future if we are to believe a 1927 newspaper article detailing Frank's introduction to motion pictures. According to the item, Lackteen

> made his debut [as a motion picture actor] under the direction of Frank Crane. It was some years ago, in Montreal, Can., where Frank was spending a vacation in between finishing his education and preparing to follow his brothers in the woolen business.
>
> Hearing that a motion picture company was going to make pictures nearby and wanting to see how it was done, Lackteen became one of the watching crowd. Crane saw the young man and immediately recognized Lackteen as a distinct type. Crane offered him $1.50 a day to work in the picture and, as it was all fun and part of the vacation, Lackteen accepted. He took to picture acting like a duckling to water and the woolen business never saw Frank.

While it is apparently accurate to state that the "woolen business never saw" Frank Lackteen, this initial appearance in a still-unidentified film didn't persuade Lackteen to abandon his "day job." Despite reputed appearances in two 1916 productions, *The Yellow Menace* and *Less Than the Dust*, Lackteen described his occupation as "common laborer" and his employer as the Dodge Motor Company in his World War I Draft Registration Card, dated June 5, 1917. He gave his address as 112 Victor Street in Highland Park, which tallies with the address set out for his brother Michael in the 1917 Detroit, Michigan, City Directory. Frank also indicated in that registration card that he was "single" and the "sole support" of his father. By early 1918, Frank's brother Tom had married Elizabeth Klaab (February 12) and Tom, Michael and father Sam had moved to 170 Gerald Avenue in Highland Park, but it cannot be stated that Frank still resided with them. According to publicity materials in a 1928 newspaper article:

> In 1918, [Frank] Lackteen was in New York and his lean face and thin body attracted the attention of a casting director for the World Film Corporation, who was in search of a half-breed Indian for a role in *Human Driftwood*. Lackteen was induced to have a screen test made and the result was a career in films.

There are problems with this item. The only film with the title *Human Driftwood* was released in April 1916, and was produced by the Shubert Film Corporation. However, *Human Driftwood* was filmed in Fort Lee, New Jersey, and distributed by the World Film Corporation (according to the Internet Movie Database), so that some truth may be disclosed in this article. If so, it adds another credit to Lackteen's appearances on film.

According to the Files of Jerry Blake website, Frank relocated to Hollywood around 1920. Circumstances certainly argue for that result, but the apparent absence of an enumeration of any member of Lackteen's family in the 1920 Federal Census makes confirmation of any such move problematic. Frank's brother Tom is still listed in the Detroit City Directory for 1920, but Tom next appears in Cleveland, Ohio, in 1921 as the defendant in a divorce proceeding initiated by his wife Elizabeth on October 11 of that year. Elizabeth was granted a divorce from Tom Lackteen on February 8, 1922, on the grounds of extreme cruelty. What may make this relevant to the life and career of Frank Lackteen is that the events played out in Ohio. In Frank's 1928 Declaration of Intention to become a U.S. citizen, Frank stated that he was married,

Lackteen (right) and *Atomic Submarine* director Spencer Bennet may have worked together for the first time in this 1925 serial.

that his wife's name was Sarah, and that she was born in Akron, Ohio. Since little else is known about the prosaically named Sarah, it might be permissible conjecture that Frank encountered Sarah through his brother Tom or the chance circumstance of Tom's residence in Ohio. Since there is no evidence of the date and place of Lackteen's marriage to Sarah currently available, this may remain "best evidence" for now.

Whatever we cannot say conclusively about Frank's marriage, it is clear that the 1920s afforded Lackteen the opportunity to become one of the preeminent silent film villains. Lackteen was a mainstay in Ruth Roland Pathe serials such as *White Eagle* (1922), *Leather Stocking* (1924) and *The Fortieth Door* (1924). The names of the characters that Lackteen portrayed during this period reflect the ethnic background of the roles in which the actor was cast: Pablo, Crouching More, Malay George and Hamid Bey are typical.

One newspaper item suggests that Lackteen may have advocated the "method acting" technique, by which an actor seeks to create an identification with his character:

> Frank Lackteen, noted Indian character screen player, believes in reverting to type when engaged in making a picture. Lackteen plays the part of Pawnee Killer in the Metropolitan production *The Last Frontier*, which was filmed on the Navajo reservation in Arizona... As soon as he arrived at Gap, where the company was stationed, Lackteen had the red men build him a "hogan" to be used as a sleeping quarters.
>
> The "hogans" are the winter residences of the tribes when it is too chilly to roll up in a blanket and court Morpheus. They resemble the igloos of the Eskimos of the far north, excepting that adobe is used in their construction instead of ice cakes. To the Indian this shack is a symbol of

Lackteen delivers a big boot to serial queen Ruth Roland in a 1922 serial.

luxury despite the fact that interior furnishings are conspicuous by their absence. Terra firma fills the bills so far as beds are concerned and a blanket or two completes the sleeping equipment.

Shortly after the completion of his role as Kaohla in 1926's *The House Without a Key* (the first Charlie Chan film), Lackteen suffered a real-life tragedy: His father "Sam" Lackteen died on January 29, 1927, at the age of 74. "Sam" died in Los Angeles, which argues that Frank's father had been residing with him prior to his death.

Within a year, Frank Lackteen took time out from his screen appearances to file papers in the U.S. Court for the Southern District of California declaring his intention to become an American citizen. Lackteen's Declaration of Intention, dated January 11, 1928, contains much personal information of interest:

- Lackteen stated that he was 5'10½" tall, weighed 145 pounds, and had black hair and brown eyes.

- According to this document, Lackteen was born in "Beyrouth, Syria" on August 29, 1895, and was residing at 1332 Sanborn Street in Los Angeles with his wife Sarah.

- He asserted that he had emigrated to America from Marseilles, France, and had arrived by ship at the port of New York on or about June 24, 1905.

Frank's brother, barber Tom Lackteen, had clearly relocated to Los Angeles. Tom filed his papers seeking U.S. citizenship in the same court on the very next day, listing his residence as 1809 Montana St., Los Angeles. By May 29, 1928, brother Michael Lackteen (also describing himself as a "barber") had also applied for citizenship in the same district court. Interestingly, an earlier application for citi-

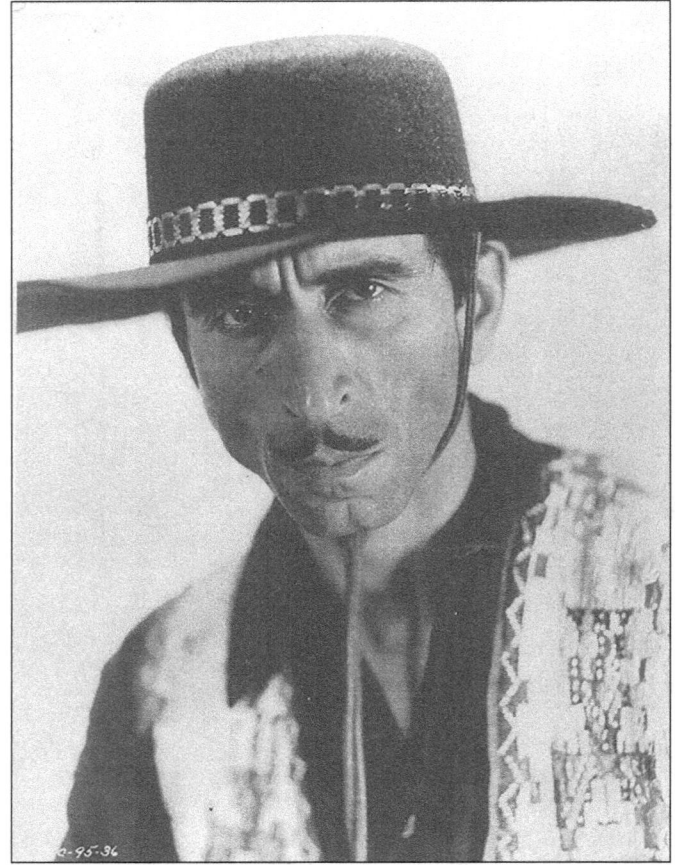

zenship filed by Michael in the Southern District Court on June 16, 1926, had been denied on the grounds that Michael's loyalty to the United States was "not satisfactory."

The advent of the sound era in Hollywood produced the first of a series of professional reversals for Frank Lackteen. As the _Files of Jerry Blake website points out, Lackteen's "strong accent confined him to playing exotic foreign villains in talkies – just as serial producers were beginning to phase such villains out of their chapterplays." Indeed, years of negative stereotyping of various ethnic groups by Hollywood that particular races "had characteristics suiting them for criminal pursuits!" (as reported by William K. Everson in *The Bad Guys*) led to the adoption of the Production Code in 1930. The Code advised against the unfavorable portrayals of the "citizenry of other nations."

By 1930, Lackteen had also sustained a personal reversal as well: He

John Davidson, another specialist in serial skullduggery, gets the drop on Lackteen in *Perils of Pauline* (1933).

Lackteen with Tom Tyler and Noah Beery Jr. in the serial *Jungle Mystery* (1932).

Buck Jones notices that Lackteen bears the Sioux mark of a "squaw stealer" in *Treason* (1933).

Lackteen and Dennis Moore grapple in *Bombs Over Burma* (1942).

Lackteen menaces a Mountie in the 1937 chapterplay *The Mysterious Pilot*.

Vulturous Lackteen opposite Bill Elliott, star of the 1938 serial *The Great Adventures of Wild Bill Hickok*.

and Sarah had ended their marriage. The 1930 Federal Census lists Frank as divorced and residing with brother Mike at 1605 Sunset in Los Angeles. Brother Tom lived nearby at 1915 Berkley with his wife and two young daughters.

At that point in his career, Frank had been relegated to playing a series of uncredited bit parts in productions such as *Captain Thunder* and *Monsieur Le Fox* (both 1930). However, better times – both professionally and personally – were on the horizon. Lackteen landed a showy role as villainous half-breed Buckskin Joe in Universal's 1932 serial *Heroes of the West*. On June 5, 1932, Lackteen married 23-year-old New Jersey-born Muriel Elizabeth Dove in Los Angeles; one of the witnesses to the ceremony was fellow actor Walter Miller.

Frank moved through the serials *Jungle Mystery* (1932) and *Tarzan the Fearless* (1933) as well as larger productions such as *The Three Musketeers* (1935) and *Anthony Adverse* (1936); he was often uncredited in those higher-budget films. The year 1936 also brought a personal highpoint: His only known child, Muriel Elizabeth Dove Lackteen, was born in Los Angeles on June 25. In 1937, Lackteen landed a substantial part in *Radio Patrol*, another Universal serial. A significant role in the 1937 Columbia serial *The Mysterious Pilot* followed.

In late 1939, Lackteen followed up on his longtime dream of becoming a citizen: The actor filed a Petition for Naturalization with the U.S. District Court in Los Angeles on December 4. The petition includes information which differs in a number of particulars from Lackteen's 1928 Declaration of Intention:

- Lackteen acknowledged that his birth name was Mohammed Hassan Lackteen.

- He asserted that he was born in "Kubalias, Syria" on August 19, 1897.

- He contended that his last foreign residence had been "Kingston, Jamaica, West Indies" and that he had emigrated from there to New York in 1905.

- He reported that he had resided in Los Angeles continuously since 1928(!).

- He concluded his petition with a request

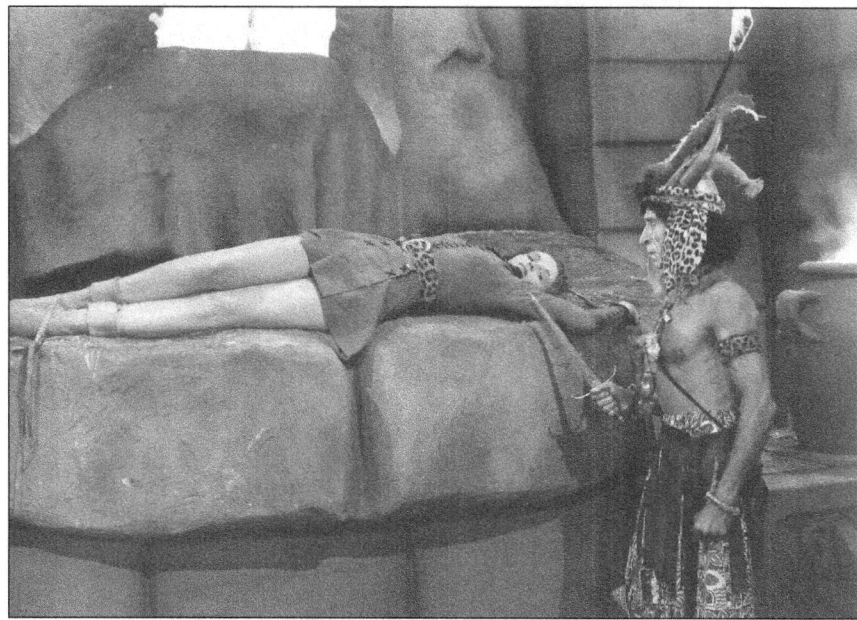

In his book *The Bad Guy*, cinema scholar William K. Everson called Lackteen "a serial witch doctor from time immemorial." Here he is in two shots from Republic's *Jungle Girl* (1941).

which he is arguably best known: Shamba the witch doctor in Republic's 1941 serial *Jungle Girl*. Lackteen was a stand-out amid the trio of heavies (also including Gerald Mohr and Trevor Bardette) menacing Frances Gifford (as "Jungle Girl" Nyoka) and Tom Neal. In seeming celebration, he became a naturalized U.S. citizen on December 12, 1941.

Over the next few years, Lackteen alternated between serials, shorts and largely uncredited roles in bigger-budgeted films. Frank's brother Tom (Abdellah) Lackteen died in Los Angeles on August 10, 1945. (According to Tom's World War II Draft Registration Card, he had been disabled for some time.)

In 1945, Frank undertook the first of several well-remembered roles in Columbia's Three Stooges shorts: Nikko, assistant to Vernon Dent's psychotic Prof. Panzer, in <u>A Bird in the Head</u>. A number of bits followed, when personal tragedy dogged Lackteen again. Frank's brother Michael ("Mahmoud") died in Los Angeles on June 26, 1947.

Lackteen persevered, portraying gangster "Red Watkins" in support of Kenneth MacDonald's "Lefty Loomis" in the 1948 Three Stooges short *Shivering Sherlocks*. Interspersed among other bits in the late 1940s was Lackteen's brief but memorable appearance as "Haffa Dolla" in the Three Stooges short *Malice in the Palace* (1949).

Lackteen moved into television in the early 1950s, appearing in episodes of *Dangerous Assignment*, *The Roy Rogers Show*, *Hopalong Cassidy* and others, while he maintained his work in film. One uncredited portrayal led to a real rarity: a short interview with Lackteen himself! Entertainment columnist Harold Heffernan encountered the actor on the set of *King of the Khyber Rifles* and filed this report under the headline **Public Unaware of Stars' Diet Struggles**:

that his name be changed to "Frank Samuel Lackteen."

The 1940 Federal Census found Frank and his family living in a rented house at 1724 North Berendo Street in Los Angeles. Lackteen's birthplace is listed as "Syria"; according to the census, the actor worked 12 weeks in 1939 and earned a total of $2000.

Shortly thereafter, Lackteen was cast in the role for

> It's simply marvelous, of course, to be a big-time movie star, reaping the glamor and the rich

Alex Gordon gave Lackteen the role of an Indian chief in *Flesh and the Spur* (1956) and then used him whenever possible, right to the end of both their careers.

rewards that travel with top-ladder fame. But almost no one gives a thought to the plodding nonentity struggling behind the spotlight, many of whom suffer just to "keep in condition" for their careers.

We were reminded of this on the set of 20th-Fox's *King of the Khyber Rifles* during a chance visit with a fellow named Frank Lackteen. Ever hear of him getting a screen credit?

Neither did we.

For 36 years, however, Lackteen, a gaunt, hollow-cheeked, cadaverous-looking individual, has literally starved for his art. He works to eat and he diets to keep working. Except that he enjoys his work as a featured film actor, he figures now he could quit it all and be even.

Lackteen is a Persian-Arabian who has established something of a record in Movietown by playing more than 500 roles as Indians, Asiatics and Spaniards. He attributes that good fortune to that hungry look.

Ever since he played Mary Pickford's Hindu servant in *Less Than Dust* in 1917, directors have typed him in similar roles. His high cheekbones, sunken eyes and jowls have earned him enough money, he says, to eat his way right out of the business.

"The irony of it all is that I'm a good cook, specializing in rich pastries," he sighed. "If I eat my cooking, my hollows fill up and I look like a thousand other out-of-work actors."

In *King of the Khyber Rifles*, he plays "Ahmed," tribesman who befriends Tyrone Power, Terry Moore and Michael Rennie. A veteran of Ruth Roland's old serials, Lackteen was born near Damascus and came to Hollywood in 1919 under contract to Pathe.

Apparently, Lackteen was able to stick to his diet; he continued to add to his film and television résumé throughout the 1950s. He made small but noticeable appearances in such films as *The Ten Commandments* and *Flesh and the Spur,* both 1956. In an altogether fitting fashion, Lackteen also portrayed the part of Chief War Eagle in the last American serial, Columbia's 1956 *Blazing the Overland Trail.* Otherwise, Lackteen turned his attention increasingly to television, appearing in episodes of *Broken Arrow, Casey Jones, The Adventures of Wild Bill Hickok* and *The Adventures of Rin Tin Tin* (all in 1958).

After Lackteen's uncredited appearance in *The Atomic Submarine* and a small part in *Three Came to Kill* (1960), the actor apparently retired from films. He returned briefly to the screen in 1964 at the request of Alex Gordon to portray small roles in Gordon's Westerns *Requiem for a Gunfighter* and *The Bounty Killer.*

Frank Lackteen died from respiratory failure on July 7, 1968, at the Motion Picture and Television Home and Hospital in Woodland Hills, California. He was buried in the Pierce Brothers Valhalla Memorial Park in North Hollywood. His widow Muriel died on February 11, 1978; his daughter, Muriel Elizabeth Dove Lackteen died on March 1, 1987. Both were residing in the Los Angeles area at the time of their deaths.

The Pressbook

Ad Mat No. 302　　3 cols. x 7½"　　(315 Lines)　　302

Ad Mat No. 103　　1 col. x 3½"　　(49 Lines)　　103

Ad Mat No. 203　　2 cols. x 3"　　(84 Lines)　　203

Ad Mat No. 301　　3 cols. x 3½"　　(147 Lines)　　301

The Full Line of
POSTERS and LOBBIES
is available through
NATIONAL SCREEN SERVICE

INSERT CARD

ONE SHEET

THREE SHEET

22 x 28 LOBBY CARD—B

22 x 28 LOBBY CARD—A

Also Available SET OF EIGHT FULL-COLOR 11 x 14 PHOTOS

★ EXPLOITATION ★

REVELL'S ATOMIC SUB MODELS GREAT FOR CONTESTS, DISPLAYS, TIE-INS
100,000 Revell Dealers Alerted

Revell, Inc., world's greatest manufacturers of model kits, are extending, through their 100,000 retail outlets, full cooperation on a local level. Here's how to take advantage of their "Atomic Submarine" tie-in:

Arrange with your local Revell dealers to sponsor a contest for boys between the ages of 8 and 15 for the neatest and best models made from Revell's two atomic subs, the Nautilus and the George Washington. Start your contest at least two weeks prior to opening to enable you to exhibit the winners in your lobby or a store window. Revell dealers will provide window space in which to display production stills and other advertising accessories. Get local U.S. Navy recruiters to act as judges. Latch on to any TV program or newspaper columns that have to do with hobbies. Revell will furnish, on request, colorful banners for lobby displays as well as stills for special newspaper publicity.

Revell has arranged a special discount price for exhibitors wishing to use their submarine model kits as prizes, not only for the contests but also for giveaways to youngsters at a special performance. The Nautilus, an 89c retailer, can be bought for $4.86 per dozen, while the George Washington which sells for $1.98, can be bought for $10.80 per dozen. All orders must be accompanied by money order or check. All shipments will be made via Railway Express, COLLECT. The minimum order is one dozen. Shipments of dozen lots via express run from 65c to $1.25 per dozen, according to distance. Please order direct from REVELL PUBLIC RELATIONS DEPT., REVELL, INC., VENICE, CALIF.

Contestants should be required to send in, with their sub models, a brief essay of 50 words or less starting with — "I WANT TO SEE 'ATOMIC SUBMARINE' BECAUSE . . ." Award Revell kits to the winners and theatre passes to the runners-up.

RADIO TRANSCRIPTION

A radio transcription especially designed to fill theatre seats is available to you at no cost. The only stipulation required is that when ordering you advise us of your playdate so that we will know how to ship. The transcription contains radio spots with strong selling copy about the picture theme, one of the most dangerous missions ever undertaken by a submarine, atomic or otherwise. Recent surveys indicate that radio listening is at an all time high despite the inroads made by television. Radio is the only means by which you can reach the thousands or more auto radios, not forgetting the great amount of portables in use. Order radio spots from Allied Artists, 4376 Sunset Dr., Hollywood 27, Calif., or from 165 West 46th Street, New York 36, N. Y.

U.S. NAVY ANGLES

Create a Navy atmosphere in your lobby and on your theatre front by hanging Navy signal flags, pennants, etc. Dress up staff in Navy blues or whites. Invite local ex-sub-mariners and frog-men and their wives and or sweethearts on opening night. Make a special exhibit of the Revell model atomic submarines. If your theatre is near a Naval installation, see if you can get a color guard to appear on your stage.

U.S. ATOMIC SUBS IN SERVICE

Make up a special 40" x 60" listing all the U. S. atomic submarines now in service. Attract attention to the board by captioning it—THE U. S. ATOMIC SUBMARINE HONOR ROLE. Most folks do not realize the number of subs involved.

THE NAUTILUS, THE SEA WOLF, THE SKATE,
THE SKIPJACK, THE SARGO, THE SWORDFISH
THE GEORGE WASHINGTON,
THE SEA DRAGON, THE TRITON,
*THE TIGER SHARK.

*This atomic powered sub is fictional. It is the "star" of Allied Artists' "The Atomic Submarine," the very first story about our undersea fleet of atomic powered submarines.

"ATOMIC SUBMARINE" IS A FIRST

Many motion pictures have been made about the U. S. Submarine service, but Allied Artists' "The Atomic Submarine" is the very FIRST about the nuclear operated undersea craft. Be sure to stress this fact in all your publicity, advertising, and in your lobby.

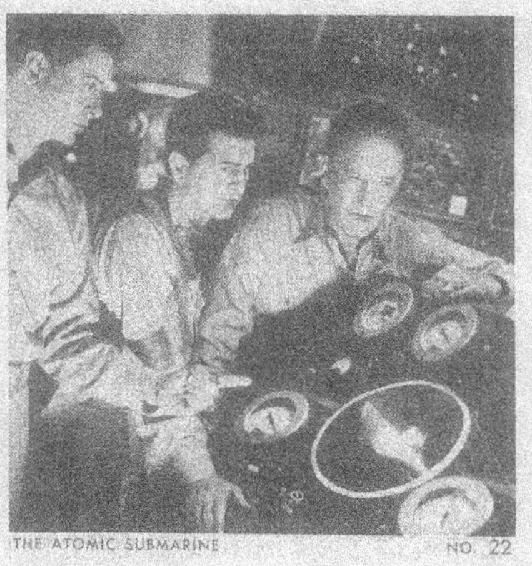

THE ATOMIC SUBMARINE NO. 22

Trouble ahead looms on the U.S.S. Tiger Shark's visio radarscope in this scene from Allied Artists' "The Atomic Submarine," the screen's first big picture of the nuclear operated subs. Pictured here (left to right) are Arthur Franz, Paul Dubov and Dick Foran, the sub's officers, assigned to meet and destroy a new type of atomic enemy craft in polar waters. The film, currently at the .... Theatre, stars Franz, Foran and Brett Halsey.

WAR UNDER ARCTIC ICE SHOWN IN "THE ATOMIC SUBMARINE"

(Advance)

What happens when an unknown enemy's latest nuclear weapon goes on a rampage of death and destruction on American submarines and surface craft in the arctic sea lanes, is dramatically pictured in Allied Artists' "The Atomic Sumbarine," scheduled to open .... at the .... Theatre. Starred in this exciting film are Arthur Franz, Dick Foran and Brett Halsey.

"The Atomic Submarine" is the movie screen's first big picture about atomic undersea craft, and it is a real thriller. The picture relates the story of the dangerous mission of the atomic sub, the Tiger Shark, assigned to search out and, if possible, destroy the unknown enemy object which has been raising havoc with sea craft in polar waters. The Tiger Shark, manned by a specially selected crew including two scientists, carefully zig-zagging between treacherous icebergs, does not have to wait long. When a bright, radio-active type splotch appears on the sub's visio radarscope, they realize they are against a weapon about which they know very little. A game of "hide and seek" follows, with the Tiger Shark officers biding their time to go into action. What happens when that moment comes, will give theatregoers a possible idea of the future atomic war, a sight that is both frightening and fascinating in its horror.

Also for the first time on the screen, Alexander Laszlo, noted composer and conductor, introduces his "electro-sonic" music score, a new type of note wizardry that sets the mood for the weird events depicted in the film. Another visual treat, designed by the picture's special effects specialists, is the terrific under-sea clash between the sub and the enemy as they are locked in mortal combat.

Alex Gordon produced the picture with Spencer G. Bennet as director and with an excellent cast of supporting players including Paul Dubov, Bob Steele, Victor Varconi, Joi Lansing and Tom Conway.

The Cast

Reel	ARTHUR FRANZ
Wendover	DICK FORAN
Carl	BRETT HALSEY
Sir Ian Hunt	TOM CONWAY
Dave	PAUL DUBOV
Griff	BOB STEELE
Kent	VICTOR VARCONI
Julie	JOI LANSING
Admiral	SELMER JACKSON
Murdock	JACK MULHALL
Helen	JEAN MOORHEAD
Carney	RICHARD TYLER
Chester	SID MELTON
Powell	KEN BECKER

Halsey Former CBS Page Boy

Brett Halsey, starred in Allied Artists' "The Atomic Submarine," was a Columbia Broadcasting System page boy when he was 19. His appearance caught the eye of Mary Livingstone (Mrs. Jack Benny). She immediately contacted her friend Bill Goetz of Universal-International aind arranged an interview. Two days later, Halsey had a two year contract with U-I in his pocket. During the two years there he appeared in 14 pictures.

In Allied Artists' "The Atomic Submarine," opening .... at the .... Theatre, Halsey is seen as a scientist, assigned to the regular crew of the Tiger Shark one of Uncle Sam's newest nuclear-powered undersea craft. First, not too popular with the crew who called him an "egghead," his know-how as the inventor and his quiet manner wins them over.

THE STORY

(Not for Publication)

Admiral Terhune (Selmer Jackson) U.S.N., calls a meeting after the seventh atomic submarine and four surface sessels have either disappeared or been destroyed in the arctic sea lanes. Present are Capt. Dan Wendover (Dick Foran), skipper of the Tiger Shark, atomic submarine; Dr. Clifford Kent (Victor Varconi) and Sir Ian Hunt (Tom Conway), scientists. Wendover is ordered to take the Tiger Shark into polar waters to determine the cause of the disasters and possibly put an end to them, with Dr. Kent and Sir Ian to go along as advisors. In the crew are Commander Richard (Reel) Holloway (Arthur Franz), Lt. David Milburn (Paul Dubov), the ship's navigator and Reel's friend, and Carl Nelson (Brett Halsey), inventor of a depth explorer. Later, while cruising in arctic waters, the Tiger Shark is jarred by a tremendous crash as a nearby freighter is destroyed and icebergs around them break up. Wendover, keeping his eye on the TV monitor, sees what he belives to be an enemy object responsible for the losses in the arctic. The Tiger Shark submerges to await whatever may come. When the strange circular craft draws close, Wendover orders his submarine plowed into it. After the crash, the submarine and unidentified craft are locked together. They begin to sink. The Tiger Shark must be cut loose if all its crew is to be saved from a living death. How this is done, but not before three lives are lost, brings the film to its exciting climax.

Versatile Star In New Film

Dick Foran, one of the screen's most versatile players, is starred as a submarine skipper in Allied Artists' "The Atomic Submarine," now at the .... Theatre, with Arthur Franz and Brett Halsey also starred.

The picture, produced by Alex Gordon, is Hollywood's first big story about atom submarines. It relates the thrilling tale of the dangerous mission of the Tiger Shark, assigned to find and destroy an enemy "weapon" which has been wrecking American shipping in arctic waters. Top Navy brass are convinced that a foreign power has designed this diabolical weapon with the intention of forcing all the nations of the world to submit to its superior know-how of atomic warfare.

The special effects, created by Jack Rabin, Irving Block and Louis DeWitt, are used in the battle scenes between the Tiger Shark and the unknown "thing" underwater.

Directed by Spencer G. Bennet, the picture boasts a cast of fine players including Paul Dubov, Bob Steele, Victor Varconi, Joi Lansing and Tom Conway.

RARE BEAUTY

Joi Lansing, one of the most beautiful and talented actresses in Hollywood, has a top featured role in Allied Artists' "The Atomic Submarine," starring Arthur Franz, Dick Foran and Brett Halsey. Miss Lansing has appeared in over 100 television network shows, as well as appearing in many of the season's big film hits, her most recent being with Frank Sinatra in "Hole In The Head." "The Atomic Submarine" opens its local engagement on .... at the .... Theatre.

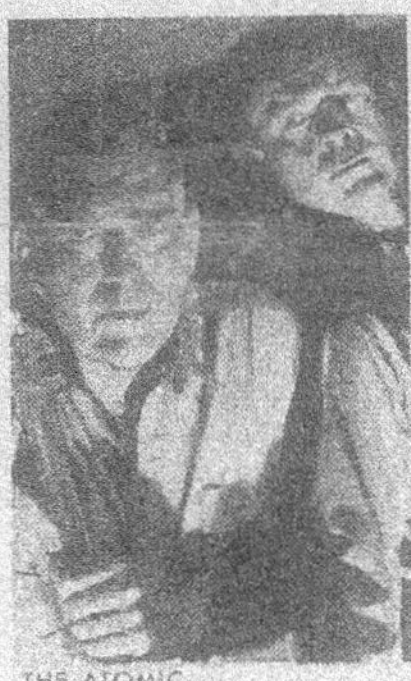

THE ATOMIC SUBMARINE NO. 2

Dick Foran (left) and Arthur Franz are shown as they appear in Allied Artists' "The Atomic Submarine," now at the..... Theatre. It's the screen's first big story of the U.S. atomic submarine fleet and tells the story of the U.S.S. Tiger Shark, assigned to patrol arctic waters in search of an unknown foe which has been wrecking American shipping. Franz, Foran and Brett Halsey are starred.

Credits

Produced by Alex Gordon; Co-Producer, Henry Schrage; Associate Producers, Jack Rabin, Irving Block and Orville H. Hampton; Directed by Spencer G. Bennet; Written by Orville H. Hampton; Special Effects Designed and Created by Jack Rabin, Irving Block and Louis DeWitt; Electro-Sonic Music Composed and Conducted by Alexander Laszlo; Music Editor, Neil Brunnenkant; Director of Photography, Gilbert Warrenton; Production Manager, Edward Morey, Jr.; Film Editor, William Austin, A.C.E.; Art Directors, Don Ament and Dan Heller; Assistant to Producer, Ruth Alexander; Assistant Director, Clark Paylow; Set Decorator, Harry Reif; Properties, Max Frankel; Chief Set Electrician, George Satterfield; Sound, Ralph Butler; Narrator, Pat Michaels; Saucer Voice, John Hilliard; Production Associate and Dialogue Supervisor, Jack Cash; Wardrobe by Roger J. Weinberg and Norah Sharpe; Makeup, Emile La Vigne; Script Supervisor, Judith Hart; Sound Editor, Marty Greco.

TO-MORROW'S WAR PICTURED IN "THE ATOMIC SUBMARINE"

(Review)

The important part that atomic submarines, equipped with underwater ballistic missiles, might play in future wars is vividly pictured in Allied Artists' "The Atomic Submarine," which opened at the .... Theatre yesterday. The film, the very first about atomic subs, is a genuine thriller from beginning to end. It is not only top entertainment, but also gives a frightening idea of things which may come.

After several submarines and four surface vessels have either disappeared or been destroyed in the arctic sea lanes, the newest of atomic submarines, the Tiger Shark, is assigned to polar waters to determine the cause of the disasters and, if possible, put an end to them. Zig-zagging between dangerous icebergs under the North Pole, the officers on the Tiger Shark, spot the unknown enemy object on their visio radarscope. Even then, they do not exactly know what it is. First they try their regulation torpedoes, without success. They now realize they are in a death struggle with an unknown enemy. Taking a million to one chance, they succeed in converting a torpedo into an underwater guided ballistic missile. What happens before they fire the missile, and the events that follow, make "The Atomic Submarine" one of the most thrilling films you have ever seen.

Excellent performances are given by stars Dick Foran as the Tiger Shark's skipper, Arthur Franz as his commander, and Brett Halsey as an "egghead" inventor. The fine supporting cast includes Paul Dubov, Bob Steele, Victor Varconi, Joi Lansing and Tom Conway.

Special mention should be given to the unusual "electro-sonic" score by Alexander Laszlo which sets the mood for the weird and thrilling events, while the special effects by Jack Rabin, Irving Block and Louis DeWitt are outstanding. Kudos should also be handed to producer Alex Gordon and director Spencer G. Bennet.

FIRST TIME

After six months of hard work and intense research, special effects specialists Jack Rabin, Irving Block and Louis DeWitt were able to bring to the screen for the first time a do or die undersea struggle between a U.S. atomic sub and an unknown enemy object beneath the North Pole. "The Atomic Submarine," produced by Alex Gordon for Allied Artists, stars Arthur Franz, Dick Foran and Brett Halsey, and opens .... at the .... Theatre.

ELECTRO-SONIC

The electro-sonic music score for Allied Artists' "The Atomic Submarine," now at the .... Theatre, composed and directed by Alexander Laszlo, noted pianist and conductor, presents a new concept in film music. In this score composer Laszlo incorporates sounds emanating from electronic sources which produce an eerie effect.

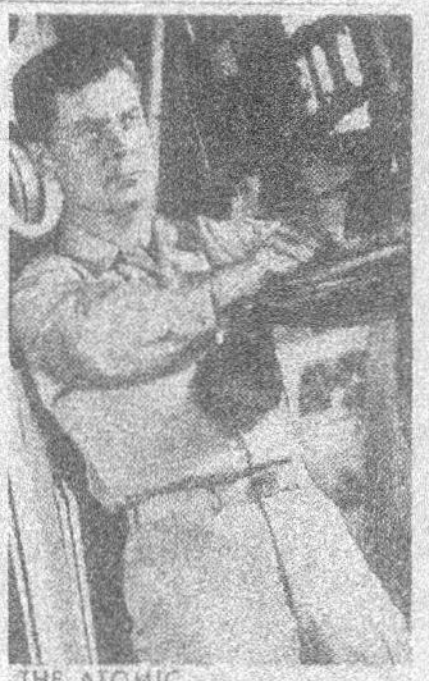

THE ATOMIC SUBMARINE NO. 1

Arthur Franz, is pictured in his role as Commander of the U.S. Tiger Shark, an atomic submarine, in Allied Artists' "The Atomic Submarine," starring Franz, Dick Foran and Brett Halsey. The film, opening .... at the .... Theatre, is the screen's first big story of this comparatively new branch of the Navy, and is a thriller.

Tom Conway In "The Atomic Submarine"

Tom Conway was induced by producer Alex Gordon to step out of retirement for the role of a British scientist in Allied Artists' "The Atomic Submarine," currently being screened at the .... Theatre.

For several years, Conway and his brother, George Sanders, were starred in two different detective series at the RKO Studios. Conway was known to millions of movie fans as the Falcon, while brother George, the Saint. Both series were extremely popular with movie audiences all over the world.

In "The Atomic Submarine," Conway is seen as one of the two nuclear scientists requested to join the crew of the Tiger Shark, an atomic submarine about to embark on a highly dangerous secret mission in arctic waters. The other scientist is played by Victor Varconi, also a name well known to movie goers. The picture is a thriller and tells of the exciting clash between the submarine and an unknown death-dealing object, believed to be a new type super-atomic weapon, the invention of an unknown enemy. The "weapon" is a triple-threat of death and destruction in the air, on land or under the sea!

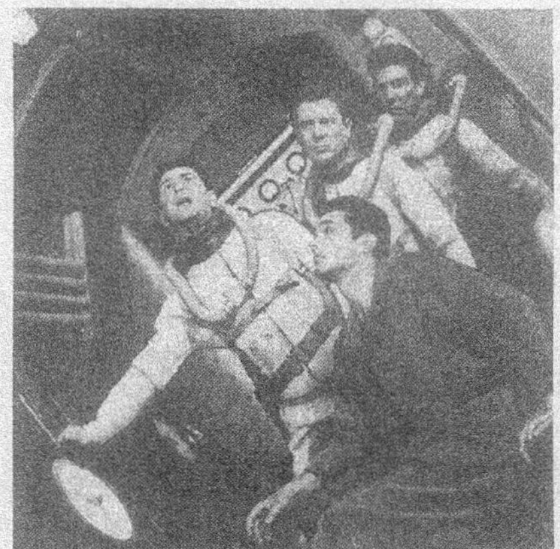

THE ATOMIC SUBMARINE NO. 21

Paul Dubov, Brett Halsey, Arthur Franz and Ken Becker, are pictured (left to right) as they face destruction in Allied Artists' "The Atomic Submarine," coming .... to the .... Theatre. The visio radarscope warns of the approaching enemy object that threatens their destruction. Starred in this thriller are Franz, Dick Foran and Halsey.

COMPLETE CAMPAIGN MAT

ALL THE AD AND SCENE CUTS BELOW AVAILABLE ON ONE BIG BARGAIN MAT!
ORDER "THE ATOMIC SUBMARINE" SPECIAL MAT NO. 1 FROM NATIONAL SCREEN

NOTE: Any of These Mats May Be Ordered Singly at the Regular Price. Order by Number Under the Cut.

Ad Mat No. 205   2 cols. x 6¼"   (175 Lines)

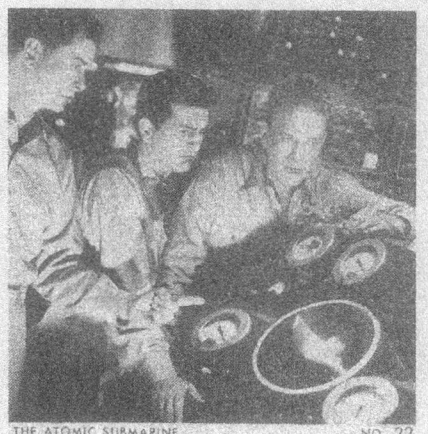

Ad Mat No. 202   2 cols. x 2¼"   (63 Lines)

Ad Mat No. 104   1 col. x 5½"   (77 Lines)

Ad Mat No. 101   1 col. x 1"   (14 Lines)

Ad Mat No. 102   1 col. x 2"   (28 Lines)

www.ingramcontent.com/pod-product-compliance
Lightning Source LLC
Chambersburg PA
CBHW081221170426
43198CB00017B/2677